The Land Is Shrinking

THE JOHNS HOPKINS STUDIES IN DEVELOPMENT

Vernon W. Ruttan, *Consulting Editor*

Asian Village Economy at the Crossroads:
An Economic Approach to Institutional Change,
by Yujiro Hayami and Masao Kikuchi

The Agrarian Question and Reformism in Latin America,
by Alain de Janvry

Redesigning Rural Development:
A Strategic Perspective,
by Bruce F. Johnston and William C. Clark

Energy Planning for Developing Countries:
A Study of Bangladesh,
by Russell J. deLucia, Henry D. Jacoby, et alia

Women and Poverty in the Third World,
edited by Mayra Buvinić, Margaret A. Lycette, and William Paul McGreevey

The Land Is Shrinking:
Population Planning in Asia,
by Gayl D. Ness and Hirofumi Ando

Gayl D. Ness and Hirofumi Ando

The LAND Is Shrinking

Population Planning in Asia

 The Johns Hopkins University Press

Baltimore and London

© 1984 by The Johns Hopkins University Press

All rights reserved

Printed in the United States of America

The Johns Hopkins University Press, Baltimore, Maryland 21218

The Johns Hopkins Press Ltd., London

Library of Congress Cataloging in Publication Data
Ness, Gayl D.
  The land is shrinking.

  (The Johns Hopkins studies in development)
  Bibliography: p.
  Includes index.
  1. Asia—Population policy.   2. Birth control—Asia.
I. Ando, Hirofumi.   II. Title.   III. Series.
HB3633.A3N47   1983   304.6'6'095   83-48048
ISBN 0-8018-2982-8

For our children

        Yumi

        Shanta

        Yan

        Eric

        Marc

        and for all the world's children—with hope

"Life without hope is . . . suffocating."

André Malraux, *Man's Hope*

Contents

Chapter 4.   Asia: State and Region in the Ecological Adjustment

Chapter 5.   The Political-Ecological Perspective: Implications and Controversies

Afterword: Reflections on Japan from a Political-Ecological Perspective, by Minoru Muramatsu

List of Figures

List of Tables

Preface

T he rural poor in east Java have a poignant
expression for our era's major ecological
change:

The land is shrinking,
the children keep coming,
and it is hard to breathe.

It is no easier to breathe in the cities, where the land provides not
crops, but jobs, and all too few of those. Streets are crowded with young
people searching and waiting for work, and with even more playing children, whose very numbers threaten to engulf opportunities before they
emerge. Not only in Java, but everywhere in the Third World, previous
ecological equilibria have been disturbed and the resulting rapid population growth holds the specter of larger masses living in even greater
poverty.

This has happened before, of course, but today something new has
been added. If the streets teem with the young, they also teem with a new
political and bureaucratic elite, national and international, searching specifically for solutions to mass poverty and rapid population growth. It is
easy to be cynical about this new elite and its population and development programing, for most of its work goes on in the comfort of conference rooms and first-class hotels. Like much of development planning, it
can be described by paraphrasing John S. Mill's indictment of nineteenth-
century British colonialism: it is merely a form of indoor air-conditioned
relief for an unproductive administrative middle class. Nevertheless it is
important to see something else in these bureaucrats and the conference
rooms that protect them from the heat of the streets. Their existence as

an administrative class for an emerging world community is an important fact of modern life from which some hope can be derived.

Although rapid population growth has occurred before, never before have governments been so deeply involved in confronting the growth. Never before have they had both the will and the capacity to perceive, assess, and react to this major ecological change. Today we are in the midst of what we call a political-ecological adjustment to rapid population growth. The ecological adjustment has occurred before. It is its political aspect that presents the image of something dramatically different in the world's population history.

The bare outlines of our political-ecological perspective can be stated simply and briefly. We begin with the hardly controversial proposition that rapid population growth in the high-fertility countries today represents a new and disturbing ecological change for the world as a whole. As in any such radical ecological change—for example, when an ant hill is disturbed—the affected population predictably reacts with pervasive and often frenetic activity. In today's human population we find a major focus of that frenetic activity in the political organization that has emerged over the past few centuries. In the political-administrative instruments of the modern state we find first a perception of rapid population growth as a new problem and then a series of actions to deal with that problem. We see these actions primarily, but not exclusively, in political decisions to adopt national antinatalist policies to be implemented primarily by national family planning programs, which aim to have an impact on fertility through the distribution of the new contraceptive technology. We argue that the timing of the decision, the character of its implementation, and the impact it has on mass reproductive behavior are significantly affected by the strength of the political-administrative systems that govern the process.

The general concept of political strength is the subject of much controversy, and it presents no less difficulty for us than it does for anyone else. We take a modest and narrow approach, however, to identify what is important for the current ecological adjustment. The world is organized into nation states governed by modern bureaucracies, and the states are in turn organized into a loose international community with its own bureaucratic administration. At the nation-state level, governments accept wide responsibility for populations in administratively defined territories. The bureaucratic form of administration gives the modern government a power unparalleled in history for organizing the population within its territory.

Modern states construct goals, largely for what has come to be called national economic development, and they mobilize resources for the achievement of those goals. From this perspective, political strength implies governmental acceptance of development goals and the creation of administrative capacities to mobilize resources and to establish priorities of action to achieve these goals. It also implies the creation of administrative capacities to perceive the changing condition of the population in its territory. That many of the world's states have been lacking in the commitment to economic development or in the administrative capacity to move their populations in that direction does not imply that this conception of strength is useless. It only indicates that political-administrative strength varies.

Our basic proposition is that where this type of political-administrative strength is greater, there will be an earlier antinatalist policy decision, a more effective programmatic implementation of the decision, and consequently a greater impact on the population's reproductive behavior. This is the bare outline of our political-ecological perspective. Note that it does not attempt to explain all fertility levels or all fertility decline. Our aim is more modest. We are, in effect, attempting to make sense of two conditions, which we believe to be interrelated today: rapid population growth in the Third World and widespread antinatalist policy decisions. We attempt to do this through a series of comparisons.

In chapter 1 we spell out the details of our political-ecological perspective. Chapter 2 deals with major differences between Asia and the other high-fertility regions—Africa, Latin America, and the Islamic (or southern and eastern) Mediterranean world. We argue that the processes of imperialism, colonialism, and nationalism produced in Asia a region of relatively strong states. This makes the region more advanced in perceiving and reacting to rapid population growth and its intense ecological pressures. Thus, Asian nations have led the world in making early antinatalist policy decisions and in translating those decisions into public programs designed to reduce human fertility.

In chapter 3 we turn our attention to India and China, two giants in the world's population growth and pioneers in the political-ecological adjustment. With a historical comparison we can trace the processes by which India came to develop a deliberately weak political-administrative system, while China was led to develop a deliberately strong system. Both states adopted antinatalist policies for the same reasons, in very much the same way, and at roughly similar times. The differences in the strength of the political-administrative systems had a marked effect on the manner in which those decisions have been implemented and also on the impact they have had on mass reproductive behavior. The data on internal variations in China are lacking, but their availability for India permits a limited test of our perspective through an examination of state differences in implementing the national family planning program. We find that states that have more effective political-administrative systems are those that have done better in recruiting family planning acceptors or in inducing populations to limit fertility.

In chapter 4 we move to a broader comparison of the twenty-one remaining major states of Asia, the region defined by the United Nations' Economic and Social Council for Asia and the Pacific (ESCAP). The larger number of cases here permits the use of some quantitative modeling to test the utility of our perspective. The number is not large enough, however, for extensive quantitative analysis. We are thus led to weave an analysis out of multiple regression equations and narrative descriptions of individual countries moving through the past three decades. Again we find that the stronger states have made earlier antinatalist policy decisions, have translated these into more effective family planning programs, and have had a more profound impact on reproductive behavior. Deviant cases appear and can be explained by specific developments in the political-administrative system, by the specific levels of population density, and by other internal differences within countries.

In chapter 5 we provide a recapitulation of the overall argument, which permits us to make two types of more extended statements. First we note that our political-ecological perspective raises a series of questions. These can be taken as a research agenda that we hope will lead us to a better understanding of the course of fertility changes in today's high-fertility countries. In the second, we use our perspective to comment on the series of controversial issues that remain today. Here we begin with our perspective and go beyond, drawing on our experience with Asian population planning over the past decade to comment on the nature of the world's population problem, on international assistance in population affairs, and on the character of today's national family planning programs.

In an afterword to this volume the distinguished Japanese demographer Minoru Muramatsu considers the specific case of Japan from our perspective. As the first industrializing nation in Asia, Japan stands somewhat between the West and the East in the pattern of its ecological adjustment. In some respects Japan follows the West in that kinship units reacting to pervasive economic changes provide the organizational locus for adjustments to rapid population growth. In other respects Japan is like the rest of Asia in the powerful role the political-administrative system played in the recent rapid downturn of fertility.

There is a moral to this analysis, which some will find pleasing, others objectionable. The world's current rate of population growth cannot continue for long. It will decline. What will vary considerably, however, is the degree of human misery that will attend the reduction in growth rates. If mass reproductive behavior does not change in the Third World, we can expect a fulfillment of Malthus's dismal predictions of increased human misery. If it does change, as it did in the industrial nations, we can at least hope for an ecological adjustment that will mitigate some of the misery and increase the opportunities for human betterment. In large part the responsibility for what happens to mass reproductive behavior lies with modern governments, in individual nations and in the world community as a whole. The technological and organizational instruments that are currently available can help to produce reproductive change with minimal levels of misery. Whether or not they will be used, whether or not they are currently used to the benefit of populations, depends very much on the strength and capacity of modern national and international governments. Thus we are led to state a normative position that holds modern governments responsible for much of the betterment or the misery that will attend the pending ecological change.

This book begins with an examination of Asia. It is here that we have our primary experience, and it is also here that we find the political-ecological adjustment in its most advanced stage. In Asia we can describe a process that is unique to our era and that portends changes in reproductive behavior that we believe will come to the rest of the developing world. We also recognize, however, that world regions differ, especially in the specific institutional histories that shape our era's distinctive pattern of ecological change. Describing and understanding these regional differences are important tasks that remain to be done. Here, they are only briefly introduced in the first chapter.

We must make an important disclaimer before proceeding. This work does not attempt to explain all human fertility at all levels: past, present, or future. We do not focus on the determinants of the demand for fertility-limiting techniques or behavior, which are the subject of much demographic analysis. We focus rather on what has come to be called the supply side of modern fertility-limiting behavior. Our aim is to understand some of the major political changes that distinguish our era and to show how these have an impact on national and international actions that today are directed toward the condition of the world's rapid population growth.

Acknowledgments

We have been studying Southeast Asia together for more than fifteen years, and population problems in Asia for more than ten years. This is sufficient time to accumulate debts that can never be repaid or even fully acknowledged. Nonetheless, we try. We have learned much from the many government officers, family planning personnel, and people in streets and villages about the conditions of rapid change, poverty, and hope. These are the nameless and numberless to whom we owe a great deal. There are, however, others whose distinctive contributions have greatly shaped our views. From the late Tun Abdul Razak, Prime Minister of Malaysia, we learned the importance of pressing high expectations of results on a colonial bureaucracy. From Rafael M. Salas, current director of the United Nations Fund for Population Activities, we have learned much about the management of human resources in the nearly impossible organizational setting of the international bureaucracy. From Carl Frisen and Sook Bang, earlier leaders in ESCAP's Population Division, we learned something of the subtle maneuvers by which the international bureaucracy generates movement toward the service of what the Filipinos so aptly call the little people. These have been valuable lessons provided by experienced teachers. If we have not learned them fully or well, it is scarcely the fault of the teachers.

We have also gained much from our respective professional colleagues. Universities provide an unusual amount of freedom and intellectual stimulation. The University of Michigan, with its impressive strength in population research, the social sciences, and Asian studies, has offered an unparalleled setting for study. Our colleagues in the Population Planning Center, the Center for South and Southeast Asian Studies, the Population Studies Center, and the Department of Sociology provided a rich resource for our investigations. The United Nations Fund for Population

Activities provided a similar setting in the nonacademic world. There we found a group of committed and competent young professionals who were a tribute to what the United Nations can be in the area of organized development assistance.

The Compton Foundation provided a welcome grant to support a research seminar during the summer and fall of 1980. Some of the political analyses and interpretations found in chapter 4 emerged from that seminar, as did a proposal to go beyond our results in further research. The members of the seminar included Alidoost Yadollah (Iran), Kirsten Alcser (United States and Denmark), Ann Alvarez (United States and the Philippines), Salleh Ismail (Malaysia), Jessica Musoke (Uganda), Ali Nawab-Safavi (Iran), and Boon-Ann Tan (Malaysia). Professor Perla Makil from the Philippines joined us for the summer of 1981. We owe a great deal to the interest, industry, and enthusiasm of our students, and to the help of the Compton Foundation.

Our colleague Ronald Freedman and the reviewers for The Johns Hopkins University Press read the entire work and provided many valuable suggestions for changes. Other students and colleagues read portions and valiantly attempted to save us from a variety of follies.

It is customary to relieve one's colleagues and mentors from responsibility for errors or follies. We are reluctant to do so as completely as custom dictates. Our colleagues are very much a part of the experience that has produced this book. They deserve much of the credit; but, alas, they will also have to share some of the blame.

It might seem contradictory that we dedicate a book essentially on family planning to children—ours and the world's. Mamdani's indictment from *The Myth of Family Planning* is unfortunately still current. He argues that family planners dislike the smile on a child's face. We do not agree with Mamdani. Rather, we believe that children today can have hope only if they are wanted; that there is much tragedy in men and women having children they know they cannot care for, however much they may be wanted in some other sense; and that governments of the world today have major responsibilities for helping people to bring their opportunities closer to their wants, and their wants closer to those of their fellows. This is essentially the vision through which we believe there lies some hope.

The Land Is Shrinking

1

Perspectives on Population Growth

Population planning in Asia today represents a massive political-ecological response to rapid population growth.

This growth in Asia, as in the rest of the Third World, is well documented and needs little introduction. Mortality has declined while fertility has remained high, producing population growth rates that range from 2 to 3.5 percent per year. This general pattern is similar to that experienced by the industrialized countries over the past two centuries, but the speed, source, and magnitude of today's change are unique.

In the industrialized countries mortality gradually declined over a period of more than a century. The decline was accompanied by a gradual increase in the standard of living, and the resulting rates of population growth were seldom greater than 1 percent per year. In Asia and the Third World today, the mortality decline has come in decades rather than centuries. It has been produced largely by the importation of a new medical and public health technology, and the resulting growth rates are substantially, and to many observers alarmingly, higher than they were in the past.

Many of the implications of this unique pattern are well understood, or at least extensively discussed. How populations respond to this growth, however, is far less well understood. In this work we shall explore what we consider to be a decisive element of the response: *the political-ecological adjustment*. We concentrate on Asia because this type of response originated and is most advanced in Asia. Further, we shall argue that the broad lines of the Asian adjustment are generating a similar response in the rest of the high-fertility world.

It is obvious that there must be a solution to the current rapid increase, for it cannot continue long into the future. At 2 percent per year, the world's roughly 4 billion people will grow to about 1500 billion in only

1

three centuries. Continued for 2,000 years, a period equal to the span of the Christian era, this growth rate would produce sufficient human material to cover every bit of known matter in the entire universe. Clearly, the growth must slow and eventually cease. Just as clearly, this will require a profound change in the character of human social organization.

Population growth will cease either through a rise in mortality or through a decline in fertility.[1] We have seen both responses in the past and in the present. Irish mortality rose during the great famine of the mid-nineteenth century; European fertility declined at the end of the nineteenth century and the beginning of the twentieth. In the 1970s there were widespread famine and mortality increases in the Sahel; fertility has declined in much of the Third World, and for the past decade or less it appears on the verge of more general decline. At present a great deal of political effort is directed toward promoting that decline.

If both mortality and fertility changes can be seen as responses to rapid population growth, they are not alike in their political implications. Broad social values and political commitments unambiguously support lower mortality. Life is valued, death is not. Agreement is readily reached on the desirability of reducing mortality and keeping it low. There may be sporadic resistance to some specific technique of mortality control, but even this tends to be short-lived. For the most part, efforts to reduce or control mortality are not politically problematic.

Fertility is a far more complex issue, and its control is usually, if not always, politically problematic. Human reproduction is surrounded by universal and persistent social structures and deeply embedded social values. Kinship systems and differentiated gender roles interlock with fertility, and all are closely connected with the specific distribution of wealth and power in human societies.[2] Thus, fertility change will usually have important political implications. This is especially true today, when organizations and governments make strong and pervasive efforts to intervene directly in reproductive behavior to limit fertility.

Direct government action to reduce fertility has not come easily or quickly. In retrospect, of course, it may appear that the change from pronatalism to antinatalism in official policies has come quite rapidly, but today the pace appears slow and the conflict protracted. It touches on deeply held values, political strategies, and narrow technical issues. Where do we strike the balance between the needs of the community and the rights of the individual? How do we balance the value of life recently conceived with that of the well-being of mother and family? If fertility must be controlled for the well-being of both community and individuals, what strategies are the most effective for reducing fertility? Will increased economic development and human welfare alone be effective, or must there be direct interventions as well? Can direct political programs for fertility limitation have a depressing impact on fertility? Does fertility limitation require administrative procedures so strong that they constitute coercion, or is it possible to have the desired impact through persuasion, education, and information? These are only some of the many issues that arise as communities and their political institutions face the problem of rapid population growth and attempt to adjust to the pressures produced by that growth. It is this that makes the political aspect of the current political-ecological adjustment so compelling.

PERSPECTIVES

Social scientists have paid a great deal of attention to the current condition of rapid growth. Most of this attention has been dominated by a social demographic perspective. Social demographers obtain information on individuals and seek to understand behavior by examining relationships between variable conditions shown by those individuals. For example, it is often observed that people who are more highly educated, live in urban areas, and work in nonagricultural occupations have fewer children than do people who are less well-educated, live in rural areas, and work in agricultural occupations. Much theorizing goes on in the attempt to explain how it is that education, location, and occupation are linked to the individual action of lower fertility. The unit of observation is the individual, and the unit of analysis is the individual, alone or aggregated on different individual characteristics.

This perspective is associated with and dominated by a specific method of observation: the census or the sample survey. The areal sample survey is certainly one of the most powerful research tools developed by modern social scientists. It has been used to provide fine insights into virtually all aspects of human behavior, and it has been used with especially important policy effects in addressing the problem of rapid population growth. One need only mention the *Knowledge, Attitude, and Practice* (KAP) survey and the *World Fertility Survey* to call attention to the extensive and valuable information generated by the survey technique in the population field.[3] It is important to observe, however, that this research technique lies behind the social demographic perspective, shaping and constraining it to focus attention on individual behavior.

The social demographic perspective contains another, less obvious characteristic. It sees *norms* as the major organizing element for human behavior. Norms are nonrational principles or determinants of action built into individuals through the process of socialization. They are nonrational in the sense that they are not calculated; rather they are followed because they are seen to be "right," or "correct," or "expected" by the individual. To put it another way, they are patterns of action infused with value and at least to a certain extent unquestioned.

The place of norms in the social demographic perspective is graphically illustrated in Ronald Freedman's excellent review, *The Sociology of Human Fertility*.[4] In Freedman's "Model for the Sociological Analysis of Fertility," norms of family size and norms of marriage, conception, and parturition stand between mortality and the social and economic structure on the one side, and human fertility on the other.[5]

It is difficult to overestimate the power and influence of this model and the larger perspective of which it is an integral part. Norms can be considered some of the most important conceptual discoveries of modern sociology, and their use in explaining human fertility has been of great consequence. In his own pioneering work in Taiwan, Freedman demonstrated how this perspective and the survey technique helped to produce a profound change in national population policy.[6] The technique and perspective have also been extensively used to shape and monitor the implementation of this and similar policy changes. The implementing programs are essentially designed to distribute the new fertility-limiting technology in a deliberate attempt to reduce a population's fertility.

It is also important to recognize, however, that the social demographic perspective is not the only one available for dealing with the population growth issue. Further, some of its strengths may lead to the neglect of important characteristics of the modern condition of rapid population growth. It is only a slight exaggeration to say that social demographers direct attention almost exclusively to individual fertility, individual contraceptive acceptance, and individual use of fertility-limiting behaviors. With this perspective, social scientists neglect the organizational elements of modern programs. Thus, policy-relevant research may well lead policy makers to overlook the administrative machinery over which they have direct control. All of this is of little consequence when the problem is that of understanding fertility and fertility decline in the past, but it is of great importance when we attempt to understand current conditions.[7]

It would be both unnecessary and foolish to reject the social demographic perspective. It can, however, be complemented with another: the ecological perspective.[8] Ecological analysis is concerned with the interaction between the organism and its environment. Three fundamental assumptions underlie this perspective. First it assumes that organisms constantly adapt to their environments. Second, this adaptation is assumed to be collective rather than individual. It is populations, not simply individuals, that adapt to their environments. Finally, it is assumed that all populations adapt not simply as aggregates of individuals, but as collectivities with some form of organization.

The ecological perspective applied to human populations, human ecology, makes a number of important observations. First, the human species has become dominant in the world ecosystem over the past million years or so. Dominance implies a great increase in numbers, which results from the human capacity to extract and utilize energy from the environment. This great human capacity is the result of an extensive development and elaboration of organizational forms for collective cooperative action.

Three types of resources flow between the organism and its environment: matter, energy, and information. All organizational forms, including those responsible for human dominance, are basically accumulations of information. Information can be compiled in a number of ways, the most important dimension of which concerns its fixedness or flexibility. Information of relatively fixed amounts and content can be accumulated and stored in the organism's genetic structure; or this process can be highly flexible, depending on the organism's development and its interaction with other organisms. In what are usually called the higher forms of life, and especially in the human animal, information is extremely varied and flexible in amount and content because it is acquired and stored in symbolic form. The great advantage of symbols is that they can be arranged in different combinations, thus providing for greater efficiency in storage, retrieval, and application.

It is important to observe that information in virtually any form, but especially in symbolic form, is a unique resource. Both matter and energy conform to the laws of conservation. They can be neither destroyed nor created; they can only be transformed. Information, in contrast can be destroyed and created. Especially in its symbolic form, it can be created and expanded almost infinitely. It is this uniqueness of information as a resource and the human capacity for symbolic information acquisition and storage that have produced human dominance in the world ecosystem.

Human forms of organization vary immensely. There are few universals in the ways that humans are arranged together for action. Symbolic interaction permits almost endless variation in the meanings that humans give to their actions, and thus also to the rules they create to produce what we call social organization, or the observable regularities in roles and relationships. This also implies that human populations vary immensely in the type and amount of information available for the ongoing process of adaptation to the environment. Thus two interrelated concerns in human ecology are identifying the dimensions of variance in human organization and analyzing the ways in which human organization is systematically related to adaptation to the environment. Some patterns of organization will appear more effective in that they permit greater degrees of human dominance, over both other forms of life and other forms of human organization.

In short, while the social demographic perspective tends to neglect organizational forms and to concentrate on individual behavior, the ecological perspective brings organization to the center of attention.

A POLITICAL-ECOLOGICAL PERSPECTIVE

If the ecological perspective considers organization to be primary, it does not specify which organizational forms should be at the forefront. This has given much ecological analysis something of an ad hoc character. The issue is solved empirically rather than theoretically; whatever organizational form appears to be most important for the specific question at hand becomes the object of focus. Thus, to apply an ecological perspective to the current issue of rapid population growth, we must turn to historical processes to determine which organizational forms should be the center of attention.

We have seen that the modern character of population growth differs from that of the past in its speed, source, and resulting growth rate. It differs in another respect as well. It occurs in a world ecosystem that has come to be dominated by bureaucratic forms of organization. Max Weber was the most prominent, but certainly not the only, early twentieth-century scholar to call attention to this phenomenon and to identify some of its central elements.[9] More recently, Charles Tilly has focused attention on the rise of the state as the central phenomenon of the past four centuries. In this process it is the modern bureaucracy in both military and civil administration that provides the organizational underpinnings of the modern state.[10]

This observation places the differences between past and present patterns of rapid population growth in a new perspective. The expansion of world trade from the sixteenth century and the agricultural and industrial revolutions of the eighteenth and nineteenth centuries greatly increased the resources that could be extracted from the environment. This permitted, or was at least accompanied by, a gradual decline in mortality and a rise in population growth rates. Rapid population growth eventually slowed, of course, through a decline in fertility, completing what we now call the demographic transition. It is important to see this fertility decline as an ecological adjustment carried out by small units—individuals and families—reacting to changing economic opportunities through migration, delayed marriage, and reduced fertility within marriage. It is even more important to note that this decline in fertility often occurred against government wishes for high or sustained fertility. When political units did act to limit fertility, it was small communities that acted to restrict marriage, not to limit fertility within marriage. Marriage was still socially defined as a relationship that included the right to reproduce. Within marriage, reproduction was expected, protected, and more or less inviolate. When marital fertility did decline, it was because of a deep normative change. The small family came to be generally valued, and fertility within marriage came to be viewed as something that could be controlled.

Thus, demographic transition theory speaks of the change from "natural" to "controlled" fertility.[11]

Twentieth-century patterns are radically different. The expansion of world trade has continued, and even accelerated. Agricultural and industrial revolutions continue, also with greater speed, and they have been accompanied by a revolution in medical technology as well. This has produced the rapid decline in mortality and the higher rates of population growth the world currently experiences. There is another and even more important revolution accompanying this process. Population policy has undergone a revolution from pronatalism to antinatalism. Following from this policy revolution, governments have established family planning programs in the attempt to intervene directly in marital fertility, to increase the use of modern fertility-limiting technology, and deliberately to bring about a decline in population growth rates.

This makes demographic transition theory far less relevant for the present than it was for the past.[12] Nonetheless, social demographers still show considerable commitment to the theory, even when that theory is undergoing vast alterations in its explanations of past changes. Thus, for example, John Caldwell's recent attempt to reformulate demographic transition theory still focuses attention on normative change. As in the past, it is the spread of the small family norm, or the Western or modern reproductive norm, that is expected to be responsible for the decline of modern high fertility.[13] We do not by any means argue that Caldwell is wrong, merely that the differences observed between past and present conditions of the demographic transition have not produced a change in social demographers' theoretical commitment to norms as the organizing mechanism for fertility change.

World bureaucratization and the policy revolution suggest that the application of an ecological perspective to the current problem calls for a specification of political forms of organization as central to the analysis. It calls for a political-ecological perspective. Today it is the political forms of organization that shape, mediate, and control much, though by no means all, of the ecological response to high population growth that is occurring. We can contrast this to the kinship organization that mediated ecological responses in the past. We might say that the past response was a normative ecological response, while the current is a political ecological response.

Political organizations are those of policing power, in the broadest sense of that term. They account for the authoritative mobilization and allocation of resources, and they apply the power of a collectivity to individual behavior. Thus, political organizations represent the community, and they raise issues of the opposition of community and individual interests and rights.[14]

In focusing on political issues, we deliberately use the term *organization* rather than *institution*. This is, unfortunately, a distinction that has escaped recent works that otherwise correctly identify environmental settings that have been neglected by social demographers and are much in need of attention. For example, Geoffrey McNicoll has written perceptively of the institutional setting of modern fertility decline.[15] Although undefined by McNicoll, institutions imply broadly accepted patterns of behavior that are, like norms, nonrational, uncalculated, and accepted. They deal with such diverse issues as kinship, resource control, or property rights, and the value of children.

In speaking of political organizations rather than institutions, we wish to call attention to different mechanisms of control in human behavior. Institutions imply a deep infusion of values, a consensus on the rules of behavior. Thus, when we speak of institutional behavior, we imply behavior that is controlled, constrained, and motivated by normative consensus, or normative integration, which we do not wish to impute to modern political organizations—especially in the Third World. The use of coercion and the central place of the army and police in maintaining governments is far too common in the Third World to permit the inference of much normative consensus.

To speak of an organization implies a greater variety of mechanisms of control, as well as a greater degree of rational deliberation in the construction of the organization. Organizations are deliberately created to achieve a limited and specified set of behaviors or outcomes. This implies that the control of individual behavior to achieve the given end is a central problem to be solved in organizational creation. Control can be achieved in one or more of three ways: through coercion, or the use or threatened use of physical force; through the manipulation of material rewards; or through the manipulation of symbolic rewards.[16] The internal compliance structures used by organizations tend to be specialized and directly related to the ends to be achieved. For example, prisons and police or military organizations use force to establish order. Factories or firms manipulate physical rewards, paying workers for calculated amounts of work to produce goods and services. Churches and schools manipulate symbolic rewards, granting praise or censure to produce new cultures or pass on existing ones.

Both the organization-institution distinction, with its implications for control mechanisms, and our specification of political organizations in the mediation of the current ecological response focus attention on the types of control available and used by national governments. We shall argue that the types of control available result from relatively long and complex processes of political history. It will be necessary to examine the histories of individual governments to determine what these types are and how this affects the process of population planning. For example, we shall examine the political histories of China and India and show that they gave China far greater capacities for mass control than they gave to India. China's political past also produced a far greater potential for powerful control mechanisms in population planning, which some observers consider was at least in part responsible for China's remarkable success in fertility reduction. When India attempted to use a comparable level of control for fertility reduction during the Emergency, the result for the government was loss of power and authority.

The ecological responses mediated by political organizations are no less complex than the normative responses of individuals, but they are in some sense more visible. Political organizations establish *policies*, or formal statements of the aims of the collectivities over which they claim control. Policy formulation leads to the establishment of deliberate implementing actions, usually in the form of public programs designed to achieve the policy aims. Finally, policies and their programs are supposed to have a specific impact on the condition that is their subject. In the case of modern rapid population growth, we have witnessed the formulation of fertility-limiting policies and the formation of national family planning programs as deliberate attempts to reduce fertility. Each of these three steps has been the subject of much current analysis. What conditions produce what types of population policies? How and to what extent are antinatalist policies translated into what kinds of programmatic actions? And what is the impact on fertility of these programmatic actions? Together these questions constitute what we choose to call a political-ecological perspective. In the following chapters we attempt to put these three sets of questions together to examine some of the more important population dynamics of Asia. First, a few words on each of the three questions is is order.

Policy

Definitions of population policy are almost as numerous as their observers.[17] There is agreement only on the most general level. Population policy typically denotes stated aims of government with reference to demographic variables, including fertility, mortality, and migration.[18] Our focus will be narrower, of course, since we are concerned only with stated aims regarding fertility.

Many observers have included along with stated aims the creation of specific organizations and actions designed to implement those aims.[19] This definition is based on the argument that stated aims are cheap; official policy statements can easily be made and do not constitute "real" policies. Again, we shall use a narrower concept, focusing on aims alone and leaving the issue of implementation for separate consideration. We believe that stated aims do have a significant independent meaning and can be effectively analyzed by themselves. This is a task we undertake in chapter 2.

Policies regarding fertility have undergone recent and dramatic changes from pronatalism to antinatalism. Most governments throughout most human history have been pronatalist. People have been considered a resource to be taxed, worked, and sent to war. More people have been considered better than few, and stated aims have commonly been to increase their numbers. Pronatalism has been the rule rather than the exception in political history. When India included a fertility-limiting aim in its First Five-Year Plan in 1952, it became the first country to enunciate an official antinatalist policy. It was far from the last, however. In the ensuing three decades most governments of the Third World followed India and announced policies that included some form of fertility limitation as the aim. By far the largest portion of the population of the Third World, over 90 percent, is today under the rule of governments that explicitly aim to limit fertility.[20]

The timing of these policy decisions varies considerably, even though the time span is a mere thirty years. The source of the policy change also varies. Some governments, such as those in India and China, came to the decision largely on the basis of their own internal processes. Others appear to have been highly influenced by external pressures from the world community as a whole and from specific members of that community. Policies also vary in scope. Some are narrowly focused on fertility limitation, largely for reasons of national economic development, or solely for reasons of individual maternal and child health. Other governments include fertility limitation as an integral part of complex and variegated policies for governance and change.

This rich variance raises important questions about the causes and effects of policies. It also permits analysis that can help to answer these questions. Our political-ecological perspective suggests that the causes of fertility-limiting policy formation will lie in some combination of growing ecological pressures and some type of political change or development. In chapter 2 we shall show that Asia experienced an earlier and more rapid development of fertility-limiting policies than have the world's other high fertility regions: Latin America, Africa, and the southern and eastern rim of the Mediterranean. We shall also show that Asia's advanced condition can be explained in part by its higher population density, which is a crude indicator of ecological pressure. It can also be explained by a distinctive historical process in which Western imperialism and colonialism and Asian nationalism led to strong commitments to policies of national economic development. Of especial importance in this process was the creation and growth of organizations specifically designed to produce information and to monitor the social and economic condition of the population under the control of the government.

Implementation

The most common implementing action for fertility-limiting policies has been the creation of national family planning programs. These are formal organizations specifically charged with distributing the available fertility-limiting technology. This technology has experienced something approaching a breakthrough in the very recent past. The intrauterine contraceptive device (IUD) and the oral contraceptive pill are two of the most dramatic developments, which have become widely available only in the past two decades. They have also been complemented by spermacidal chemicals, injectables, cheaper and higher quality condoms, and simpler and safer surgical techniques for sterilization and abortion. That is, the stock of cheap and effective noncoitally specific fertility-limiting methods has been significantly improved.

The technological development has itself had a deep impact on implementing actions. The technology is highly effective, portable, and inexpensive. This has encouraged governments to adopt policies and create distributive programs aimed at reaching couples in their childbearing years. If rapid population growth came to be perceived by governments as detrimental to other aims, this specific programmatic action offered the hope that something could actually be done about the problem. It also offered a type of direct action with which governments were familiar. Medical and public health programs have been part of the normal stock of government activities for a few generations. Further, the rapid declines in mortality recently experienced by most of the Third World were brought about in large part through public programs that carried a new and highly portable mortality-limiting technology to mass populations. In effect, it was easy to decide to attack fertility directly when a technology became available that was both familiar and could use familiar distributive systems.

The new fertility-limiting technology has another important aspect as well. It has a decidedly medical, and more importantly a Western medical, character. Chemicals, needles, and knives intruding into the human body have come to be developed and extensively controlled by the medical profession. Further, this profession is unique in having what can be called public access to private parts. All societies define the genitalia as in some sense private, though there is immense variety in the costumes and symbols used to denote private parts. The medical profession is virtually alone in having legitimate impersonal, or public, access to these parts.

This distinctive character of the new technology has meant that the medical profession and medical organizations must have an important place in the programs of policy implementation. The political-ecological perspective leads to the expectation that these location decisions in policy implementation will be political issues. Therefore, they will be in part the object of some controversy as organizations compete for resources from their environment. Finkle and Crane have shown that the role of the World Health Organization in fertility limitation can best be explained from this type of focus.[21] They show that the WHO initially resisted open consideration of fertility limitation as a part of international technical assistance, insisting that the issue was a socioeconomic rather than a health issue. Once the United Nations did make a formal decision for fertility limitation in technical assistance, however, the WHO urged that it, and the medical profession it represented, should have substantial control over the programing.

Like policies, programs vary considerably, presenting both problems and possibilities for analysis. National family planning programs differ in the character of the distribution they undertake. Some use passive clinical tactics to make the new technology available; others are much more active in attempting to persuade people to use the technology. Some use monetary or other material incentives, and some have used coercion. That is, the observable distributive tactics employ the full range of control mechanisms available to organizations. This has become an important public issue, of course, and most explicit policy today proposes that distribution be noncoercive and that acceptance be voluntary.[22] There remains, however, real variance in the control tactics used in family planning, and this calls for analysis.

Programs also vary in the range of the fertility-limiting technology they use. Few use the full range available. As we show later, India relies primarily on sterilization techniques, while Malaysia depends almost exclusively on the oral contraceptive. Taiwan and Korea began their programs in the early 1960s with heavy reliance on the IUD. They later experienced increases in the use of the oral contraceptive, though they are still distinctive for their extensive use of the IUD along with orals. This variance has gone almost completely unanalyzed by the social scientific community that lavishes so much attention on family planning programs and fertility change. There is also variance in the use of abortion for fertility limitation. Muramatsu shows in the afterword to this work that Japan's extensive use of legal abortion in its immediate post-World War II period of rapid fertility decline was in part a deliberate policy. It was a policy decision facilitated by less cultural resistance to abortion than we find in many societies. He also shows that the abortion policy was related to the unavailability of alternatives. Japan's fertility declined before the major breakthroughs in the new contraceptive technology.

Our political-ecological perspective leads us to examine the variance in family planning programs and to search for the determinants of this variance in the political and administrative systems of which they are an integral part. This represents a set of problems located on what has come to be called the supply side of the fertility problem, but to deal with this set of issues, it is better to turn to impact, the third step in our approach.

Impact

There has been much debate, discussion, and analysis concerning the impact of family planning programs on fertility. The conceptual and methodological problems of identifying a specific impact from a particular program are formidable, and it is fair to say that they have not yet been solved. The technical problem of disentangling effects has its counterpart in the lines drawn in the debate. The simplest line is between the supply side and the demand side of fertility-limiting behavior.[23] On the demand side is the argument that individual social and economic conditions determine the individual demand for fertility limitation. It is argued that fertility will not decline until individual demand increases. This will require major social and economic changes that are somewhat comparable to the urbanization, industrialization, education, and rising living standards that were often associated with fertility decline in the past demographic tradition.

This argument was explicitly developed in policy and ideological terms at the Bucharest Conference in 1974, where it came to be known as the redistributive position. It was earlier stated in more scientific form by Kingsley Davis in a 1967 article in *Science* magazine.[24] Davis also pointed to one of the issues that subsequently became an important element in both development and fertility policy, the role of women. When social conditions provide women with viable alternatives to childbearing, fertility will decline. Thus, education and employment for women and their general emancipation become important programmatic elements in the implementation of fertility-limiting policies. This, of course, complicates the analytical problems of identifying impact, for educational and employment policies and programs are usually undertaken for other than demographic reasons. There is more in policy and program impact on fertility than simply antinatalism and family planning.

The supply side argues that there is already a substantial unmet demand for fertility limitation. Three types of evidence are used to support this position. One is the observation of the extensive use of abortion, despite its illegality, pain, and danger to many women.[25] The second comes from many surveys that show substantial proportions of women who report not wanting any more children, and yet who do not practice fertility control.[26] The third comes from the observed rapid growth of family planning program acceptors soon after program formation in many countries.[27] The major proponents of the supply side argument are found in national and international population and family planning organizations. R. T. Ravenholt, for many years director of the United States

Agency for International Development's Office of Population, became one of the most outspoken advocates of this position.

The sides of this argument can be distinguished conceptually, but individuals and states have shown both ambivalence and dramatic switches in the positions they have taken. During the 1950s much development effort was dominated by an enthusiasm for growth, and there was little interest in the supply side of the fertility issue. This changed radically in the 1960s, when family planning and the supply side gained great momentum, only to be reversed again at Bucharest in 1974. During the 1950s the United States rejected supply side appeals, while the Scandinavian countries, India, and Sri Lanka made strong arguments for assistance in family planning. Individuals have made some of the most dramatic shifts. For example, at Bucharest Karan Singh of India and the Chinese delegates countered the Western nations' zealous promotion of family planning programs with the argument that "development is the best contraceptive." Just two years later, as minister for health and family planning during India's Emergency, Singh argued that the urgent need for fertility limitation was too great to wait for development, and that more direct, and more draconian, measures were required. Today it is the Chinese leaders who appear to see great urgency and to be solidly on the supply side of this debate.[28]

The ideological element of the debate will not be resolved, it will only lose salience, as it did in the past. It is striking to note that the ideological elements of the debate at Bucharest were very similar to the lines drawn between Malthus and Godwin nearly two centuries earlier. It is often forgotten that Malthus directed his first essay at the optimistic and reformistic vision of William Godwin, and that this touched off a debate that raged for two decades into the nineteenth century, drawing lines between conservative and progressive orientations to the world.[29] Godwin represented the progressive, falling on what would be called the demand side today. He proposed extensive reforms in social institutions, especially for greater equality in the distribution of wealth and power. With such reforms, and what he believed to be the inevitable progress of the human race, the problem of rapid population growth would be solved through the rational and humane actions of individuals. Malthus argued that population growth would obstruct human progress and that the solution lay in individual restraint: later marriage and abstinence in the marriage bed. This does not place Malthus on the supply side of the current debate, of course, since he opposed what he considered vicious artificial actions that permit the enjoyment of sex without accepting its responsibilities. Nonetheless, the historical development from Malthus did move directly to family planning, supplying information and services to permit individuals to limit their fertility more effectively. In any event, the Malthus-Godwin debate that raged in England for the first part of the nineteenth century was not resolved; it simply lost salience, arising again only in the current setting of rapid population growth.

The analytical element of the debate continues and may perhaps be at least partially resolved. Freedman and Berelson, Berelson and Mauldin, and Srikantan[30] have used multiple regression techniques in cross-national studies to show that family planning programs do have some independent impact on fertility decline, but that the effect is not as great as that of the level of social and economic development. We have used the same strategies in chapters 3 and 4 to suggest that among the states of India and among the countries of Asia roughly the same combination of effects can be observed. The level of social and economic development, or the conditions on the demand side, have a substantial independent impact on fertility decline. The strength of family planning programs, however, can also be seen to bring about fertility decline. As in the previous studies, the family planning impact is substantial, but it is not as great as that of social and economic development. Although this moves toward some resolution of the analytical elements of the debate, questions remain.

Hernandez has reviewed most of the empirical studies that attempt to show some independent effect of family planning programs and has concluded that they are all conceptually and methodologically flawed.[31] If family planning programs do have an impact on fertility, it is yet to be conclusively demonstrated. There is, however, a growing compromise position, which holds that both advanced levels of social and economic conditions and a well-developed family planning program have had substantial influence in reducing fertility in many parts of the Third World.[32]

The following study provides support for the compromise position, but we do not claim the support is in any sense conclusive. This is largely because we do not attempt to develop a full theory of fertility decline. Our aim is more modest; we are concerned with the neglect of political and organizational factors in current population analysis. We attempt to make up for some of that neglect with the development of an explicit perspective that brings these issues to the center of attention. We hope to show here that this perspective can help to make sense of what we consider to be major events of our time: the antinatalist policy revolution and the pervasive growth of national family planning programs.

COMMUNITIES

The unit of ecological analysis is the ecosystem. This is the system within which populations and environments interact in a dynamic and adaptive process. The boundaries of the ecosystem, like the organization through which adaptation takes place, are defined more by empirical than by theoretical considerations. They are, in effect, the boundaries of the populations that are the object of the analysis. They are unspecified in theory, except with reference to populations and to the organizational mechanisms by which populations adapt to their environments.

The political-ecological perspective implies that the ecosystem's boundaries will be defined with reference to political organizations. For the world as a whole, we can identify two types of communities that are of especial concern. These are the modern nation state and the emerging world community. This does not by any means exhaust the list of effective communities that can set the boundaries of our units of analysis, but we believe they are by far the most important.

If the adaptive actions of political organizations are visible, this is because they are the explicit policies of nation states, translated into programs by the common administrative apparatus by which states carry out their actions. The policy revolution that we have witnessed is a revolution of the stated aims of national governments, and the programs that are designed to achieve those aims are national family planning programs. Thus, the nation state constitutes one of the most important communities within which we can observe ecological responses and adaptations.

It is not the only community of interest, however. Out of the interactions of nation states, we have seen the emergence of a world community organization. This is a multidimensional community, to be sure, with bilateral, regional, and worldwide groupings and a wide variety of types of organizations that operate within specific ecological niches. We cannot begin to capture the immense complexity of this entire community, but we can begin to assess the ecological responses to rapid population growth by focusing attention on those subcommunities and organizational networks that have been most actively involved in the current response.

One of the most important of the international communities, of course, is that defined by the existence of the United Nations. We shall be concerned with the role of that organization in the ecological response, and also with its Specialized Agencies and regional economic commissions. In addition, there is a relatively limited range of industrial states, foundations, and voluntary associations that have been active in population planning. They will play a substantial role in the story we shall tell of the Asian experience.

There is an alternate conceptual strategy for defining the boundaries of the ecosystem. What can be called a world economy perspective has recently gained considerable vogue.[33] Its proponents view the world, especially with the rise of Western dominance since the sixteenth century, as a system increasingly integrated by a capitalist economic system. It is marked by a subset of core industrialized states whose wealth is dependent upon extraction of capital from poorer, periphery states, and who depend in part upon another subset of semiperiphery states for both stability and the transfer of capital.

The world economy perspective has a great deal to recommend it. In taking us beyond the boundaries of individual states, it provides some explanations for the failures of some national economic development activities and focuses much-needed attention on the character of the larger world system in which states act. This is similar to our point of view in one important respect, that of power distributions. The world economy perspective tends to see the stratification of nation states much as Marx viewed the stratification of peoples. Power is based on the control of production; it is held by the wealthy and used for their own protection in a persistent struggle against the poor. Thus, wealthy nations are seen at the top of the world economy, using their power to extract wealth from poor nations and to keep them poor against their demands and struggles for greater equality. We see power distribution as more multipolar and more fluid, with different coalitions forming around different issues in a less easily defined manner.

In population planning, the world economy perspective provides a distinctive and provocative point of view.[34] Population planning appears as a strategy of the wealthy core states to maintain control over the poorer periphery states. It aims not at an adaptation that can increase human productivity and welfare among the poorer populations, but at sustaining the wealth of the core states, which in turn requires the continued poverty or underdevelopment of the periphery.

It is not difficult to find evidence to support this view of population planning, as Bondestam and Bergstroem have done. We find it far from compelling, however, because it fails to explain important similarities and differences in both national and international policies and programs. United States foreign assistance policy from 1966 to 1974 is explained, but not the policy prior to 1965, nor even that of the most recent period. It is not easy to explain the earlier Scandinavian pressure for assistance, nor the more recent Swedish positions. The reversal of India from Bucharest to the Emergency might be explained with reference to fascism and dependence on Western industrial states, but the government's subsequent loss of power at the polls fits less well. Similarly, the changing positions of China do not fit well with a perspective that sees population planning largely as an instrument of control in the persistent war of the poor against the rich. Nor does such a point of view help to explain the homogenization of official population policies and actual programs that the world has experienced over the past three decades.[35]

It may well be that a world economy position will ultimately make better sense of current Third World population dynamics than our political-ecological perspective, but we do not believe it does so at present. Certainly one way to determine which concept provides the most understanding is to pursue each as far as it will take us. We begin here with the attempt to comprehend the political-ecological perspective in Asia.

2

Population Policy: The Antinatalist Revolution

THE RELEVANCE OF POLICY CHANGE

W e have argued that the change in official government policy from pronatalism to antinatalism is sufficiently profound to warrant its characterization as a policy revolution. Although at close perspective the change may appear slow, in the broader historical context it has indeed been revolutionary. In effect, it has taken only a single generation to reverse political orientations that are as old as government itself. Here we wish to show that this revolution has been in large part centered in Asia, and that it has grown out of a long historical process that has given Asia a leading position in what we call the political-ecological adjustment.

The first step in this adjustment involves policy change. It is often noted that policy statements are easy to make and do not necessarily imply that relevant implementing actions will follow. Therefore the mere observation of stated changes in policies will be an insufficient base from which to draw serious inferences. This may be true, but we find the argument less than compelling because we can show that even these statements of aims are systematically related to other significant environmental conditions. That is, they are ecologically relevant facts. We shall show in three ways that these policy changes are not simply randomly distributed. First, we can show that as a region Asia moved more rapidly to policy changes than did other major high-fertility regions—Latin America, Africa, and the southern and eastern Mediterranean world. Second, we can show that population density, a critical ecological variable, is systematically related to the policy changes we observe. Finally, we can show that the content, which constitutes the public image of the policy changes, differs between regions in ways that are understandably related to the specific values and institutions of the regions.

18

LOGISTIC MAPPING

The specific political organizational actions for population policy making are almost infinitely varied. It is possible, however, to bring some order to this variety by using the simple three-part classification developed by the Population Council for its annual assessments of the world's population programs.[1] Nations can have both a public antinatalist policy and a program to promote fertility limitation; they can support programs without having an official antinatalist policy; or they can have neither policy nor program. Thus, the three positions can be roughly ranked (a) Official Antinatalist Policy and Program, (b) Program Support without Official Policy, and (c) Neither Antinatalist Policy nor Program.

We can use the model of the logistic curve to examine the movement over time of populations organized under these three policy categories. The curve describes a general process by which populations fill up new territories, or by which the human species has often developed and adopted new technologies, which change the character of its environment. Thus, the logistic mapping of political events provides an instrument suitable for the analysis of political-ecological adjustment. We present a series of logistic curves in figure 2.1, which indicate that Asian populations entered into the political-ecological adjustment earlier than did populations in other regions of high fertility.

The logistic curves in figure 2.1 and the distributions in table 2.1 show that Asia entered the process of antinatalist policy formation earlier than did the other regions. India was the first country to include an explicit antinatalist policy in its five-year development plans. It was followed shortly by Pakistan and China.

The years 1966–1967 represent a major watershed in policy formation at the level of the world community. It was then that the United Nations passed a formal resolution that legitimized the inclusion of fertility limitation programs in technical assistance. It was also in those years that the United States, the major world donor of technical assistance, reversed its previous policy and provided funds for fertility limitation.

By 1966, twelve out of twenty-two Asian nations had themselves made antinatalist policy decisions. In contrast, only four of the twenty-six Latin American nations, three of the forty African nations, and three of the eighteen Mediterranean nations had made similar decisions.[2] Thus, not only was Asia earlier than the other high-fertility regions, but it reached its conclusions before the world community had made this change. We infer from this that Asian nations made their antinatalist policy decisions largely from forces internal to the nations themselves. To a far greater extent, such decisions in the other regions were the result of influences from the larger world community. Not only were Asian nations earlier in this process, they were also leaders in moving the rest of the world

Figure 2.1   Percent of High Fertility Countries with Fertility-Limiting Programs
by Major World Region and Date of Policy Decision

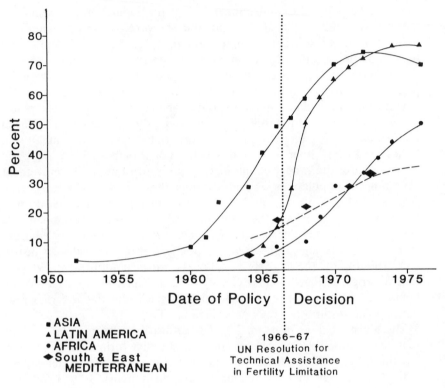

Source: See Table 2.1

community to make this significant policy adjustment. As we shall note
later in this chapter, Asian nations benefited considerably from world
community decisions, since these helped to mobilize resources for Asian
fertility-limiting programs.

It seems clear, then, that Asia has led the high-fertility world in making
the change to official antinatalist policies. Implementation and impact are
other matters, however, which we cannot deal with effectively at this
regional level of aggregation. It has been observed that between 1965 and
1975 Asia had more rapid declines in both crude birth rates and rates of
natural increase than the other regions.[3] We hesitate, however, to link
this with policy decisions or program implementation, since the variance
within the regions is substantial, and policy is by no means the sole, or
even the major, determinant of fertility. In subsequent chapters we shall

TABLE 2.1
The World's High-Fertility Countries, with Dates and Types of Population Policy Decisions by Major World Region

	Countries with Fertility Limitation Policies or Programs			
Year	Asia	Latin America	Africa	South and East Mediterranean
1952	India A			
1960	Pakistan A (Bangladesh 1971 A)			
1961	S. Korea A			
1962	China A Fiji A Vietnam A	Cuba B		Tunisia A
1964	Taiwan B (1968 A)			
1965	Sri Lanka A Singapore A Hong Kong B (1973 A)	Chile B	Mauritius A	Turkey A Egypt A
1966	Malaysia A Nepal A	Jamaica A Honduras B	Kenya A S. Africa B	
1967	Iran A	Barbados A Nicaragua B Trinidad and Tobago A		
1968	Indonesia A Papua New Guinea B	Bolivia B (1976 A) Costa Rica B Domin. Rep. A Ecuador B Venezuela B El Salvador B (1974 A)	Zimbabwe B	Morocco A
1969		Panama B Guatemala B (1974 A)	Benin B Gambia B Ghana A	
1970	Philippines A Thailand A			
1971		Haiti B		Algeria B
1972	Laos A (1976 C)	Paraguay B	Mali B Uganda B	Iraq B
1973			Liberia B Zaire B	
1975		Brazil A Mexico A	Lesotho B Zambia B Togo B	
1976		Peru B	Senegal B	
Subtotal	17	20	15	6

TABLE 2.1—*Continued*

	Countries without Fertility Limitation Policies or Programs		
Asia	Latin America	Africa	South and East Mediterranean
Burma, Bhutan	Bahamas	Angola	Bahrain
Kampuchea,	Guyana	Burundi	Dem. Yemen
(Laos 1976)	Surinam	Chad, Congo	Jordan
Mongolia	Uruguay	Central Af. Rep.	Kuwait
N. Korea	Bolivia	Eq. Guinea	Lebanon
		Cameroon	Libya
		Ethiopia	Oman
		Gabon	Qatar
		Guinea	Saudi Arabia
		Ivory Coast	Syria
		Madagascar	U. A. Emirates
		Mauritania	Yemen
		Malawi	
		Mozambique	
		Niger, Rawanda	
		Sierra Leone	
		Somalia	
		Swaziland	
		Upper Volta	
Subtotal 6	5	21	12
Grand Total 22*	25	36	18

Sources: The list of countries is derived primarily from the United Nations list, to which North Korea, Taiwan, and Vietnam have been added. Dates for decisions have been taken largely from Nortman, *Factbook,* years 1970 through 1978.

*Laos appears twice in the subtotals, but is counted only once in the grand total.

A Indicates countries that have made official antinatalist policy decisions and provide programmatic support for fertility limitation.

B Indicates countries that provide public support for fertility limitation but have not made an official antinatalist policy statement.

C Indicates no antinatalist policy and no program support.

attempt to examine these linkages in greater detail when we compare countries, but at this regional level it is best to be content with explaining the clearer and less ambiguous differences in policy decisions.

A POLITICAL-ECOLOGICAL PERSPECTIVE ON ASIAN POLICY CHANGE: DENSITY, LEGITIMACY, AND NEW NATION STATUS

In explaining Asia's more advanced position in the political-ecological adjustment we can also provide a more detailed exposition of the adjustment itself. Our explanation contains three major arguments, which focus on population density, the legitimacy of public fertility limitation policies, and, most important, the specific set of historical conditions subsumed under the rubric of the distinctive new nation status found in Asia. It is especially in the latter that we see the roots of the distinctively political aspect of current ecological adjustment.

Population Density

In ecological analyses, density is a variable of great significance. Density of a species usually increases under favorable environmental conditions. As it increases, fundamental changes often occur, especially in patterns of reproductive behavior. In the organization of animal behavior these changes can be quite dramatic, as Calhoun has shown in his experiments with rats, and as others have demonstrated with humans.[4]

In table 2.2 we show population densities for the 108 high-fertility states listed in table 2.1. Densities in persons per square kilometer are shown for states with and without population-planning programs by region.

There are three important conditions to observe from this table. First, median and mean levels of population density are considerably higher for Asia than for the other three regions. Second, for all states together median and mean densities are higher among those that have adopted fertility limitation policies than among those that have not. Finally, this relationship holds for each of the regions considered separately. The only exception to this pattern is in the Mediterranean states, where the mean, but not median, density is higher among the states without population policies: 70, as against 32 for those with policies. This higher mean level, however, is largely produced by the relatively high density of Lebanon (268) and Bahrain (391). If these are excluded from the calculation, the mean is only 18, which is considerably below the mean for the states with population policies.

This analysis suggests the hypothesis that population policy decisions reflect an adjustment to high population density. Thus, Asia's more advanced position in the political-ecological adjustment may simply be caused by its higher level of population density. There are three problems raised by this hypothesis, however. First, high population density does not appear to be either a necessary or a sufficient condition for the policy decisions, since the ranges of densities overlap considerably among states with and without appropriate policies. States with quite low density levels (for example, Malaysia) have made the political decision to control population growth, and others with high levels (for example, North Korea) have not.

Second, from an ecological perspective many different patterns of adjustment are possible in the face of high and growing density. Populations can experience rapid outmigration, a rise in the death rate, a decline in

TABLE 2.2
Population Density (Persons per Square Kilometer) for 101 High-Fertility States by
Population Policy Decision and Region (1975)

	Asia	Latin America	Africa	Mediterranean	Total
States with antinatalist policy or program	$(N = 17)$	$(N = 20)$	$(N = 15)$	$(N = 6)$	$(N = 58)$
Range	20–4,066	5–566	1–426	7–49	1–4,066
Median	88	29	24	35	39
Mean	573	99	52	32	223
States without antinatalist policy or program	$(N = 5)$	$(N = 5)$	$(N = 21)$	$(N = 12)$	$(N = 44)$
Range	1–128	3–17	1–157	1–391	1–391
Median	45	12	13	16	16
Mean	40	10	25	70	36
All states	$(N = 22)$	$(N = 25)$	$(N = 36)$	$(N = 18)$	$(N = 101)$
Range	1–4,066	3–566	1–426	1–391	1–4,066
Median	86	26	22	30	30
Mean	424	82	36	57	138

Source: United Nations, *1975 Statistical Yearbook,* table 18, pp. 67–68 for density data; and table 2.1 above for country program information. (Means used are unweighted means.)

fertility, or some combination of the three, either independent of or directed by the political organization. Thus, the density-policy link must be mediated by other socioeconomic and political conditions.

Finally, we must determine the causal connections between population density and any specific adjustment through changing behavior patterns. Since the political-ecological adjustment implies a decision process by the population's authoritative organizations, we should expect the organic links to include processes of organized perception and decision making. Spelling out these connections in detail leads us to a fuller exposition of the political-ecological adjustment.

Legitimacy

Asia does not contain salient values that render illegitimate public programing for fertility limitation. This is especially important in contrast to Latin America. In an extensive review of national value systems and population control in Latin America, J. M. Stycos has shown how pervasive is the opposition to family planning.[5] He distinguishes three major elite groups concerned with social change: conservatives, social reformers, and revolutionaries. Conservatives, who might be expected to promote family planning to reduce pressures for change, oppose family planning largely from a commitment to orthodox Roman Catholic values.

Stycos states that revolutionaries oppose population control either from a strict Marxian opposition to the Malthusian formulation, or from an equally strict Marxian objection to any type of social reform that reduces pressures for a more radical change. Finally, Stycos says, the reformers have been the most supportive of fertility-limitation, but even this group shows some opposition, due to suspicions of the motives of the United States in its emphasis upon family planning in recent foreign aid programs. Thus, conservative religious values, revolutionary values, and anti-United States sentiment draw together a wide variety of highly diverse elite groups in opposition to explicit fertility-limiting policies.

Latin American opposition is reflected in the peculiar distribution of countries by the type of policy. Figure 2.2 shows that Latin America currently has a high proportion of countries with support, but no public policy, for fertility control. Chile provides an excellent example of a progressive government that made an implicit commitment to fertility limitation programing as early as 1965, but found it prudent not to make a specific public policy pronouncement to this effect.[6] Without the value constraints of Latin America, Asian governments have shown little reticence in officially proclaiming what they intend in population programing.

Stycos also notes that Latin American leaders have changed rapidly and significantly in favor of fertility limitation in the past decade. This is reflected in our logistic mapping in figure 2.1, which shows a rapid shift to support for family planning in Latin America after 1967. At the same time, Stycos questions how effective the commitment of Latin American leaders will be. He observes the underlying opposition and the incomplete commitment that is reflected in the small number of statesmen willing to give public policy support to family planning. He sees the programs, even as late as 1970, to be "more symbolic than substantive," and he argues, as we do, that "successful family planning programs require a substantial degree of commitment on the part of strategic groups in the leader class." Finally, Stycos argues that in Latin America the general public is in a greater state of readiness than are the leaders for serious collective fertility limitation policies.[7]

The major religions of Asia—Hinduism, Buddhism, Confucianism, Taoism, and to a lesser extent, Islam—have either been silent on the issue of fertility control or at least have not presented the same highly organized and dogmatic opposition that is associated with Roman Catholicism. Whether the Chinese religions or some other set of values is primarily responsible for the apparently persistent desire of families for sons, and the extent to which this poses an obstacle to family planning programs, is not known. Freedman has found a preference for sons among urbanized and industrialized American populations, and the Asian preference may be as much the result of longstanding attachments to land as the result of any religious element such as ancestor worship. In any

Figure 2.2   Proportion of Countries with Different Population Policy Positions
by Region (1975)

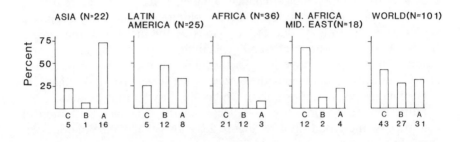

(Positions: C – no stated antinatalist policy, and no program

B – population control program but no stated
antinatalist policy

A – stated antinatinatalist policy and program)

Source: See Table 2.1

event, even in this case, the obstacle operates at the level of the individual and the family and not necessarily at the collective or political level.
That is, on the substantive issue of fertility control there appears to be a
clearer separation of secular and sacred power systems in Asia than in
Latin America.

Where Islam has presented a political obstacle to family planning programs, as it appears to have done in Malaysia,[8] the issue is less a religious
one and more one of ethnic conflict in the arena of the state. In Indonesia, Islam as an organized value force appears to have tempered only
slightly a strong central political commitment to family planning programs. In Pakistan and Bangladesh, and more recently in Iran, Islam, *as
it is interpreted*, may have a dampening effect on family planning. Still,
the obstruction appears more the result of local interpretations and does
not emanate from a central political unit, as it does in Roman Catholic
environments. Thus, overall Asia has the advantage that religious value
systems have not presented serious obstacles to public programing for
fertility limitation.

New Nation Status

We find the most important explanation and the fullest exposition of the
political-ecological character of the current adjustments to lie in the dis-

tinctive character of Asian nations as new nations. In this we follow Shils's[9] early usage in part, but we diverge from his views in arguing that new nation status in Asia is quite different from that in Africa. Further, we argue that this difference is important in determining the character and timing of the political-ecological adjustment.

New nation status as we conceive of it here represents not a static condition, but a dynamic cumulating set of conditions increasingly favorable to the political-ecological adjustment we observe. These conditions appeared over time as part of a pervasive historical process, the growth and demise of modern colonialism in Asia. In this process, conditions led to and built upon one another in a cumulative fashion to produce both a specific historical process and a current set of conditions that are distinctive to Asian nations, and which help account for the type of adjustments now being made.

We present this historical process in ideal-typical fashion to analyze the distinctive elements responsible for the adjustment, but we recognize that not all nations followed this process in the same way or at the same time. Thailand and Iran remained at least nominally independent through the rush of colonialism at the end of the nineteenth century, though they were deeply affected by the forces of colonial expansion. Additional variations within the region will become apparent and will receive special attention later, but we can proceed most fruitfully by considering the process as an ideal-typical abstraction in which the important distinctions to be made are those with Africa and Latin America.

In summary, we argue that (a) the greater penetration of modern colonialism in Asia produced (b) a more powerful mass nationalist movement, which led to (c) a strong political and organizational commitment to economic development and centralized development planning (usually, but not necessarily, in a nonrevolutionary setting), which in turn led to (d) the development of political-organizational competence and activity in economic planning, which finally led to (e) political decisions for family planning coming from economic planning centers, justified largely by macroeconomic arguments, and calling for the use of government organizations to promote fertility control. This is essentially the character of the political-ecological adjustment we observe in an advanced state in Asia. It will be useful to present the steps in this process in somewhat greater detail.

The penetration of modern colonialism. Broad distinctions can be made between two different organizational carriers of imperialism. Monarchic mercantilist organizations, conquistadors, and the crown carried imperialism from the Iberian peninsula to Central and South America. In contrast, capitalist companies from northwestern Europe were the organizational carriers of imperialism to Asia and Africa. The predominance of the latter distinguishes modern (nineteenth- and twentieth-century) colonialism. The former especially marks the colonial experience of Latin America, which came to an end in its specifically political form early in the nineteenth century before the great rush of modern colonialism carried by capitalist companies.

Although the capitalist companies of Europe began trading activities in Africa and Asia early in the seventeenth century, the process of penetration was much more rapid in Asia. By the middle of the nineteenth century, Western penetration into Africa was limited to a small area in South Africa and a few additional coastal positions. By the same time in Asia, both India and the Netherlands Indies formed vigorous centers of colonial penetration from which the highly accelerated territorial acquisition of the late nineteenth century brought all of Asia under Western political domination.

Modern colonialism everywhere, but again in a more advanced state in Asia than in Africa, proceeded to build organizations of dominance with a powerful economic rationality. It is here that we see a clear indication of what Max Weber called the overwhelming technical superiority of bureaucratic organization. Revenue collection, land registration, police and military operations, trading activities, and finally massive mining and plantation systems all proceeded in increasingly bureaucratic, that is, calculable, fashion.

Even prior to the modern thrust of colonialism, the differences between the capitalist and the monarchic-mercantilist organizational carriers can be seen in the sugar economies of Central America. Territories under the control of capitalist companies, such as Barbados, Trinidad, and Jamaica, moved more quickly to an exclusive sugar plantation economy than did either Puerto Rico or Cuba, which were organized under monarchic mercantilist organizational forms.[10]

Modern colonial penetration brought four major changes in social organization in all cases, though again, in varying degrees in different territories. First, conceptions of legitimate authority changed from what Stokes has called the divine right of kings to the divine right of masses.[11] The consent of the governed was a political legitimizing formula born and nurtured in the metropolitan nations of the West. It was carried, albeit in altered form, to the colonial territories by the modern administrative structure (government, courts, and schools) established by the colonial masters. The new concepts of legitimacy ultimately provided ideological weapons for colonial nationalist movements, striking the metropolitan powers where they were most vulnerable. Such concepts greatly aided the struggle for independence and were themselves reinforced by the winning of independence. They thus set the stage for mass mobilizations, both during the struggle for independence and in the political orientations of the postindependence period.

The revolutionary transformation of legitimizing formulas is seen nowhere more dramatically than in India. The attempt in the Sepoy Mutiny to reestablish the old Moghul court rule in 1857 failed utterly. A generation later the Congress Party was born, whose first demands were for more places for Indians in the *colonial* civil service. These initial demands grew logically and inexorably into demand for self-government.

Second, the specific organization of dominance changed with the colonial penetration. The change involved a growth in both the extent and the scope of power exercised by the central authority over the population. It made little difference whether the colonial masters found collaborators among the indigenous ruling groups, in whose name the new masters exercised indirect rule, or whether the indigenous rulers were eliminated and replaced by direct colonial authority. Everywhere colonialism brought a greater thrusting of central authority into previously isolated areas. The scope of dominance also increased as authoritative organizations became increasingly differentiated. This extended the "legitimate" functions of government far beyond those limited to revenue collection and defense to include such things as education, public health, public works, and extensive economic controls.

Third, colonial penetration changed the character of elite organization. Where traditional authoritative structures were left more or less intact, the elites of these structures gained increased opportunities for action through education, travel, and economic advancement. In addition, modern colonialism brought dramatic economic development, however unbalanced and foreign-dominated, and this meant new opportunities for upward mobility for the lower classes. Finally, colonialism often brought immigration of new ethnic groups, producing even more opportunities for upward mobility and thus an increasing differentiation of elites. This overall enlargement and differentiation of elites brought demands in the colonial territories for broadening the scope of opportunities, thus reinforcing the demands for continuing expansion of government. It also produced considerable variance in the specific mixture of demands for modernization found in the new states in the post-independence period. This will be seen to have had a powerful impact on specific political decisions on population policy.

Finally, colonial penetration changed the economic base of large portions of the populations in colonial territories. In many cases, colonialism destroyed traditional native productive and trading networks. In virtually all instances these were, however, replaced by a far more powerful extension of modern networks. Plantation economies, modern mining activities, the increasing commercialization of agriculture, and the penetration of modern manufactured products were all a part of market development, which broke the economic isolation of large portions of populations previously organized in primarily subsistence economies.

The rise of modern nationalism. Modern nationalism in Asia and Africa was a natural outgrowth of modern colonialism. Nationalist movements in all cases built upon the new social and economic organization that colonialism produced and focused collective activity on targets provided by the colonial authorities in the form of modern bureaucratic administration. Further, the nationalist movements took over the ideologies and political theories of the metropolitan masters and developed these in two directions. Toward the masses the new indigenous elites used Western ideologies for the mass mobilization that would be required to achieve independence. Toward the colonial masters the new elites used Western ideologies in the demand for self-government.

To the extent that colonialism broke down local isolation and drew heterogeneous primordial groups into a single administrative structure, it provided a social base on which nationalist leaders could mobilize large populations. To be sure, nationalist mobilization efforts often contained elements of primordial identities, and it has not been uncommon for these movements to fracture into conflicting ethnic or linguistic groups following independence. Even this fracturing, however, serves to underscore the fact that the nationalist struggle for independence did indeed weld together disparate groups in a modern form of organization.

Nationalist elites likewise are products of modern colonialism. Whether their roots lay in the high or low status groups of the precolonial period (contrast the Brahminical background of Nehru with the untouchable background of Ambedkar), the new elites emerged through the educational institutions and occupational positions created by colonial rule. The economic growth produced by colonial rule provided the resources for the development of this new elite. The growth also created resources that could be channeled into modern means of communication—newspapers and later the radio—by which the new elites could come into contact with one another and could also build up a mass base of followers.

The administrative structures built by the colonial rulers provided attractive targets for the activity of the nationalist movements. Here were effective structures of authority in which nationalist elites could first demand positions on the grounds of technical capacity, the grounds on which recruitment to modern bureaucratic forms of organization was allegedly based. Early nationalist struggles were aimed simply at gaining more positions in the colonial government services for indigenous elites. In the final stages of nationalist independence struggles, the movements aimed not at destroying the colonial administrative structures, but at taking them over intact and staffing them with native elites.

If colonial penetration produced nationalist movements, where the penetration was greater these movements were stronger and more developed. The contrast between Asia and Africa is striking. Asian nationalist movements have longer histories and have been both stronger and more developed throughout the twentieth century than were comparable movements in Africa. It is instructive that an American survey of nationalism entitled "The Nationalist Epidemic," published in 1934, contains sections on Japanese, Chinese, Indian, Filipino, and Near Eastern nationalism, but has none on nationalist movements in Africa. Likewise, a British survey, published by the Royal Institute of International Affairs in 1939, contains a chapter on nationalism in Asia but makes virtually no mention of nationalism in sub-Saharan colonial Africa.[12] To all intents and purposes, the only nationalist movements in colonial territories worthy of note before 1945 were those in Asia and to a much lesser extent in the Near East.

Nationalist movements in the colonial territories were the forerunners of political independence. Thus, the dates of independence reflect in large part the different ages and strengths of these movements. The high tide of independence occurred in Asia between 1945 and 1957. India achieved political independence early, as did Burma and the Philippines, each representing the success of relatively older and stronger nationalist movements. By 1959, when the weaker nationalist movements in Malaysia and Singapore had achieved political independence, the process was largely completed for Asia. Only then did it begin in Africa, with 1960 as the year with the largest number of territories becoming politically independent.

This is not to argue that it was only, or even primarily, movements internal to the colonial territories that produced independence. External factors were involved and were even decisive. The entire global conflict of World War II, and especially the conflict in the Pacific, constituted a historical event that triggered the breakup of the overall colonial system.[13] The war, however, provided only the external force that tipped the balance of the struggle in favor of the nationalist forces. It was thus an event that accelerated the ongoing cumulative process from nationalism to independence; it does not account for the earlier emergence of nationalism in Asia.

The commitment to development. The ideological and political underpinnings of the nationalist movements generated strong commitments to central planning for national economic development and population welfare. The undertaking is roughly similar regardless of whether the independence movement was evolutionary, as in India, or revolutionary, as in China.[14] There are, of course, considerable differences in the specific interpretations of the world on which the commitment is based and in the specific tactics by which the national policy is to be implemented. Nonetheless, the basic agreement on central planning for national economic development and popular welfare is the same in each case.

The process of transition from colonial to independent nation status provided the setting in which the commitment to economic modernization was crystallized and given its specific organizational manifestation. Here there is considerable difference between the evolutionary and revolutionary processes. Since most of the Asian nations proceeded to independence in a more evolutionary than revolutionary manner, we shall be concerned with the outcome of the evolutionary process at this point. Later we shall be more concerned with the outcome of the more radical and revolutionary process.

In the evolutionary process, the transition to independence involved a progressive participation of Asian nationals in the colonial government and in the broader modern communications network that was generated by the colonial government. This larger network of authority and communication provided a specific setting that determined the processes by which Asian leaders would mobilize forces for independence. The mobilization for the most part took the form of a public and open organization of the masses, the generation of political support in the metropolitan country, and the presentation of arguments to the colonial and metropolitan governments.

Mass mobilization was advanced by arguments concerning the greater level of popular welfare that could be provided by an independent government. Promises of general goals, such as economic development, industrialization, and the eradication of poverty, were combined with specific promises of more education, more jobs in high-paying industrial enterprises, and more and better health services. As such promises were effective in mobilizing popular support, they further committed the nationalist movement to these specific goals.

Mobilization of intellectuals both in the colonial territory and in the metropolitan power took a number of directions. One involved the invidious distinction between colonial and independent status as determinants of economic modernization. As early as 1900 Indian nationalists pointed out to themselves and to their friends in England that Japan had become a major, wealthy industrial nation after only one generation of independent economic modernization, while India remained economically backward after two centuries of tutelage under the most industrialized nation of the world.[15]

Further, Asian nationalists participated, through their Western education, in the general theoretical and empirical discrediting of laissez-faire capitalist models of development that was current in intellectual circles of the 1930s. They also took part in the Marxist-Leninist interpretations of capitalism and imperialism that arose on the European continent during and after World War I.[16]

Finally, the events of World War II deepened the commitment to central planning as a major strategy for achieving national economic development and welfare. The bitter rivalry between communist and capitalist models of development was greatly attenuated by the composition of the victorious allies in the war. The Soviet Union emerged in 1945 as a model of great attractiveness. Central planning and rapid development of heavy industry became the most favored strategy for achieving economic development.

The colonial situation itself must also be seen as one generating a favorable disposition to central planning on the part of the nationalist elite. Governments in the colonial territories enjoyed positions of overwhelming dominance. Whether this resulted from a prior colonial destruction of indigenous centers of initiative, or from the colonial emergence in a setting of weak initiative, the colonial situation was one in which the major impetus in most matters lay with government. From health, education, and welfare through commerce, agriculture, and industry, private sources of action were weak, especially among native populations. In addition, colonial governments usually used as part of their legitimizing arguments some form of responsibility for the well-being of their people. For the colonial rulers, and thus easily for the new nationalist leaders, government had a rightful responsibility for exercising initiative to advance local and national interests.

The emergence and crystallization of this commitment to central planning for economic development for popular welfare can be observed in such public forums as the legislative council debates that commonly preceded the granting of independence. Nationalist leaders used these forums, as well as the wider forum of modern mass communications, to make arguments for government responsibility, for the necessity of central planning, for promoting economic development to eradicate poverty, and for the general advancement of the popular welfare.[17]

The organizational implementation of the commitment. The commitment to central planning for economic modernization was implemented along with independence by the creation of organizations for economic planning. Central planning agencies, national economic councils, and economic planning units proliferated immediately after independence as the new indigenous leaders took control of the administrative apparatus left by the departing colonial powers. The bureaucratic structures implanted by the colonial powers were not just targets for the nationalist leadership; they also served as models on which to build new instruments for the achievement of the new national goals. Thus, the new development organizations usually sprang forth from existing colonial structures. There were ready-made offices, positions, desks, and files that could be taken over and used to implement the new goals of the independent leadership. In all cases, however, it was necessary to make some basic changes in the structures and goals of government. This proceeded along two discernible lines: changing the administrative location of the planning agency, and creating a specific economic competence in the agency.

Colonial economic agencies were typically located in the offices of the finance secretary. Indeed, the major instrument for coordinating colonial administrative structures lay in the office of finance. This typically gave to colonial economic administration a highly conservative fiscal bias. The health of the economy tended to be judged by the magnitude of annual revenue surpluses or deficits, so planning typically took the form of conservative estimates of revenues and at least mildly exaggerated estimates of expenditures. Financial secretaries commonly calculated revenues and were conservative in their results. Expenditures, on the other hand, represented requests from the various differentiated agency heads. Since agency heads usually expected to be granted amounts less than requested, the prudent head tended to inflate budget requests. For the most part, deficit financing was negatively valued, and the time span for organizational control was the fiscal year. All of these features supported a highly conservative fiscal policy. If economic planning were to be an exercise in the achievement of long-term national economic goals, it would be necessary to remove planning from the direct and specific control of the finance office and place it under national political direction.

Thus, with independence the new offices for planning were typically moved out from under the direct control of the finance secretary and given a location in the center of political control. The new offices were made directly responsible to the head of state, the president or prime minister. The finance officer was, of course, included in the higher levels of planning, but only as one, and not necessarily the most powerful, voice. Now it would be possible to establish long-term goals for the nation. This also implied that financial constraints would be viewed on different time schedules. Deficit financing could more easily be accepted since political leaders used time horizons that were greater than the annual fiscal year. It was often argued, for example, that budgets could be balanced over the long term, over trade cycles or generations. Annual deficits could be accepted, since they would lead to long-term increases in output, which would ultimately balance government budgets. Thus, the five-year plan can be seen as the powerful symbol generated in political centers to free planning considerations from the constraints of the fiscal year.

The rise of new planning organizations in new administrative locations radically changed the bases of staff recruitment. For the colonial finance secretary, a good general education combined with long experience in colonial finance was sufficient, but the new planning agencies required the services of technically competent economists. Thus, the normal bureaucratic development of the planning agencies provided for a rapid growth of competence in economic analysis, and the new agencies quickly came to be directed and staffed by economists.

The increased number of economists in planning activities also meant that demands would be placed upon the entire administration for data that could be used by trained experts to monitor the long-term behavior of the economy. Thus, the new agencies typically implied a rapid increase in surveys, censuses, and standard reporting procedures that increasingly moved to cover the entire economy. For the colonial administration, the most complete data sources typically covered foreign trade and little more. For the planning agencies, the operation of the entire economy and society became objects of scrutiny.

Finally, the creation of economic competence in planning activities meant that economic measures would be used to evaluate the performance of the overall system. The goal of planning became economic development, with output per capita as the measure of development. Growth rates and the overall performance of the system, in annual and five-year intervals, were measured in terms of growth in output per capita. It is true that the earliest plans laid heaviest emphasis upon the numerator of this measure, increasing output; but since goal achievement would be measured by the complete fraction, the stage was set for the emergence of population growth, the measure's denominator, as an important condition to be evaluated and controlled.

The decision for fertility limitation programing. Decisions for fertility control programing in Asia came largely from centers of economic planning.[18] Further, the decisions came as the planning agencies accumulated data that shifted the emphasis in the measurement of system performance from an exclusive concern for output to a concern for population growth. The census reports from around 1960 and the socioeconomic surveys accumulating at this time were largely responsible for this shift in emphasis.[19] Early enthusiasm for economic development was dampened as governments found that massive public investment and national development programs were not increasing output as rapidly as was originally hoped. Even when output was increasing, the rate of growth was not sufficient to achieve development targets, especially given the high rates of population growth that were only then becoming visible.

In addition, the population projections made during the 1950s were often found to be conservative. Census returns showed higher rates of population growth than were expected. Thus, it was early in the 1960s that economic planners came to see population growth as a major obstacle to the achievement of economic development goals.[20]

At that time, it was inevitable that political elites, directing new governments committed to economic development, would readily make the decisions to engage in large-scale public programs for fertility reduction. The decision in the final analysis was greatly facilitated by the appearance of new contraceptive methods, especially the intrauterine device and the oral contraceptive, which were inexpensive, (apparently) effective, and highly suited to the administrative structures controlled by the new political elites.

At this point a brief summary of our historical argument is in order. We have attempted to show that there was a continuous historical process of political change and organizational growth that gave Asian nations the specific capacity to make fertility reduction a major political aim. Policies were shaped out of the events of the time, using the organizational capacities for collective perception and decision making that had been built step by step in continuous reaction to present and immediately past conditions. From this ideal-typical perspective, of course, the process appears far more uninterrupted and understandable than it actually was. There were fits and starts, movements toward conquest, liberation, development planning, and population planning that were halted, diverted, or rapidly advanced. These more intimate details have been brushed aside in our attempt to interpret a broad sweep of history and to provide a plausible link between that history and the specific condition of population planning that we see in advanced form in Asia. In what follows we attempt to test this interpretation by drawing out something approaching propositions, which can then be tested against the processes of population planning in Asia itself.

EVOLUTIONARY AND REVOLUTIONARY PATTERNS

The process we have described has largely been a gradual, evolutionary one. Colonial forces created new social groups, new administrative forms, and new political processes over decades. The struggle for independence has been portrayed as a gradual political struggle, with little in the way of pitched battles marking the violent rendering of an old system. Not all independence processes in Asia have been so gradual, of course. We have also seen rapid and radical revolutionary changes in which new social forces have come to power through great upheavals. China is the major example, about which there is considerable information on population policies. Vietnam and Cambodia share some of the revolutionary character of China, but we have less information on their population policies. Thus, we can at this time move our analysis forward only through a detailed comparison of China and India, which is the subject of chapter 3. Our argument here is that the basic processes of political mobilization, commitment to economic development, perception of rapid population growth, and the political adoption of antinatalist policies were similar throughout the region.

Throughout Asia, then, in both evolutionary and revolutionary states, we have seen roughly the same organizational developments produce a powerful political-ecological adjustment to the condition of rapid population growth. Through a variety of specific historical paths, the organizations of the state have assumed great, and in some cases exclusive, power for the mobilization of populations. Those state organizations have penetrated deeply into the forces that affect and control major social change. From this penetration, from the deep commitment to goals of change, the governments have moved inexorably to perceive rapid population growth, and then to define this condition as a problem to be overcome. Like poverty, economic backwardness, and low productivity, this problem was defined as one that required major organized action. Thus, the political-ecological adjustment we observe is a form of collective response to rapid population growth, which grows out of prior collective aims for organized and centrally directed social change.

It is in this overall pattern of change that Asia shows historical uniqueness as a region. In Africa many of the same forces have been in operation, but they have come later and they have been much weaker. In Latin America, a quite different form of colonialism produced a different form of nationalism and independence movement. In both Africa and Latin America, then, the impetus for a political-ecological adjustment has come far less from within the regions and much more from outside. To explore the broad outlines of this argument, we must move to a consideration of the world community that has emerged in response to the condition of rapid population growth.

THE POLITICAL-ECOLOGICAL ADJUSTMENT
AND THE WORLD COMMUNITY

The above discussion has dealt with statelike units of analysis, territories marked by administrative boundaries that define the limits of authority. In this analysis there is an implicit assumption that states are relatively discrete and autonomous units. They are assumed to control both their boundaries and the populations that lie within them. More important, however, is the assumption that it is the state that is the critical decision-making unit in which the current population adjustment is being made. This is appropriate to the argument that the current adjustment is being worked out in authoritative organizations of resource mobilization and allocation.

At the same time, we recognize that the assumptions behind this form of analysis are only partly justified. A critical portion of our argument is that there is an emerging world community, which increasingly impinges upon each of its statelike members, especially with respect to patterns of modern social and economic transformation. Further, with respect to the population adjustment, Asia has played a leading role in the emergence of this new world community.

Over the past decade it has become commonplace to observe the interdependent relations among all populations on the planet. Titles such as *Spaceship Earth* dramatically proclaim this interdependence.[21] In human ecology itself it is common to observe that a world with a large number of relatively isolated communities has been replaced by a world in which all communities and populations are tied together in mutual interdependence.[22]

Just as smaller communities have experienced the rise of authoritative organizations, so the world community has witnessed a rise of its own organizations for authoritative resource mobilization and allocation. The United Nations and its agencies are the most conspicuous of these, but we should also include in this larger organizational network private international organizations and the states themselves that are tied together in bilateral and multilateral relations. All of these organizational units constitute a network that controls the mobilization and flow of resources in the world community. The process of adjusting to the condition of rapid population growth constitutes one of the most pressing concerns and one of the areas of most urgent activity of the world community's political organizations. As in Asia, the world's population adjustment is increasingly a political-ecological one; and in this adjustment, Asia has played a leading role.[23] The relationship between Asia and the world's political-ecological adjustment has, however, been marked by a pattern of mutually supportive development.

In broad terms, this has involved the legitimacy of the issue itself and the flow of technical, human, and financial resources applied to it. Asia's advanced position in the political-ecological adjustment has helped justify public intervention into reproductive behavior. The legitimation has supported the mobilization of world community resources, which have flowed back into Asia and also into the rest of the high-fertility world. The pattern of resource flows shows a variety of stages in the political-ecological adjustment; but here again, Asia appears in a more advanced stage and is laying out possible paths that will be followed in the rest of the high-fertility world. The following pages spell out this process in somewhat greater detail.

Reproductive behavior has until recently been considered a private affair that should be immune from public intervention. As late as 1958 the United States' President Eisenhower vetoed the utilization of foreign assistance for fertility control programs on the grounds that reproductive behavior is a private matter and should not be the subject of state action. This was also basically the position of the United Nations until 1966. Given this background, it was especially important that fertility control gain legitimacy as a public activity in the world community. Without such legitimacy, the political-ecological adjustment would remain largely confined to Asia, and would be considerably weakened even there.

Asian leaders exerted significant influence both privately and in the United Nations in valdiating public fertility control activity. They provided strong and rational voices in the discussions that led to the United Nations General Assembly resolution of December 1966,[24] which dramatically changed the position of the world community on public activity concerning reproductive behavior. Asian leaders were also prominent in the privately sponsored *World Leaders' Declaration on Population*, which gained signatures of heads of state throughout 1966 and 1967. By the end of 1967, the thirty heads of state who had signed included eleven from Asia, four from Latin America, five from Africa and the Middle East, and nine from developed economies of Europe, North America, and Oceania. Without Asian leadership, both inside and outside the United Nations, it is doubtful that the world body would have made its dramatic reversal in 1966.

Asian leadership also provided important legitimacy for public population programing around the critical period of the World Population Year, with its great debates in Bucharest in August 1974.[25] This conference, the first world conference of state representatives on population affairs, crystallized the ideological debate over fertility control. The ideological character of the debate came as a surprise to the population control proponents of the industrialized nations, who apparently expected the Bucharest conference merely to endorse their own sense of urgency over rapid population growth and to approve their world plan of action, which contained heavy emphasis upon promoting public fertility control programs.[26]

At Bucharest, Third World states, led by Algeria, denounced the emphasis on fertility limitation as a tool of development and argued forcefully for greater equality in the distribution of the world's wealth. Thus fertility limitation, or family planning, came in part to be opposed to equality in the specific aims of modern social transformations.

Although Asian states took part in the ideological debate, they have not been at what can be called the center of conflict. On the contrary, in its own deliberations Asia appears beyond the ideological debate and is involved in the more practical problems of promoting better public development activities, including fertility control programs. Thus, in the Second Asian Population Conference in 1972, the public statement by Rafael Salas, Executive Director of the United Nations Fund for Population Activities, on the limited achievements of family planning programs and the need for greater attention to programs of social and economic justice produced no ideological debate.[27] Rather, it was accepted as a statement of fact and necessity, reflecting what most Asian governments had discovered through extensive experience with population control programs. In a sense, Asia had moved beyond the point of ideological debate by facing the intractable problems of attempting to promote broad social and economic transformations.

Following Bucharest, the Asian nations met in Bangkok for a post-World Population Conference session in January 1975. This meeting was to operationalize the World Plan of Action within the Asian context. There was also a second and more diffuse objective, however. Many Asian delegates expressed disappointment with the Bucharest meeting, which they felt did not provide sufficient opportunity for them to present their needs, nor did it really speak to their problems. They felt they were beyond the fruitless ideological debates that engaged the less technically competent and more political leaders from other states. The draft plan of action that was prepared in Bangkok did indeed ignore the more political rhetoric of Bucharest and speak in much greater detail to the specific problems of Asian states and to the actions that could be taken to meet those problems.[28]

Thus Asia's advanced position in the political-ecological adjustment, which has implied much direct experience in the organization of both broad development and more specific population programs, has reinforced the legitimacy of public population programing. It has done this in part by directing attention away from ideological debates and toward the difficult problems of producing major social changes through public programs.

With increasing legitimacy, greater resources were mobilized in the world community for the adjustment to rapid population growth. The growth of these resources was initially slow, but soon the pace quickened considerably. In the first three years of its operation, 1967–69, The United Nations Fund for Population Activities (UNFPA) received pledges of only US$4.9 million. By the end of 1978, total pledges were more than one hundred times this amount, standing at US$516.6 million. The annual and cumulative pledges for the period are shown in table 2.3.

A large share of these new resources of the world community has been directed back to Asia, in support of the political-ecological adjustment being made there. New resources have also gone to the rest of the high-fertility world, but the pattern of allocation is different from that in Asia, suggesting different stages in the overall process of the political-ecological adjustment. The clearest and most precise set of data for this analysis is provided by the financial allocations of UNFPA. Although the flow of resources is highly complex, with both human and financial resources included in the pledges of technical assistance, the allocation of financial resources provides a useful and simple index of this large and more complex flow. From the UNFPA allocations, there are a number of important observations to be made.

First, as we show in table 2.4, in the initial stages of world community involvement, 1969–71, over half of the financial allocations went to Asia. There are, however, different ways to assess this pattern. Asia has a much larger population than do the other two regions: over 2 billion people,[29] against about 300 million in Latin America and just under 500

TABLE 2.3
Financial Pledges to UNFPA, 1967–78 (in US$ millions)

Pledges	1967–69	1970	1971	1972	1973	1974	1975	1976	1977	1978
Annual	4.9	15.4	27.9	30.6	42.4	54.1	63.2	79.1	91.7	107.3
Cumulative	4.9	20.3	48.2	78.8	121.2	175.3	238.5	317.6	409.3	516.6

Source: UNFPA Annual Reports for respective years.

million in Africa and the Middle East. If allocations were made simply on the basis of population size, Asia would be seen to gain considerably less financial help than Latin America or Africa and the Middle East ($5.76 per capita versus $10.67 and $15.25, respectively). The United Nations does not, however, deal with individuals, but with member governments, the organizational representatives of their populations. Further, in the early stages of the political-ecological adjustment to rapid population growth, the United Nations interacted primarily with states that had made a decision for some form of population control program. The allocations per country with a population program, therefore, provide a more accurate picture of the resource flows, and these show that Asia obtained more than twice as much as Africa and the Middle East and about four times as much as Latin America. Thus, Asian political support in legitimizing population control programing has brought financial support to the region for furthering the growth of such programs.

Table 2.4 also permits one other interesting observation. Of the total allocations to each region, Asia has received a larger portion for country programs than for regional projects. This permits the interpretation that Asia's more advanced stage in the political-ecological adjustment allows a large volume of resources to be specifically directed to national family planning service delivery projects. The greater use of regional projects in Latin America and Africa and the Middle East may be interpreted as activity in support of the initial legitimation of public population programing. Tables 2.5 and 2.6–2.9 permit us to test this interpretation and to suggest that there are different stages in the political-ecological adjustment.

In table 2.5 we go beyond the initial years examined in table 2.4. At this point, the cases become sufficient to call for separation of two regions of the high-fertility world. Asia and Latin America remain the same, but Africa becomes sub-Saharan Africa, separate from the southern and eastern portion of the Mediterranean. This division brings greater homogeneity to the regions, although it still leaves the Mediterranean world with only six countries in which fertility limitation policies operate. In table 2.5 we also shift to the use of actual rather than allocated amounts. Allocations indicate the orientations of the provider, but here we are more interested in the absorptive capacities of the recipient regions, and this is more accurately reflected in actual expenditures.

TABLE 2.4
UNFPA Allocations to Country and Regional Projects, 1969–71

	Asia	Latin America	Africa & Middle East
Number of countries	24	26	57
Countries with programs	18	18	22
UNFPA allocations			
Total $millions	12.1	3.2	6.8
Country projects	8.7 (72%)	1.9 (59%)	3.7 (54%)
Regional projects	3.4 (28%)	1.3 (41%)	3.1 (46%)
Allocations per country with program	$672,000	$178,000	$309,000
Approximate allocations per capita	$5.76	$10.67	$15.25

Source: UNFPA, Report 1969–72, appendix B, pp. 41–53.
Note: The figures here differ considerably from those in tables 2.5 and 2.6 for two major reasons. First, these data show allocated amounts, which are often for projects that extend over a number of years in which the actual expenditures per year will be lower than the total allocation. Tables 2.5 and 2.6 show the annual actual expenditures. Second, the figures in this table include amounts allocated to the Specialized Agencies (FAO, WHO, UNESCO, ect.) for programs in a given country as well as those allocated to regional activities and to direct country projects. The figures in tables 2.5 and 2.6 include only actual expenditures for projects funded directly to the country through UN or UNDP offices, not through the Specialized Agencies.

From table 2.5 we can see that Asia has retained its dominant position in UNFPA resource use, though there is also some decline in dominance. Throughout the decade it received over half of all resources, declining from 60 percent to just under 50 percent of total funds. This dominance is striking when one recognizes that total UNFPA funds grew to about twenty times their original levels. The other three regions continue to show far less resource use. The Mediterranean region fluctuated around 15 to 20 percent, while Africa and Latin America grew during the decade from about 10 to near 20 percent. The most striking change comes in the Mediterranean region, where a few programs in operation commanded 30 percent of the modest UNFPA funds available before 1970. The region as a whole, however, did not have the absorptive capacity of Asia. Thus, as the UNFPA funds grew, the region's total allocation dropped steadily from 30 to under 20 percent. For the overall pattern, however, we can see both Asian dominance and leadership, with the other regions following behind in their growth of resource use for population programing.

Tables 2.6–2.9 and figure 2.3 show a functional distribution of the UNFPA expenditures, from which we can infer something about the stages in the worldwide political-ecological adjustment. For all areas, the two largest functional categories of expenditures are basic data collection and family planning services. The former are primarily for population censuses. Family planning services expenditures are self-explanatory, rep-

Table 2.5
Actual UNFPA Contributions to Country by Region (US$1000)

Region	1969–71	1972	1973	1974	1975	1976	1977	1978	Total
Africa	253	701	1,644	3,778	6,177	6,625	6,737	14,980	40,895
	7.4%	10.8%	14.5%	13.9%	16.1%	14.5%	14.0%	18.9%	16.0%
Asia	1,842	3,907	6,206	12,010	17,390	18,271	21,181	38,228	118,084
	53.5%	59.9%	54.9%	44.3%	45.2%	40.0%	43.9%	48.3%	46.5%
Latin America	314	678	1,836	6,890	9,598	12,778	10,372	16,335	53,803
	9.1%	10.4%	16.2%	25.4%	24.9%	28.0%	21.5%	14.3%	21.0%
Mediterranean	1,035	1,234	1,621	4,409	5,316	8,006	9,987	14,643	46,251
	30.0%	18.9%	14.3%	16.3%	13.8%	17.5%	20.7%	18.7%	18.1%
Total	3,445	6,520	11,309	27,087	38,482	45,679	48,277	79,185	259,983
	100%	100%	100%	100%	100%	100%	100%	100%	100%

Source: UNFPA internal accounts computer printout.

TABLE 2.6
Functional Distribution of Actual UNFPA Expenditures in Country Programs in Africa As of 31 May 1978 (US $1000)

Areas of Activities	1969–71	1972	1973	1974	1975	1976	1977	1978	Total
Basic population data	83 32.9%	269 38.3%	878 53.4%	2,715 71.9%	4,494 72.7%	4,524 68.3%	3,123 46.4%	8,127 54.3%	24,214 59.2%
Population dynamics	15 6.0%	92 13.1%	201 12.2%	229 6.1%	238 3.9%	197 3.0%	444 6.6%	752 5.0%	2,167 5.3%
Population policy		4 0.1%	56 3.4%	36 1.0%	21 0.0%	14 0.2%	37 0.1%	103 0.7%	271 0.7%
Family planning	155 61.1%	230 32.8%	281 17.1%	306 8.1%	1,119 18.1%	1,271 19.2%	2,290 34.0%	3,029 20.2%	8,682 21.2%
Communication & education		106 15.1%	155 9.4%	192 5.1%	244 4.0%	311 4.7%	522 7.8%	2,472 16.5%	4,004 9.8%
Multisector activities Program development			73 4.4%	299 7.9%	61 1.0%	308 4.6%	321 4.8%	496 3.3%	1,558 3.8%
Total	253 100.0%	701 100.0%	1,645 100.0%	3,778 100.0%	6,177 100.0%	6,625 100.0%	6,737 100.0%	14,980 100.0%	40,895 100.0%

TABLE 2.7
Functional Distribution of Actual UNFPA Expenditures in Country Programs in Asia As of 31 May 1978 (US$1000)

Areas of Activities	1969–71	1972	1973	1974	1975	1976	1977	1978	Total
Basic population data	111	219	503	1,182	1,017	1,005	1,018	3,594	8,649
	6.0%	5.6%	8.1%	9.8%	5.9%	5.5%	4.8%	9.4%	7.3%
Population dynamics	60	36	9	44	277	345	541	949	2,262
	3.2%	0.9%	0.1%	0.4%	1.6%	1.9%	2.6%	2.5%	1.9%
Population policy	19	18	47	159	25	350	247	436	1,301
	1.0%	0.5%	0.8%	1.3%	0.1%	1.9%	1.7%	1.1%	1.1%
Family planning	1,563	3,256	4,327	7,659	12,757	13,268	15,534	25,797	84,160
	84.8%	83.3%	69.7%	63.8%	73.4%	72.6%	73.3%	67.5%	70.8%
Communication & education	72	244	926	2,277	2,612	2,392	2,401	4,269	15,194
	3.9%	6.3%	14.9%	19.0%	15.0%	13.1%	11.3%	11.2%	12.8%
Multisector activities	1	21	29	22	20	32	100	114	340
	0.1%	0.5%	0.5%	0.2%	0.1%	0.2%	0.5%	0.3%	0.3%
Program development	17	112	366	666	681	877	1,340	3,068	7,127
	0.9%	2.9%	5.9%	5.5%	3.9%	4.8%	6.3%	8.0%	6.0%
Total	1,842	3,907	6,206	12,010	17,390	18,271	21,181	38,228	118,984
	100.0%	100.0%	100.0%	100.0%	100.0%	100.0%	100.0%	100.0%	100.0%

TABLE 2.8
Functional Distribution of Actual UNFPA Expenditures in Country Programs in Latin America As of 31 May 1978 (US$1000)

Areas of Activities	1969–71	1972	1973	1974	1975	1976	1977	1978	Total
Basic population data	223	258	461	1,847	1,769	4,402	976	423	8,358
	70.8%	38.0%	25.1%	26.8%	18.4%	18.8%	9.4%	3.7%	15.5%
Population dynamics	35	65	307	717	455	687	739	1,394	4,401
	11.3%	9.7%	16.7%	10.4%	4.7%	5.4%	7.1%	12.3%	8.2%
Population policy		39	43	35	42	54	35	50	301
		5.8%	2.5%	0.5%	0.4%	0.4%	0.3%	0.4%	0.6%
Family planning	36	166	842	4,180	7,041	8,935	8,337	8,868	38,404
	11.3%	24.4%	45.9%	60.7%	73.4%	69.9%	80.4%	78.2%	71.4%
Communication & education	19	150	180	111	289	700	285	600	2,334
	6.1%	22.1%	9.8%	1.6%	3.0%	5.5%	2.7%	5.3%	4.3%
Multisector activities	2				2				4
	0.5%				0.0%				0.0%
Program development									
Total	314	678	1,836	6,890	9,598	12,778	10,372	11,334	53,803
	100.0%	100.0%	100.0%	100.0%	100.0%	100.0%	100.0%	100.0%	100.0%

Table 2.9
Functional Distribution of Actual UNFPA Expenditures in Country Programs in the Southern and Eastern Mediterranean as of 31 May 1978 (US$1000)

Areas of Activities	1969–71	1972	1973	1974	1975	1976	1977	1978	Total
Basic population data	85 8.2%	136 11.1%	816 50.3%	1,057 24.0%	1,729 32.5%	1,997 24.9%	2,886 28.9%	2,002 13.7%	10,709 23.2%
Population dynamics	23 2.2%	28 2.3%	44 2.7%	134 3.0%	172 3.2%	184 2.3%	644 6.4%	1,337 9.1%	2,566 5.5%
Population policy		50 4.0%	22 1.3%	43 1.0%	121 2.3%	58 0.7%	196 2.0%	488 3.3%	976 2.1%
Family planning	887 85.7%	610 49.5%	590 36.4%	2,483 56.3%	2,850 53.6%	4,837 60.4%	5,304 53.1%	8,946 61.6%	26,507 57.3%
Communication & education	40 3.9%	408 33.1%	46 2.8%	349 7.9%	247 4.6%	537 6.7%	532 5.3%	810 5.5%	2,969 6.4%
Multisector activities Program development		1 0.0%	104 6.4%	343 7.8%	197 3.7%	393 4.9%	426 4.3%	1,061 7.2%	2,524 5.5%
Total	1,035 100.0%	1,234 100.0%	1,621 100.0%	4,408 100.0%	5,316 100.0%	8,006 100.0%	9,987 100.0%	14,643 100.0%	46,251 100.0%

Figure 2.3   UNFPA Support (US$ million) for Country Programs and Proportion of Funds Supporting Basic Data Collection and Family Planning Services, by Year and Major World Region.

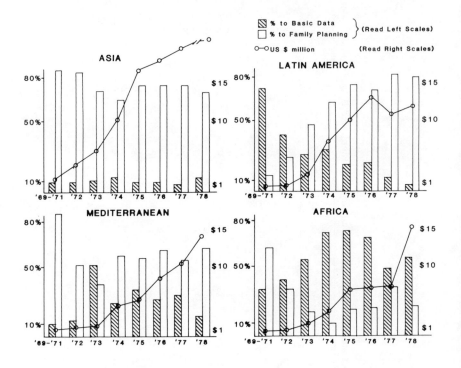

Source: See Tables 2.6–2.9

resenting funds going directly to the support of contraceptive distribution. Figure 2.3 abstracts the major movement from the expenditure data in tables 2.6–2.9, to show changes in total UNFPA expenditures, together with changes in their functional distribution to the two major categories.

It is here that we can see evidence of something approaching a set of stages in the political-ecological adjustment. We argued that for Asia, development goals were established, which called for monitoring of socio-economic dynamics; and from this monitoring, political leaders were led to adopt antinatalist policies. Since Asia made the fundamental policy decisions before the UNFPA was in the business of resource allocation, it already had in place a network of national family planning services whose resource needs were visible, large, and rapidly growing. Thus, the great majority of UNFPA funds could go directly to these service programs, even though those funds grew rapidly through the decade. In Latin America, initial funds went primarily to building the perceptive capacities that would lead to policy decisions and programmatic actions. Given the relatively high development of such perceptive institutions already in place in Latin America, UNFPA funds could be readily absorbed and quickly translated into decisions, and subsequent funds could be directly channeled into the family planning services that were essentially designed to implement the policy decisions.

UNFPA expenditures in Africa were initially very small and were concentrated in only one or two countries that had made some form of antinatalist policy decision. This accounts for the high proportion of funds for family planning in the first few years. As UNFPA activities increased in Africa, however, the major need appeared to be in the elementary areas of data collection. As expenditures grew, it was this development of perceptive capacity that absorbed most of the resources. Even now it appears that this fundamental stage is just beginning to experience the organizational development it requires, since the UNFPA and other donors are committing large amounts of resources to a series of African national censuses.

Our political-ecological perspective would lead us to predict that this census-taking activity will be followed by antinatalist policy decisions, and thus by increased capacities to absorb funds for family planning services. It should be noted, however, that the political-ecological adjustment is in large part a political one. African census activity is not by any means politically neutral. It is probable, in fact, that the potential for ethnic or tribal conflict in the political arena is much greater in the case of African census taking than it is in other regions. This may provide the coming decade with an illustration of how a political-ecological adjustment can be arrested, by stopping the development of a population's collective or organized perspective capacities.

The Mediterranean region presents a puzzling picture, with considerable fluctuation in the functional allocations and no clear relationship between these and the growth of total expenditures. The unstable nature of the activities, however, derives primarily from the small number of countries (six) and the small number of country recipients. The single project of a national base-line survey can produce a radical change in functional allocations for a period of only one year. In addition, for many of the countries that require fundamental work in basic data collection, domestic resources are more than adequate, and UNFPA resources are not in high demand.

The UNFPA is not by any means the only international organization by which the world community is adjusting to the condition of rapid population growth. It is, however, the most specifically and legitimately *world* organization, and its activities appear sensitively attuned to advancing the political-ecological adjustment.[30] It first mobilized and allocated funds in support of states in the more advanced stage of the adjustment in Asia; it then began the delicate diplomatic work of providing support to various organized centers of population concern in Latin America and Africa and the Mediterranean world. As a United Nations activity it has respected the sovereignty of the member nations and has attempted to work with their own definitions and perceptions of their population problems. That is, it is promoting a worldwide ecological adjustment in which the major actors are the statelike units in which modern populations are organized. This is only one aspect of the rich reciprocal relation between the state and the world community. We shall have the opportunity to explore other aspects of this relation in subsequent chapters. This nexus represents a unique condition of the political-ecological population response, which we believe is certain to have far-reaching significance for the overall character of the response.

This is only the beginning of the story of the political-ecological adjustment. It is, to be sure, an important beginning; but it raises two questions to which this volume is, in part, directed. One concerns the simple question of results. Will the political-ecological adjustment process be an effective one? The identification of the current adjustment process as political does not imply that it will be successful. Statelike units may prove to be ineffective mechanisms for organizing their populations for an effective accommodation to rapid population growth. If they prove to be ineffective and still retain their sovereignty, the prospects of a Malthusian change through higher death rates will be greatly enhanced. It is our opinion that the current adjustment process will prove successful, however. We believe there are grounds for a cautious optimism that the demographic transition in the high-fertility countries will be completed through a reduction of fertility. Further, we believe the political organizations of state and international communities will play a significant role in producing this result. Some of the grounds for this optimism have been stated above, others will appear in subsequent chapters.

A second and related question concerns the type of activities, or the specific character of the adjustment that is possible and likely given its political nature. In comparisons of China and India, some observers have noted distinct differences that emerge from revolutionary versus evolutionary change. The revolutionary nationalist liberation process tends to produce what has been called an *organic* approach to the problem of rapid population growth, creating a new set of organized activities that appears to be designed to meet the problem. The more evolutionary liberation processes tend to produce a traditional *bureaucratic* approach to the problem. Population control programs of most high-fertility states have been amply criticized for being narrowly focused family planning programs. Many are little more than limited programs for clinic-based distribution of contraceptives to individual women and men at risk. It is possible that the cumulative political-organizational process itself may restrict the scope and character of the collective effort to such an extent that it will be ineffective. Further, a similar and apparently inescapable process of bureaucratization may overtake the organic processes of the revolutionary states, as revolutionary programs have often been overtaken by bureaucratization in the past, and render even these collective efforts ineffective.

Again, we believe there are grounds for a cautious optimism in the matter of the degree and effect of bureaucratization. We are beginning to see increasing activity in bringing together the variety of specialized bureaucratic agencies of development and fertility control into more integrated efforts. It is quite likely that such integration will greatly accelerate over the next decade. It is also probable that revolutionary organic efforts will become more routinized and differentiated into specialized activities, but we do not believe this will significantly detract from the impact those organic efforts will have on reducing fertility. We hope some of the grounds for this optimism will also become clear in subsequent chapters.

3

India and China

SUMMARY OF THE ARGUMENT

India and China, the world's two most populous countries, have more in common than their size. Similarities in both demographic and sociopolitical histories have placed these two countries together in the vanguard of the current political-ecological adjustment.

The similarities in demographic histories can be seen in the population growth curves shown in figure 3.1. They describe for both countries fifteen hundred years of rough stability or slow growth, with populations hovering around fifty million. This was followed by two centuries of erratic acceleration and a recent spurt to population levels that previous generations would have considered impossible.

We have seen this type of curve before, of course. It described the Western industrial countries up to the early part of this century, and today the curve is frequently used to describe the demographic history of the total world population. For the Western world, the sharply rising segment of the curve preceded a major ecological adjustment: declining fertility and the completion of the demographic transition. The curves for India and China today lead one to expect for them as well a dramatic form of ecological adjustment.

If demographic histories lead to the expectation of a major ecological change, recent history leads to the expectation that this will be a political-ecological change. Both countries are overwhelmingly agrarian and poor. Both have ancient civilizations and ruling systems. Both felt the double impact of Western imperialism and internal disorder, which brought them to the mid-twentieth century suffering the twin ills of foreign domination and internal misery. For both, the problems were compounded by rapid population growth. In both countries powerful nationalist movements

Figure 3.1 Long-Term Population Growth in India and China

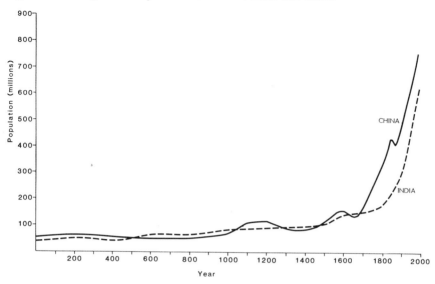

arose to confront the two problems and thereby to gain for their peoples independence and dignity together with increased human productivity and welfare. And in both cases these nationalist movements led to new forms of political organization, to the formulation of new goals of national economic development, and thence to the adoption of official antinatalist policies and the creation of nation wide fertility limitation programs. In effect, these two massive and massively poor countries are now experiencing roughly similar political-ecological adjustments to high fertility and population growth.

If the similarities in the political-ecological changes are striking, the differences are more illuminating. It is well known that the two countries are taking different paths to the modern world, paths that especially entail the use of different forms of political organization. China has chosen a deliberately strong form of political organization, India a deliberately weak one.[1] They thus demonstrate once again a distinctive feature of the human species: the flexibility or variability of its forms of social organization. This in turn raises two central questions for human ecological analysis: How do different forms of organization arise? And what impact do they have on the way populations interact with their environments? The extreme differences in political organization between India and China provide an excellent opportunity to address these questions. These differences can be seen to have direct and powerful implications for almost everything they do as nations, and certainly for the character of their collective efforts to control high fertility and rapid population growth. These implications can be seen with dramatic clarity in their respective family planning programs.

Common and accepted images of the two countries' family planning programs are radically different. The few observers who have visited China, seen some of its local units, talked with its leaders, and studied available documents report a remarkable public program.[2] It has promoted increased age at marriage, four- to five-year spacing between births, and stopping first at two children and more recently at one. All modern fertility-limiting methods, including abortions, are available and extensively used. Paraprofessionals, the famous "barefoot doctors," provide links between clinics and the masses of the rural population, bringing both health care and contraceptive services and supplies. Married couples are organized into planned birth committees, which generate heavy and effective peer pressure to limit the number of children each couple has. At all points, political cadres oversee the activity to assure that the national goals will be realized. The impression, undoubtedly overdrawn, is one of total organization, total dedication, and total effectiveness. Observers consider it almost certain that China will reduce its crude birth rate to less than twenty per thousand by the year 2000.[3]

In contrast to China, the data on India are so voluminous and varied that it is misleading to speak of a national program as a single homogeneous entity. Nonetheless, a recent detailed field study of the family planning program in Uttar Pradesh provides a good basis for contrasting the two countries' programs.[4] Family planning in India comes under the jurisdiction of the state health services, which operate out of specialized clinics. Medical doctors direct the clinics and have something of a formal monopoly on the distribution of technical medical supplies and information. The family planning program is primarily concerned with distributing contraceptives, although there is a weak link with maternal and child health. Direct attempts to increase the age at marriage are not a concern of the program. Rather, it works primarily to deliver condoms and to recruit sterilization acceptors among both men and women. Other contraceptive methods are not extensively used, and abortion is strictly limited. Paraprofessional field workers bring information to the villagers and attempt to recruit contraceptive acceptors. The technical health activities of field workers are not extensive and are deliberately limited. The clinic medical doctors give no real or effective supervision to the field workers, who are demonstrably inefficient. Surveys of villagers indicate little or no contact with field workers despite a decade of supposed extension activity. At all levels, political leaders intervene in the implementation of the program, more to place or sustain their supporters in official positions than to assist in meeting program goals.

The overall impression of the Indian program is one of weak organization, inefficient workers, and relatively little impact on fertility. Observers consider it questionable whether or not India will reduce its crude birth rate to twenty per thousand by the year 2000.[5]

The radical differences in our common impressions of the two programs raise two types of questions. One concerns the cause of the difference; the other, the accuracy of the impressions. A political-ecological analysis will lead us to look for causes in the institutional histories by which different forms of political organization emerged and have consequently produced the dramatic differences in fertility limitation programs. Before turning to this history, however, we must say something about data and accuracy of impressions.

The impressions of programs used above show explicitly and dramatically the source of our problems. Reports on China are made by a few scattered visitors on tours greatly limited in time and coverage. Most have seen virtually the same field situations, talked with the same handful of officials and citizens, and used roughly the same highly limited documentary evidence. The Indian evidence used here came from a detailed study done by a joint Indian-American team of social scientists who spent months in carefully organized and controlled field observation and data collection. In India, the program itself, other government agencies, and scores of Indian and foreign social scientists have produced masses of studies and statistics on the family planning program. There should certainly be some question about the relative accuracy of our two impressions. We shall have more to say about this presently, but it is nonetheless reasonable to set this issue aside for the moment and to focus our attention on the different forms of political organization by which the ecological adjustment is taking place.

We must begin with a summary of the historical processes by which India developed a weak state and China a strong one.

IMPERIALISM, COLONIALISM, AND NATIONALISM: THE ROOTS OF STRONG AND WEAK STATES

The character of today's Indian and Chinese states emerged out of a long and complex historical process in which the decisive elements lay in the interaction of indigenous conditions and the external forces of Western imperialism.[6] Initial conditions were different, as were the timing and character of the imperialist penetration. As a result, both colonial and nationalist movements were profoundly divergent; and out of this divergence there arose the differences between strong and weak states.

Before the coming of Western imperialism, China was ruled by a more centralized administrative system, which had been in place for almost two thousand years. A wealthy and powerful court at the center directed a far-flung administrative system with officials unified by a Confucian tradition passed from generation to generation by education in the classics. This education constituted both a form of investment for local notable families and a culture that tied local officials closely to the centralized ruling system. That this system was dominated by foreigners,[7] the Manchus, at the time of Western imperialist penetration was of relatively little importance. They had, like other conquerors, been effectively integrated into Chinese civilization. The Manchus did, however, provide useful targets for nationalist mobilization. At least for the nationalists, it could be assumed that these foreign rulers were responsible for China's internal misery.

Ecological conditions supported the strength of the central administration. The heartland, situated in the lower reaches of the two great rivers, the Yellow and the Yangtze, was laced with extensive water-control projects that served to tie local units more closely to the center.[8] Officials administering the laws of the emperor came from powerful gentry families, whose wealth lay largely in the ownership of land. Patrilineal kinship tied persons in the provinces and at the center in a close symbiotic relationship. The gentry controlled agriculture and extracted the surplus needed to maintain the officialdom. Officials in turn maintained order and protection through the police and military and organized major water control projects that made the land more productive.

In contrast to China, the Indian land mass was ruled by a far less centralized administrative system, and even that system was in an advanced stage of disintegration at the time of Western imperialist penetration. Like China, India had experienced successive waves of foreign conquerors. The last wave, the Moghuls, coming out of Persia and Afghanistan, provided a relatively effective tax-gathering system and employed both indigenous Hindu forms of rule and local notables. The decentralized character of administration can clearly be seen in contrast with that of China in the area of water control. There was little in India to match the great canals and diking systems found in China. Rather, irrigation was a constant problem, solved more or less by the construction of tanks or manmade lakes.

A further set of centrifugal forces was introduced by the religious differences between the rulers and the ruled. Islamic rulers variously attempted either to convert the masses of Hindus or to leave them to their own devices. Left alone or not, the religious differences provided a deep fissure into which the British could eventually drive a decisive wedge, splitting rulers from their base of wealth and making possible the conquest of the entire land mass.

Western imperialism came earlier to India than to China, and it penetrated the subcontinent far more profoundly. From the battle of Plassey in 1757 to the Sikh Wars in the 1840s, the British advanced steadily throughout India. In the conquest they demonstrated not so much the force of Western technology as the force of Western bureaucratic organization.[9] This organizational superiority was equally demonstrated in the trading companies that followed the conquest and drew Hindu merchants into the growing world capitalist system.

It was not until the end of the conquest of India that Western imperialist penetration began in earnest in China. Not only did the intrusion come later, it came from a series of competing metropolitan forces. While India was conquered militarily by a single European power, China was forcibly opened by a collection of Western powers whose gunboats forced upon the country a series of treaty ports through which, it was hoped, Western economic interests could enter what has often been (and is still today) seen as a massive and massively attractive potential market. If control of the land mass by a single European power brought a cohesive administrative penetration of India, the treaty ports brought to China a later and more limited intrusion of market forces and of Western ideas detached from Western administrative structures.

The British built an administrative system in India that became something of a model of a modern civil service. Although it was an extremely small service, with about one thousand British civil servants ruling nearly half a billion Indians, it provided the framework for the establishment of a new form of the modern state. Railroads drew provinces together into a single network. Laws, banks, commercial houses, schools, and the military together wove a web of a new Indian state that was distinctively British Indian.

The treaty ports through which a portion of China was economically invaded were weak and limited when compared with the structures of penetration in India. They permitted some economic inroads, both for the purchase of Chinese materials and for the sale of Western goods. They could not, however, give Western economic interests more than limited access to internal markets. It was Chinese merchants who provided links between the foreigners and the interior, and the internal cohesion of the Chinese indigenous economy further insulated it from the extent of market and political penetration that India experienced.[10]

In both cases, however, the external penetration worked as capitalist penetration typically works in its periphery. Resources and wealth were extracted and flowed primarily to the metropolitan powers at the center. The end result was the same for both countries: foreign domination and internal poverty.

Strong and enduring civilizations could not be expected to react only with apathy or accommodation to such forceful intrusion. Western colonialism in both India and China generated powerful resistance, which ultimately took the form of modern nationalist movements. In these movements two dominant ideologies competed for leadership: Liberalism and Marxism. It was largely the differences in the interaction of external and internal forces that would determine which ideology would emerge victorious in the two countries.

For India it was important that foreign rule was exercised by only one nation, and even more by one that provided leadership in the development of Western institutions of parliamentary democracy. As Britain consolidated its rule of India, it was itself undergoing profound transformations at home from what Stokes has called the divine right of kings to the divine right of the masses.[11] What emerged was a formula in which legitimate authority could be claimed only on the grounds of the consent of the governed.

As Indians were drawn into an increasingly British India, they absorbed this legitimizing formula along with the skills, positions, and visions provided to the local elite whose cooptation made it possible for the small corps of foreigners to rule so vast a land. The coopted Indian elite came to demand, like their earlier American revolutionary counterparts, no more, but no less, than the rights of Englishmen.

A watershed in this elite's emergence can be seen in the brief span of thirty years that separated the Sepoy Mutiny in 1857 from the formation of the Congress Party in 1888. The Mutiny represented the last dying gasp of a conquered civilization attempting to turn back to its earlier rule. This attempt to drive out the British and to reestablish the old Moghul court was, however, a total failure. And just a generation later a new group of Indian leaders formed a modern political party whose stated aim was to gain more places for Indians in the Indian civil service. From a failed attempt to drive out the British and destroy their foreign ruling structures, Indians moved to a new attempt to take over those structures of rule for themselves.

This was a demand to which the British were deeply vulnerable. Indian leaders ultimately had only to demonstrate that it was they, not the British, who held the consent of the governed, in order to lay claim to legitimate authority in India. That claim was not made easily, of course. The Congress Party experienced more than a generation of very limited and gentlemanly cooperative discussion with the British. Discussion produced more and more places for Indians in the civil service, but it could not by itself produce self-rule. For this, mobilization of the masses was required.

It was decisive for India that this mobilization came to be led by M. K. Gandhi. The interaction of Gandhi's person and philosophy with the character of British rule in effect precluded the emergence of Marxism as an organizing ideology and set a liberal stamp on the nationalist movement. Gandhi is well known for his espousal of nonviolence in collective action, but it was just as important that he eschewed class warfare as the process by which India would confront the twin ills of foreign domination and internal poverty. Gandhi's approach was successful in large part because the British acceded to Indian demands for constitutional reform at the same time that they effectively used force to block the emergence of more violent and radical liberation strategies. As a result, the Congress Party moved ahead with mass mobilization led by a loose political structure with little internal discipline. It became a party that could gain votes from a rural mass still very much controlled by local landed interests.

Thus, the struggle in India against foreign domination and internal poverty gradually evolved as a constitutional struggle led by a legal party that sought evolutionary reform rather than revolution. The party was immensely successful, but only in the first of its aims. As a constitutional party it was led to develop legal and normative protections for all groups in the society. It could argue, as it did, that foreign rule was responsible for internal poverty and that only self-rule would permit the collective action needed for the elimination of poverty. Nevertheless, given the character of the metropolitan power it faced, it had to accept a liberal— that is a weak—form of state mechanism with which to exercise that self-rule. The conditions were highly suited to, and indeed only permitted, a liberal solution to the immediate problems.

Almost the opposite was true for China. It has often been observed that in China the power and effectiveness of the old ruling system, and indeed of the civilization itself, choked off attempts at reform until only radical solutions to internal problems appeared possible. There were attempts at reform, of course, and they took both violent and constitutional forms.

A series of uprisings originating in the Shantung and White Lotus rebellions in 1774 and 1775 began to shake the established order on the eve of the major Western intrusions. The next century witnessed such major uprisings as the Taiping, Nien, and Boxer rebellions, with the Republican revolution coming early in the twentieth century. All showed a similar pattern. They attempted to remove old forms of oppression, inequality, corruption, and ineffectiveness in the political and social order. All were eventually put down through some combination of Chinese military action and foreign assistance or conquest. Each was followed by attempts at constitutional reform that loosened some of the constraints of the old system, but in each case, the reforms threatened established groups and were choked off by reactionary movements that only succeeded in establishing still another dynasty.

This pattern was broken by the Maoist mobilization of the peasantry for a Marxist-Leninist inspired revolutionary movement. Chiang Kai-shek proved to be the last of the reformers turned emperor; or better, the last to attempt to take China into the world capitalist system by means of liberal ideologies and institutions. Chiang's Communist opponents were committed to a Marxist-Leninist revolution that would be led by a tightly disciplined party. They began with an attempt to mobilize the urban proletariat, following the Soviet model, and in this were completely unsuccessful. The failure led to the major innovative shift toward mobilizing the peasantry—still, however, under the control of a tightly disciplined revolutionary party. This innovation proved successful. It is neither possible nor necessary to determine whether the disciplined cadre-type party organization and the revolutionary ideology were necessary to achieve consolidation of power in the state. It is sufficient to observe that the consolidation did take place in this manner, thus giving the new government both the ideological and organizational underpinnings of a strong state.

Thus, the long and complex historical processes of imperialism, colonialism, and nationalism had profoundly different outcomes in India and China. In their interactions with the indigenous dynamics these external forces provided profoundly different supports for the type of political system that would emerge with the demise of the Western overseas colonial systems following World War II. We need not accept the outcome as inevitable to agree with Lucien Bianco that there were few times in history less suited to the use of liberal solutions to address internal problems than those found in China over the past century.[12] By extension we can also agree that there were few times in history more suited to the use of these solutions than those found in India during the same period.

Liberalism for India meant that a weak government would preside over a weak state. It would at least theoretically protect the rights of individuals and groups to pursue their interests, even against the aims of government. It would accept legal constraints against the formulation of national goals and against the mobilization of resources needed to achieve those goals. The triumph of Marxism implied a strong government and state in China. It was a government firmly committed by ideological, organizational, and military successes to the clear formulation of national goals and to the unambiguous right to mobilize resources for the achievement of those goals, regardless of the opposition of individuals or groups held over from the old order.

With this profound difference in the strength of their respective state ideologies and organizations, India and China undertook deliberate public action to address the problems of population growth and to intervene into human reproductive processes. As we shall see, the attack on the population problem, and even its fundamental identification, was not an isolated act of population planning. In each case it was an integral part of the overall process of planning for modern economic and social development.

POPULATION PLANNING: DECISION, IMPLEMENTATION,
AND IMPACT

Decision

In both China and India, the decision for an antinatalist policy was the
product of the combined activities of the national population census and
national economic planning. Censuses provided the conscious national
perception of population size and growth, which led to clear and forceful
arguments for fertility limitation. National planning provided the conscious formulation of collective goals, which included an official commitment to national efforts at fertility limitation. As with most other processes, that in China was more abrupt and revolutionary, that in India
was more gradual and evolutionary.

The censuses that provided India with her major capacity to perceive
population size and growth began in 1872. Table 3.1 shows an overview
of their results. The early efforts were rough and incomplete, but they
increased in both coverage and accuracy with each decennial count. Even
the increased capacity, however, did not move the British rulers to perceive problems in population growth, and for the first half-century of
census taking there were no Indian demographers to contest the generally
held notion that population growth implied prosperity. It was not until
after the fifth census, in 1911, that an Indian statistician, P. K. Wattal,
published a study of the census that identified population growth as a
problem, *The Population Problem in India* (1916). The study did not have
much influence at that time, in part no doubt because it was followed
almost immediately by the great influenza epidemic that wiped out virtually all of the decade's population increase. Nonetheless, it represents a
revolutionary change in thinking on India's population. It established a
course of public thinking and analysis that gradually achieved dominance.

Wattal revised and republished his study following the censuses of 1931
and 1951. The basic argument remained the same, but its scope and
precision developed considerably. In 1934, his analysis of the 1931 and
previous censuses provided an argument that India's "normal" rate of
growth was about 1 percent per year. With a population of about 350
million, this offered what he considered the "truly staggering prospect" of
India entering the twenty-first century with 700 million people.[13]

In 1934 Wattal pointed out that the previous fluctuations in decennial
growth rates had been caused by periodic famines and epidemics. India
was free of these after 1921, offering prospects for continued and even
increasing growth. He went on to analyze birth and death rates, marriage
rates, and unemployment, and was led by this to offer strong arguments
for public birth control programs. The 1958 study showed a continuation

TABLE 3.1
Indian Intercensual Growth Rates, 1871–1981

Decade	% Growth	Source
1872–1881	1.5	
1881–1891	9.6	
1891–1901	1.4	
1901–1911	6.4	
1911–1921	1.2	
1921–1931	10.4	Wattal (1934), p. 7
1931–1941	12.7	Wattal (1958), p. 25
1941–1951	13.2	
1951–1961	23.0	U.S. Bureau of Census (1978), p. 6
1961–1971	24.8	U.S. Bureau of Census (1978), p. 6
1971–1981	24.8	Census of India (1981)

Note: All figures are adjusted to the territory of independent India to make them comparable despite changes in territory.

of the "normal" rate and even offered prospects for an increase in the rate of growth.

For Wattal, for the Census Commissioner, and for other observers, 1921 emerged as a great watershed.[14] The fluctuations that produced relatively slow growth rates prior to 1921 had given way to continued growth at relatively high rates. There could be no doubt that this posed a serious problem for India, and that the solution necessarily lay in concerted collective efforts to reduce fertility.

The census intruded once again, in 1961, to produce not only an argument but also an official decision for greater urgency in attacking high fertility. For the first two five-year plans, 1951–56 and 1956–61, it was estimated that population would grow at about 1.25 percent per year. Pre-census surveys in 1959–60 showed that the actual rate for the two plan periods would be much higher, about 2.0 percent. Preliminary census figures from 1961, available when the third plan was being drafted, showed an even higher growth rate of about 2.3 percent. The adjusted figures would subsequently show a growth rate of about 2.0 percent, but the higher figure shocked Indian planners and increased their sense of urgency over the population problem. As we shall see, this led directly to a large increase in plan allocations for the family planning program, and for other changes as well that would signal greater efforts to reduce fertility through public programs.

If the increased perceptive capacities provided the arguments for reducing fertility, the development of national planning activity provided the mechanism for the decision that government should act for the entire society in reducing fertility. Economic planning had emerged as a central national activity during the 1930s. The Soviet five-year plans provided an important external stimulus that supported political developments in the Congress Party in India.[15] In 1934, Sir M. Visererarayya published his *Planned Economy for India,* which was basically a proposal for extended industrialization, with a large role for private firms. Under the presidency of Subhas Chandra Bose, the Congress Party created a National Planning Committee in 1938, with Nehru as its chairman. This brought together socialist, communist, and industrial leaders, who proposed a major effort to establish central government leadership and responsibility for directing the coming social and economic changes of the country. Eight groups with twenty-eight subcommittees were established to consider India's major problems and the course of collective action that each required. One of the subcommittees was specifically charged with addressing the population question.

Conflict with Gandhi forced Bose out of the Congress presidency in 1939, and conflict with the British put Nehru in jail. The war effort subsequently reduced Congress planning activity to a mere shadow, but the model was taken up again after the war. In 1947, when India achieved independence, the National Planning Committee published reports of most of its subcommittees, including the resolutions that each had proposed. The Population Subcommittee dealt with a wide variety of conditions and passed eleven resolutions, the fourth and fifth of which were directly concerned with national fertility limitation.

> 4. In the interests of social economy, family happiness and national planning, family planning and limitation of children are essential, and the state should adopt a policy to encourage these. It is desirable to lay stress on self-control, as well as to spread knowledge of cheap and safe methods of birth control. Birth control clinics should be established, and other necessary measures taken in this behalf and to prevent the use of advertisement of harmful methods.

> 5. We consider that the gradual raising of the marriage age and discouragement of polygamy are desirable in the interests of the limitation of family size.[16]

In March 1950, the Planning Committee was transformed into a permanent National Planning Commission with responsibility for creating five-year plans for national development. The first five-year plan for India went into effect in April 1951. It assumed an annual rate of population growth of 1.25 percent and recognized the responsibility of the state to undertake "positive measures . . . to inculcate the need and technique of family planning."[17] The resources allocated to this activity were small, only 6.5 million rupees out of a total plan allocation of 23.6 billion rupees, and were primarily for research and attitude surveys. The amount actually spent was even more modest, only 1.4 million out of a total expenditure of 19.6 billion rupees. Nonetheless, the decision for an official antinatalist policy was taken. It was publicly declared and embedded in the organization of national planning.

The decision was clearly the result of a gradual evolutionary development extending over the better part of a century. The line is not unbroken, but it is easily traced. The speed was hardly breakneck, but it did increase over time. From the systematic population counts beginning in 1872 through the rationalistic approach to national planning in the 1930s and finally to the creation of national economic plans, a process was in operation that led to a decision for a national antinatalist policy. There would be subsequent fluctuations in emphasis, but there would be no turning back from this fundamental break with past pronatalist policies. By this decision India became the first in what was to become a long line of high-fertility nations that would adopt explicit antinatalist policies in the third quarter of the twentieth century.

China's antinatalist policy decision is also rooted in perceptive capacities and planning orientations, but the historical lines of development are more broken and erratic than those in India. Census taking is not new to China, but in the modern period it has been anything but regular and cumulative. China has been counting heads for over two thousand years, but both coverage and accuracy have varied considerably with the quality of local administration, which has been deeply affected by the rise and fall of dynasties. When the government was weak, administration did not go beyond the walled towns of the provincial and county headquarters. Further, censuses were widely known to be undertaken for purposes of conscription or taxation, increasing both the incentive for and likelihood of evasion and underenumeration. The past two centuries have been no exception to the historic rule of variable accuracy, but they nonetheless show an unmistakable process of population growth.

The censuses of the period 1776 to 1850, and of 1953, are generally considered to be the most useful[18]. In the earlier period, population grew from 268 to 429 million, or under 1 percent per year. The last decades of Manchu rule were marked by sufficient strife to cause extensive loss of life and to make census figures quite unreliable. Just before the Manchu collapse in 1908, however, the government did establish a Directory of Statistics under the Ministry of Civil Affairs. The directorate conducted a census between the years 1908 and 1911, producing a figure of about 342 million as China's population.

The new Republican government published a census for 1912, giving a count of almost 420 million, with no explanation for the increase of 78 million. Chiang Kai-shek's Nationalist government tried again, beginning in 1928, to conduct a census, and it published these figures: for 1928, 442 million; for 1933, 444 million; and for 1936, 479 million. The final Nationalist count in 1947 showed a figure of 455 million. None of these could have been more than guesses, however, since the machinery for census taking simply did not exist. Nonetheless, no matter how inaccurate the latter figure, it was the only one that the new Communist leaders had available, and it represented a growth of about 6 percent over the past century. Here there were no grounds for concern about a population problem.

The bases for concern changed drastically, however, with the first Communist census of l953. This showed a total of 582,603,417 people,[19] or 28 percent above the last Nationalist census and about 36 percent above the 1850 count. More important, the census revealed that the current annual growth rate was probably above 2 percent, and that the population up to the age of seventeen constituted over 40 percent of the total. In terms of growth rate, absolute size, and dependency ratio, the demographers could see in these results the basis of a massive population problem.

These demographic perceptions would ultimately lead to a strong commitment to fertility control programs, but for almost two decades after the census they would be only one element in the policy debates. Four basic positions can be identified in the policy debates of the following years, with two forming the center of the controversy.

First, there was the pronatalist influence of the traditional value placed upon family size. It has often been noted that the Chinese have great procreative potential, deriving largely from the centrality of clan and family to Chinese social organization.[20] In the revolutionary situation, however, this tradition has not been without its detractors. Like other revolutionary leaders, the Chinese Communists defined the traditional family structure as a tool of the old order, an instrument of individual oppression and exploitation. Pronatalist forces carried by the traditional family would have no place in the ideology of the new state. The family has not, of course, succumbed to this onslaught,[21] but it has been deprived of a place in the policy debates on population.

A second major element in the debate is Chinese ethnocentrism. The traditional concept of China as the Middle Kingdom had clear pronatalist implications. A sense of Chinese innate superiority could only imply that more rather than fewer Chinese would be a good thing. It is possible that in its geopolitical manifestation this ethnocentric argument had some pronatalist influence during the Korean War, and more generally with respect to American military encirclement, but it does not appear to have been a powerful element in the debate.

The two remaining, and central, elements in the debate were vulgar versions of Malthusian and Marxian perspectives on population. Even before Malthus, the Chinese scholar Hung Lian-chi warned that a growing Chinese population would result in war and famine.[22] It was, however, the modern Malthusian argument, that progress is impossible due to the ability of population growth to outstrip output growth, which drew the ire of Marx and cast the frames of the modern debate. Marx held that surplus population, like surplus labor, is an inevitable product only of capitalism. A communist system, freed of the exploitation based on private property and capital accumulation, would have no population problem.

In the early period of Communist rule, the debate over the implications of population growth were thus cast in nineteenth-century ideological terms. Mao reacted in 1949 to a United States statement concerning the unbearable pressure of population growth on land in China with an attack in "The Bankruptcy of the Idealist Conception of History," in which he argued that China's large population was a source of strength, and all pessimistic views were "utterly groundless." A subsequent article in the *People's Daily* of 25 April 1952 described birth control as a form of genocide without bloodshed.[23]

All of these elements are interwoven in a historical dynamic. In effect, when the revolutionary tide flowed strongly, it brought high optimism for rapid increases in production and both neglect of and resistance to ideas for birth control. When the revolutionary tide ebbed and technical and organizational problems of production were major concerns, population growth was accorded higher priority as a problem, and birth control gained greater attention and resources.

It is possible to identify three periods: 1949–58, 1958–67, and 1967–present in which the revolutionary tide flowed and ebbed. Each period began with a revolutionary enthusiasm that precluded a sense of urgency about population growth; but each also ended in a cooling of revolutionary fervor, a turn toward the more instrumental issues of development, and a greater concern with the problems of rapid population growth. Throughout the flowing and ebbing of the tides, however, it is also possible to see a steady cumulation of both interest in and organizational capacity to deal with population growth. Policy statements vacillated, but underneath them birth control activity grew, although not always with the same speed.

In the initial stage, 1949–58, the Chinese Communist leaders supported a pronatalist policy, rejecting what was then defined as the Malthusian view of the interrelationship between mass poverty and population growth. The optimism brought by victory in the revolutionary war combined with the model of modernization provided by the Soviets to shape the content of population debates and policy in this period.

Following the Marxian theory of population, the Chinese leaders held the optimistic view that the country would before long achieve sufficiently rapid industrialization and modernization of agriculture to raise the living standards of the Chinese masses and eventually to reduce fertility. The leaders were further convinced that population growth was proof of benefits to be derived from the economic progress created by the Chinese form of socialism. Population size was a reflection of national power. Thus, the results of the national census of 1953 were interpreted optimistically by some political leaders, such as Pai Chien-hwa. He saw a population of more than 600 million as an economic asset rather than a liability. It was also argued that a large population was the foundation of the new socialist system. Under the People's Democracy, people were regarded as the most valuable resource, and also as the masters of their own fate.[24]

Two other factors also appear to have supported, though perhaps not decisively, China's early pronatalist policy. One was the expected impact on fertility of the attack on the traditional family. The Decree of 1 May 1950 denounced and made illegal many forms of the old traditional family, and some leaders apparently thought this would have a negative impact on fertility. If this did not support the other pronatalist forces in China, it certainly did not counter them.

The second factor supporting pronatalism was the Korean War. This brought increased mortality in war casualties, but even more, it emphasized the dangers of the then considerable military pressure on China. American military encirclement, John Foster Dulles's dream of rolling back communism, and the threatening posture of the Nationalists on Taiwan provided constant reminders of strategic dangers and supported the view that the Middle Kingdom would be safer with a larger population.

Nonetheless, the 1953 census started the movement toward a gradual change in policy from pro to antinatalism. The change was initially timid and hesitant, but it gathered momentum under the impact of the regime's increased capacities for monitoring social and economic changes. Premier Chou En-lai reportedly announced in June 1950 that China's population was about 488 million. The publication of census returns showed this figure to be about 100 million too small. An error of this magnitude was bound to have profound effects on elite perceptions. A deputy of the National People's Congress presented arguments for the spread of birth control information in 1953. He did not present a Malthusian argument, but focused attention on maternal and child health, with some emphasis as well on the larger macroeconomic obstacles posed by a large and rapidly growing population. A further series of articles in 1955 promoted the idea of birth control for maternal and child health, as well as for the purposes of relieving pressures on young men and women so that they could devote more time and energy to productive work and to political studies.[25]

It was not, however, until 1956 that the antinatalist view received explicit, official support. The initial reaction of the Chinese Communist Party was unclear until the Eighth Party Congress in August of that year; it was then that Chao Li-tzu spoke of birth control. The core of his argument lay in this statement: "We agree that appropriate birth control methods are desirable in order to protect maternal and child health and educate the younger generation which will contribute to the health and prosperity of the Chinese people. The Health Department, in collaboration with other concerned agencies, should adopt effective information campaigns and other means for this purpose."[26]

Until this statement was issued, the promotion of birth control was carried out by individuals who were active in voluntary family planning activities and had little contact with the government or the Chinese Communist Party. With this official support, the birth control program of China was steadily intensified until 1958. During 1955–1958, the Health Department conducted an aggressive information and education campaign to disseminate contraceptive information and to increase awareness of the importance of family planning among the masses. Induced abortion was legalized on medical grounds in 1954, with a further relaxation of restrictions in 1955. Sterilization was made easily available, and medical research on contraception was encouraged. The birth control program was not integrated into the first five-year plan of China (1953–1957);[27] nor was birth control included in the 1956 draft of the "Twelve-Year Plan for Agricultural Development 1956–67." It was, however, included in the revised version of the latter document published in 1957.[28]

The official acceptance of birth control was preceded by debates between intellectuals represented by the president of Peking University, Professor Ma Yinchu, and the Chinese Communist Party, especially through the magazine *New Construction*. The debates eventually resulted in a speech by Professor Ma at the People's Congress in July 1957. He argued that China's unlimited population growth would require increases in food production and a corresponding reduction in cash crop production, and that such a condition would negatively affect light industry directly and heavy industry indirectly. He also proposed that projections of the rapid population growth, and their implications for development planning, be incorporated into the second and third five-year plans. In addition, he advocated both birth control and marriage at a late date.[29]

The support of birth control by the Chinese intellectuals was not based on the neo-Malthusian theory of population. Its ideological justification was found in the Marxian thesis that planned population growth is acceptable when it is necessary because a socialist society regulates its material production, and that the citizens' rights, including induced abortion and contraception, are to be protected in a socialist society.

In 1958, the revolutionary tide flowed once again with the Great Leap Forward. With it came an attack on birth control. Although the nineteenth-century ideological elements of the population debate had been more or less cleared away with the 1955–57 pronouncements, the change of policy would nonetheless lead to bitter ideological attacks on supporters of previous policies. Not untypically, these attacks materialized rapidly with changes in policy. The 9 October 1957 issue of the *People's Daily*, the organ of the Communist Party, contained articles supporting birth control. In the issue of 14 October, however, the bitter attacks on those intellectuals who had supported birth control commenced. They continued until May 1958, when both Liu Shao-chi and Mao announced that the new revolutionary strategy needed more people. For Mao once again the people were defined as the source of energy and commitment. To reduce their growth would only deprive the revolution of their energies.

With the flowing of the revolutionary tide, optimism was once again high. Agricultural production had scored some increases, and the shift from peasant to commune organization, transforming a mass of peasantry into agricultural wage laborers, was thought capable of producing even greater increases. Against this surge of revolutionary optimism, birth control was defined as pessimistic and defeatist. It was simply incompatible with the new confidence embodied in the Great Leap Forward.[30]

Despite the pronatalist pronouncements by the Chinese decision makers arguing for increases in the labor force during the period of the Great Leap Forward, birth control activities were not necessarily prohibited. Birth control clinics were not closed down, and contraceptives and abortion were still available. This disparity between the explicit policy statement and the continued implementation of a birth control program may well suggest a fundamental dilemma which the Chinese political leaders faced at that time. The dilemma was that while recognizing the need to reduce fertility, they also realized the difficulty in disseminating family planning information and in providing contraceptive services, especially for the rural population, within a short period of time. They found it hard to change the attitude of Chinese peasants toward large families, as Premier Chou admitted to some visiting Japanese family planning experts.[31] Thus, as Leo Orleans suggests, the Chinese policy makers resorted to the alternative approach, which was to increase productivity, especially agricultural productivity, in order to ease the hardship experienced by the rural population. This was in part why the Great Leap Forward campaign subscribed to a pronatalist population policy. Thus, this shift in the government's population policy should be considered temporary.[32]

The Great Leap Forward was a disastrous failure. Industrial production fell far short of the expected goal, and the quality of industrial products was often substandard The agricultural sector also suffered from natural disasters, and agricultural production planning was hit by a massive statistical failure. Goals and achievements were greatly inflated as they were transmitted upward by cadres eager to gain favor and to protect themselves from the wrath of the true revolutionaries. Such statistical inflation could not for long hide the realities of production, however. The recognition of the failures was not long in coming, and the Great Leap Forward was abandoned in January 1961.

The failure of the Great Leap Forward forced the Chinese decision makers to reverse their economic policy. The new policy was more pragmatic; it was oriented toward strengthening the agricultural base of the economy and stimulating industrialization through surplus agricultural production. The main concern, however, was with increasing food production in large part to feed 600 million Chinese.

Family planning was reactivated at the beginning of 1962 as a means of controlling rapid population growth. While these activities received less publicity than before, they were reported to be supported by the greater involvement of high party and government officials. This political support was also augmented by the mobilization of larger financial resources than before. For instance, it is reported that large numbers of personnel were trained for family planning activities, and generous incentives were provided for induced abortion.[33]

While family planning services were extensively provided, delayed marriage was also vigorously promoted as another means to curtail rapid population growth. Numerous articles in newspapers and magazines such as the *People's Daily* pointed out to the readers the negative effects of early marriage, especially on the opportunities for political studies and technical or career development. In contrast, it was argued that delayed marriage would promote better maternal and child health and would facilitate the acquisition of technical knowledge for Chinese workers. During the years from 1962 to 1966, the recommended age at marriage for Chinese women was between twenty-three and twenty-seven, while for men it was twenty-five to twenty-nine years.[34]

Family planning activities were also intensified, and the same political justifications were used. Family planning was not intended for elimination of the surplus population, but for the promotion of family health, political study, and productivity. With strong political commitment, family planning information could be widely disseminated through hospitals, and clinics as well as through labor unions and women's groups.

The reversal in population policy after the Great Leap Forward was also supported by the increased capability of demographic monitoring. A somewhat limited census of the Chinese population was conducted in 1964. Like the 1953 census, this revealed that China had a larger population with a higher growth rate than expected.[35] This seems to be reflected in a response of Premier Chou En-lai to Edgar Snow in 1964. Chou indicated that the target of the Chinese government was to reduce the growth rate to less than 2 percent, since it had risen to 2.5 percent partly as a result of improved economic conditions in the past two years. Chou also argued that birth planning would contribute to an improvement in living standards.[36]

A slightly different interpretation of the findings was presented, however, just before the beginning of the Cultural Revolution, to discredit the improved demographic monitoring. In early 1966, Chairman Mao stated in an interview with Edgar Snow that he did not believe the report showing that the population of China was between 680 and 690 million. He further argued that the population growth rate might be declining due to the high mortality rate. It is significant that Chairman Mao held this demographic perception immediately preceding the Cultural Revolution in 1966.

The final period of population policy began when the political tranquility of the early 1960s was shattered in 1966 by a mobilization of unprecedented proportions, commonly called the Cultural Revolution. The political rampage of the Red Guards, with the encouragement of Chairman Mao, produced massive dislocation of both population and administration. It generated political turmoil that tore the country apart for three years and continued, though with diminishing force, until the death of Mao in 1976.

For the initial three years of intensive cultural revolution, there ceased to be political pronouncements concerning population growth. Once again the tide of revolutionary fervor flowed, ignoring the pessimistic calculations of population and food supply that had supported an antinatalist policy. There was no explicit reversal to a pronatalist policy, as there was during the Great Leap Forward, but the breakdown of all administrative machinery meant that family planning, as well as other public services, would be weakened and disrupted.

The final period turned with the ebbing of the revolutionary tide and the weakening of the Cultural Revolution around 1969. The army gradually brought order to the countryside, and more technocratic ideologies and groups gained ascendancy in government. Once more the emphasis on modernization returned. The death of Mao in 1976 exposed the radical group, and the "Gang of Four" became the scapegoat whose repudiation would cleanse the revolution of what were now considered irrational and subversive elements.

At the first session of the Fifth National People's Congress, on 26 February 1978, Chairman Hua Guofeng explicitly delineated the new modernization orientation.

By the end of this century, the output per unit of major agricultural products is expected to reach or surpass advanced world levels and the output of major industrial products to approach, equal or outstrip that of the most developed capitalist countries. In agricultural production, the highest possible degree of mechanization, electrification and irrigation will be achieved. There will be automation in the main industrial processes, a major increase in rapid transport and communication services and a considerable rise in labour productivity. We must apply the results of modern science and technology on a broad scale, make extensive use of new materials and sources of energy, and modernize our major products and process of production.[37]

In consonance with this renewed emphasis on economic modernization, the Chinese leaders once again recognized the economic liabilities of the country's large and rapidly growing population.[38] The new constitution, adopted by the Fifth National People's Congress, clearly reflected this concern and linked it with support for equal rights for women, the protection of marriage, the welfare of mother and child. Article 53 of the new constitution states: "Men and women shall marry of their own free will. The State protects marriage, the family, and the mother and child. The State advocates and encourages family planning."[39]

The antinatalist link to economic development was further reiterated by Chairman Hua Guofeng in his report to the Sixth National People's Congress in June 1979. This statement was even more explicit about the demographic target of the People's Republic of China and the means to achieve it:

> We must conscientiously carry out ideological, educational and technical work as well as child care and health work throughout the country so that people can practice family planning willingly, safely and effectively. Practical measures should be taken to reward couples who limit themselves to a single child and gradually to institute social insurance for aged people who are childless . . . . This year, we must do everything we can to lower the country's population growth rate to about ten per thousand and we must continue to lower it year by year in the future. By 1985 it should drop to five per thousand.[40]

The statement by Chairman Hua was being translated into a draft of new family planning and birth control law by the National People's Congress in June 1979. The new law includes economic incentive measures such as rewarding a married couple with only one child with child health subsidies, bonus work points, higher pensions, and priority in the allocation of housing in urban areas and private plots in the rural areas.[41]

It is not yet possible to tell how these drastic new measures will work, or how stable they will be in the future. Nonetheless, China is now committed to a strong antinatalist policy. Over the past decades the tides of revolutionary fervor alternately obstructed and promoted the movement to this new policy. Although the flowing of the tide brought optimism, curtailing emphasis on antinatalism, each ebbing of the tide seems to have left more and more of the ground exposed. With each successive commitment to economic development, the perception of rapid population growth as an obstacle to the achievement of national goals has been strengthened. Each successive flooding of revolutionary fervor reduced the emphasis upon, but did not reverse the previous movement toward, antinatalism. Today an extreme ebb tide has left the Chinese government as perhaps the regime most powerfully committed to fertility reduction.

The antinatalist policy decisions of both China and India thus represent a profound movement in human ecological processes. For the first time in history, these large populations, organized through modern political institutions, have embarked upon conscious and vigorous efforts to reduce fertility and population growth. The world at large intruded only little, and not always with support, into the formulation of these new efforts. The decisions were primarily made from within and reflected the emergence of new internal political and social forces. Both nations were pioneers in the world's new political-ecological adjustments to rapid population growth. There are two important similarities in the two countries' decisions for antinatalist policies, which can tell us much about the current ecological process that is at work.

First, both nations emerged in 1950 with great confidence that independence and central planning would work quick miracles with the major problems of poverty and inequality. The confidence is understandable, however naive it appears in hindsight. Elites in each nation had seen foreign domination as the major cause of poverty. Both sets of elites also saw the achievement of independence as a first step in bold new centrally directed efforts that would eradicate domination and poverty.

In both cases it was those very centrally planned efforts that led to the adoption of official antinatalist policies. In neither case was population policy itself a central element of national policy. Rather, it was derived from more deeply embedded goals of modern economic and social transformation. As those goals were given organizational and programmatic life, and especially as national monitoring capacities were developed and specifically tuned to the achievement of these new goals, population policy experienced a profound transformation. From a weak and derived position, antinatalism has in both countries come to be a primary national programmatic goal.

Second, both nations experienced deep ambivalence about antinatalist policies, and in both these were only symptoms of a more profound ambivalence over the basic goal of modern industrial transformation. The expressions of ambivalence were different, to be sure, but both strove for and feared modernization.

Gandhi, and his disciples after him, led the opposition to a fertility control program based on modern contraceptive technology. They considered modern contraceptives to be weak and hedonistic means that could not lead to good ends. The fertility control of which they approved could only be achieved through self-control motivated by a high consciousness of individual responsibility and moral action.

Mao opposed fertility control on the ideological grounds generated by

Marx's bitter diatribe against Malthus. Population problems were sympto-matic only of capitalism, where private property led to exploitation and to the view of people as commodities. In a socialist revolution, people were power. Under the guidance of the party, population constituted a force that would tear apart the evil old world and build a new and better one in its place. The revolution would preclude a population problem by produc-ing enough for all, now and into the indefinite future.

Both expressions also reflected a profound ambivalence over the course of modern industrialization. For each group of revolutionaries, the search for material power threatened the attempt to build a new type of society based on new persons. For Gandhi, material goods threatened to subvert the soul force he attempted to mobilize. For Mao, industrial production threatened to produce a new class of exploiters and to subvert the con-struction of a new type of man whose social responsibility would always triumph over the desire for individual or family gain.

In both nations the realities of rule and the intractable problems of mass poverty have reduced considerably, though certainly not eliminated, the earlier ambivalence. The alleviation of mass poverty and the external demands of national power appear to require massive and rapid industrial development. In addition, immensely powerful bureaucratic organizations have been built up around the business of planning and industrialization. The ideology of revolutionary development has a weaker organizational base, and its programmatic implications are often only negative and lack clear and precise organizational activity. Under these circumstances, na-tional industrial development has emerged as the dominant goal, and with it the demand for urgent collective efforts at fertility limitation. For now, at any rate, the earlier ambivalence presents little problem in either coun-try. It is perhaps too much to expect, however, that it is firmly and forever laid to rest.

These similarities are instructive. The decision-making processes that lead to official antinatalist policies appear moved by the same logic, re-gardless of the political evolution and the ideological content with which poor, high-fertility populations have come to address the modern world. Those political differences have, however, had a marked impact on both program implementation and the impact those programs have had on actual human fertility. It is to these, then, that we must give our attention now.

Implementation: India

Over the past three decades the organizational system for implementing India's antinatalist decision has grown massively in size, but its character has changed little. It continues to be dominated by the public health and medical bureaucracy and by the concentration on a narrow range of clinic-based contraceptive technology. It is, in effect, an organizational system designed to deliver contraceptive supplies and services to individuals seeking assistance. True to the liberal character of the entire Indian political-administrative system, and in contrast with the Chinese system, it is ill-designed to mobilize the population forcefully for any concerted effort. As we shall see, when the government did attempt to use the system for a level of mobilization it was ill-equipped to achieve, the result was disastrous for the ruling group.

The growth in the system's size has been dramatic and is easy to document. Three basic comparisons should suffice to show the growth: with total national planning, total national output, and foreign assistance.

Table 3.2 shows the allocated and actual expenditures for the seven plan periods from 1951 up to the current plan for 1978–83. The first three plans cover the fifteen years from 1951 to 1965. There followed three annual plans during the 1966–68 period when the five-year planning schedule was disrupted by economic dislocations and war. The fourth plan, 1969–74, resumed the regular five-year schedule. The fifth plan, 1974–79, was aborted in its final year by the fall of the Congress government. The plan was terminated by the new Janata government, which went on to construct its own plan for the period 1978–83.

Total plan allocations during this period grew rapidly from 23,560 million to 693,800 million rupees. Throughout the growth, four major categories of development infrastructure (agriculture, irrigation and power, mining and manufacturing, and transportation and communication) claimed about 80 percent of the total allocations. Human services consistently received about 20 percent. Within human services, family planning allocations grew rapidly from 6.5 million to 7,650 million rupees, or from about 0.03 percent of total allocations to a high point of almost 2 percent in the fourth plan period, and then back to 1 percent for the current plan.

In the first plan period, much initial work had to be done to create the tools of planning and the administrative procedures for using the resources allocated. As a result, the overall absorptive capacity of the system was relatively low: only about 80 percent of the total allocated funds were actually spent. Most of the major categories experienced roughly the same level of shortfall in spending. In family planning, the reluctance of Gandhians to move rapidly into the distribution of contraceptives, and a greater emphasis on motivation, education, and research, resulted in an even lower level of actual spending. Only 22 percent of the allocated funds were actually used. After this plan period, overall capacity for utilizing resources grew rapidly in all sectors. Family planning has, however, consistently lagged behind other organized sectors in the capacity to spend its allocated funds. The discrepancy is not large, especially from the third plan onward, but it is persistent. It reflects an aspect of the family planning organization that we shall discuss presently.

TABLE 3.2
Indian National Plans, Percentage of Funds Allocated to Major Categories, and Actual Expenditures as a Percentage of Allocated by Major Categories

| | | | | Five Years Plans and Years | | | |
	I 1951–55	II 1956–60	III 1961–65	Annual Plans 1966–68	IV 1969–73	V 1974–77	VI 1978–83
Allocated funds							
Total (mill. rps.)	23,560	48,000	75,000	66,250	159,020	372,500	693,800
% To:							
Agriculture	15	12	14	17	17	13	12
Irrigation & power	28	19	22	25	22	24	44
Mining & manufacturing	8	19	24	25	23	24	15
Transportation	24	29	20	18	20	19	15
Human services	23	20	20	15	17	16	13
Family planning	0.03	0.1	0.4	1	2	1.4	1
Actual as a percentage of allocated for:							
Total funds	83	97	114	a	99	106	b
Agriculture	81	97	102	a	85	91	b
Irrigation & power	88	97	115	a	121	161	b
Mining & manufacturing	54	126	110	a	86	82	b
Transportation	93	91	142	a	95	97	b
Human services	89	83	99	a	108	107	b
Family planning	22	43	93	a	88	93	b

Sources: Government of India, Five Year Plans, respective years.
[a] Only actual expenditures are given for the three annual plans.
[b] Only allocated figures have been given.

TABLE 3.3
Indian Family Planning Expenditures in Relation to Gross National Product at Current
Market Prices, 1951–78

Plan Period and Year	F.P. Exp. (mill. rps.)	GNP (mill. rps.)	F.P. Exp. per mill. rps. GNP
I. 1951/2–55/6 (ann. ave.)	0.28	95,452	3
II. 1956/7	0.87	112,090	8
1957/8	2.60	112,370	23
1958/9	3.15	126,500	25
1959/60	5.10	130,900	39
1960/1	9.84	139,990	70
III. 1961/2	13.93	147,990	94
1962/3	27.72	157,270	176
1963/4	21.72	179.780	121
1964/5	65.25	211,130	309
1965/6	120.00	218,660	549
Annual Plans: 1966/7	134.26	252,500	532
1967/8	265.23	296,120	896
1968/9	305.15	302,930	1,007
IV. 1969/70	361.81	335,210	1,079
1970/1	489.04	364,520	1,342
1971/2	617.56	389,720	1,585
1972/3	797.43	429,390	1,857
1973/4	494.13	534,470	925
V. 1974/5–77/8 (ann. ave.)	1,197.50	705,240	1,698

Sources: Family planning expenditures 1951–73/4, *Family Welfare Planning Yearbook* (1973), p. 83, final year adjusted with FYP V data. 1974/5–77/8 from FYP VI. GNP (at factor costs) from Government of India *Economic Survey 1980–81* (New Delhi: Government of India Printer, 1981), table 1.1, p. 65.

Family planning expenditures have also grown rapidly as a proportion of total national output. Table 3.3 shows the growth in family planning expenditures and in gross domestic product. By examining family planning expenditures as a proportion of total Gross National Product, we correct for price rises and show the change in the real commitment of societal resources to public efforts at fertility reduction. Since family planning costs are such a small portion of total output, they are shown in million rupees in column two, and million rupees per GNP in column four. It is this last column that provides the data to assess the growth of government allocations to family planning. The pattern is clear and undebatable. Except for two years, 1963–64 and 1973–74, there is a continuous and substantial rise in real national resources committed to the national family planning effort.

Finally, table 3.4 indicates that this financial effort has largely been a domestic one. For the first three plan periods, when India spent about 272 million rupees for family planning, it was virtually without foreign

TABLE 3.4
Domestic and Foreign Aid Expenditures on Indian National Family Planning, 1951–77 (in million rupees)

	1951–65	1966–73	1974–77	Total
Indian expenditures	150	3,584	4,790	8,524
Foreign assistance	0	736	599[a]	1,335
Total	150	4,320	5,389	9,859
% Foreign	0	17.0	11.1[a]	13.5

Sources: Indian expenditures from table 3.3. Foreign assistance: 1966–73, Visaria and Jain, India (1976), p. 29; 1974–77, UNFPA (1978), p. 184.
[a]UNFPA series on foreign assistance shows 216.4 million rupees for 1977–78. If this amount is not included, the foreign assistance will be only 382.6 million rupees, reducing the foreign percentage to 7.4 for 1974–77 and to 11.8 for the entire period.

financial assistance in this area. Following the world decision for public intervention into reproductive behavior, India was the target of what may be likened to a crash program in foreign aid for fertility reduction. In the eight years of the annual plans and the fourth plan, foreign contributions amounted to 736 million rupees and accounted for 17 percent of the total funds spent in India. The United States was quickly on the scene, providing half of the total foreign funds. Sweden was not far behind, with almost a third. Over a score of other international organizations joined the scene as well. Political conflicts between India and the United States resulted in a cessation of United States assistance, with no new obligations made after 1972. Since that time, the various United Nations funding and technical agencies and the Scandinavian countries have been the major contributors, and the foreign proportion has dropped to only 11 percent of total expenditures. The United States is now in the process of negotiating new aid agreements, but it is expected that the relative levels of family planning assistance will probably remain less than one-fifth of the total Indian financial effort.

While foreign financial assistance has not been insignificant, it must be seen in its proper perspective. From 1965 onwards, India received a great deal of urgent advice, as well as technical and financial assistance, for its national family planning program.[42] UN, U.S. AID, and World Bank missions all strongly pressed India for more action. The IUD was imported in 1965 and was hailed as a major technological breakthrough that would solve India's problems—if not overnight, then certainly in the near future. In 1966 the United States tied its food aid to Indian investments in family planning. Then came the flood of funds, amounting to something in excess of 100 million rupees per year from 1968 to 1973. There was also a flood of international governmental and non governmental organizations with activities in India. The most recent UNFPA Inventory lists assistance projects of thirty international private and government organizations with activities in India.[43] All of this neither determined nor altered, but only complemented, the efforts of dominant movements within India to act with more determination to limit fertility.

We have already noted that the 1961 census produced its own internal shocks, which are clearly reflected in the pattern of real expenditures. The last column in table 3.3 shows that expenditures almost doubled from 1961 to 1962, more than doubled from 1963 to 1964, and then almost doubled again in the following year, all before the flood of foreign assistance began. Foreign assistance was important, but primarily because it gave added fiscal weight to the internal organizational forces that were identifying India's population problem with increasing precision and were charting a course of increased public action for attention to that problem. As will be apparent shortly, in non-monetary aspects the foreign assistance has not by any means always been so benign.

India's great mobilization of financial resources was used to build a large, specialized bureaucratic system for the distribution of modern contraceptives. The model to be followed was already suggested in Wattal's analysis of 1934 and the Planning Committee's population resolutions of 1939 and 1947: government-established birth control clinics. There were 147 at the end of the first plan (1955) and 1,800 by the end of the second (1960); 12,138 in 1965, 40,360 by 1972–3, and 82,546 reported in 1976.[44] These were at first only specialized birth control clinics, then gradually contraceptive services came to be offered by most of the centers of the medical and public health system. The ratio of population per outlet dropped precipitously from about 2.8 million in 1956 to 7,600 per outlet in 1976. By 1972, the Family Welfare Planning Yearbook listed 50,491 full-time personnel in family planning at the district and clinic levels, and by 1976 the number had grown to 56,477.[45]

At its core, this distributive system is an integral part of the national medical and public health system. The Ministry is at the top of Health and Family Planning, with comparable state ministries directing district family planning bureaus that in turn provide services through urban and rural primary health centers, subcenters, and family welfare planning centers. Beyond this, core resources are directed to family planning outlets in a large number of public corporations, voluntary organizations, government and private hospitals, and thousands of small private retailers who sell condoms subsidized through the government's Nirodh program. It is neither necessary nor feasible to provide a detailed picture of all of the elements of this system. Many accounts of the Indian family planning program include an organizational chart, which is a familiar map of lines of authority and specialized responsibility.[46] This type of map with boxes and lines has come to symbolize the rational bureaucratic approach to the large scale enterprises our era uses to address large scale problems.

This vast, complex, and variegated system can best be characterized as a public bureaucracy dominated by a Western-oriented medical profession, delivering a narrow range of contraceptive techniques to individual users on demand, and employing individual motivation and mass communication techniques to create demand.[47] It is a system that is familiar in the organizational landscape of rich industrial capitalist nations, that is reflected in tattered and threadbare fashion in poor nations, and that diverges in significant ways from the systems found in new revolutionary socialist nations.

From the program's inception in 1951 through each of the five-year plans, there has been a clear and explicit commitment to link family planning with the public health and medical system. Fertility limitation began as the responsibility of the Ministry of Health and has remained as such, although there has been considerable differentiation and specialized development of the family planning organization at levels both of central government and state capitals. This has implied two interrelated conditions: the dominance of the Western-oriented medical profession and a concomitant reluctance to use private market, nonmedical networks for contraceptive distribution.

The Indian medical profession has acted much as have its counterparts in other pluralist nations. It eliminated the "licenciate," or the middle level of less well-trained doctors which the British had created, in an attempt to meet Indian needs. It blocked the integration of traditional practitioners into the public system; and it resisted, albeit unsuccessfully, the expansion of state medical schools. When schools were expanded under pressure from the states, the profession ensured its dominance by resisting any changes in the content of training away from Western individualistic and curative orientations. Although the profession has not resisted the expansion of nurses' training, it has successfully insisted upon medical control of the application of oral contraceptives, IUDs, and, of course, sterilization. When the state attempted to correct the heavy urban bias in the distribution of doctors, the medical profession successfully fought a proposal for compulsory service of medical graduates in rural areas.[48]

In effect, the evolution of a pluralist political system from British to Independent India implied the protection of professional groups, permitting them to use whatever political power they could mobilize. In India, as in other pluralist systems, the medical profession has been highly successful in gaining sufficient political power to establish and protect its monopoly over a wide range of activities. Such professional control is typically far more effective in promoting the interests of the professionals than in advancing services for the clients.[49]

India's reluctance to use the private market and nonmedical networks for contraceptive delivery can clearly be seen in the experiences with the IUD, the pill, and the condom. All three have involved foreign assistance, not always happily. The IUD was introduced into India in the early

1960s. Professional medical norms dictated careful testing of the device before it could be officially adopted. Between 1962 and 1964, the government conducted about fifty clinic trials all over India, and it had access to the growing international literature on the device.[50] The health minister, Sushila Nayar, favored a cautious approach, applying the device only where adequate medical facilities were available for effective insertions and follow-up. This was, however, just at the beginning of the world's new enthusiasm for fertility limitation in foreign aid. India was then host to a United Nations expert team, which it had requested in January 1965.[51] The team apparently took a more urgent view of the population situation and was far more confident of the IUD than was the health minister. After a reported full day of discussion, one of the UN team members succeeded in persuading the minister to abandon her cautious approach and to press for a vigorous program of IUD insertions.[52] The result was at best disappointing; to some it appeared disastrous.

The IUD was first offered as a program method in 1965, and it gained 812,713 acceptors in the first year (through March 1966). In 1966–67, there were 909,726 acceptors. The promised breakthrough appeared assured. In the following year, however, the new acceptors fell drastically to about 669,000; in 1968–69, to 478,000; and the numbers remained considerably below 500,000 per year until 1975. [53] In the first two years, the IUD provided about 40 percent of the total program acceptors. The precipitous drop brought it to less than 10 percent by the early 1970s. This can scarcely be called a failure, except of initial expectations, but it was surely that, and the reasons for even this failure of expectations are instructive.

Effective use of the IUD requires good clinical services and a strong orientation toward clients. Insertions must be carefully done after thorough screening for contraindications. Clients require both careful treatment during insertion and adequate follow-up services to take care of the inevitable side effects. There is ample evidence that careful, client-oriented services can produce extensive popular acceptance of the IUD.[54] India apparently lacked the capacity to provide such services, or at least in sufficient amounts to recruit more than about half a million acceptors per year. The early enthusiasm led to ambitious targets, with the inevitable pressures that produced overzealous recruiters. Overworked government doctors were apparently unable to provide the mandatory careful individual service, and clinic and extension facilities were incapable of providing the follow-up support needed for successful IUD programing.

These observations are widely made with respect to the weakness of the IUD program, but there is another observation that is not made. India has apparently been unwilling or unable to use private medical practitioners to insert IUDs on the basis of a government-provided fee for service, although it is well known that this strategy proved highly effective in both Taiwan and South Korea. It is not clear in this case why India has not made greater use of its private medical sector, but the condom experience indicates a possibly pervasive and nonrational distrust of the private sector.[55] At any rate, the lessons that other countries have to teach about the use of private doctors for IUD insertion have not been taken up by India.

The lesson concerning foreign experts was fully learned, however. Another round of confrontations emerged over the use of the oral contraceptive. In these cases, it was the Americans who pushed with great vigor. U.S. AID's population office made strong and repeated recommendations for the Indians to adopt widespread distribution of the pill. Private American drug company representatives toured India and attempted to open outlets for the distribution of their products.

Indian resistance has been near complete. The government has undertaken numerous studies of the pill under central medical supervision, yet still remains skeptical of both its safety and utility. Foreign drug company representatives have been officially ejected from the country. Today the family planning program remains almost completely without the pill as a contraceptive method for general distribution. It appears that in this case a very specific conflict with and rejection of American pressure may lie behind the nonuse of the pill as a standard program device.[56]

Rejection of the private market, however, has not been complete. India has pioneered in the distribution of condoms through private commercial channels and has developed a distribution model that has been taken up by a number of other countries.[57] In 1968, the Department of Family Planning decided to undertake a program of subsidized commercial distribution through six of the country's major marketers of light consumer goods. The government recruited marketing executives and paid their salaries, underwrote advertising costs, and provided subsidized condoms to the distributors.[58] The distributors selected an appropriate name, Nirodh, a valued Sanskrit word meaning "prevention," and designed a marketing campaign with strategies that had proved effective in the sales of other products. Sales increased rapidly, from 53 million condoms in 1970–71 to 115 million in 1973–74.

This unprecedented collaboration between government and private distributors in family planning has not, however, been without considerable strain.[59] The program was originally conceived by a foreign marketing expert working with the Ford Foundation in India. He reports extensive difficulties in bringing the government to accept the demands of private marketing. Executive salaries were both higher and more variable than civil service commissions usually find tolerable. Executive demands for rapid information feedback, for autonomy in decisions on packaging and distribution, and for heavy advertising outlays—greater than sales revenues in the early stages—were accepted by Indian bureaucrats only with the greatest reluctance. After rapid increases in sales, the government cut advertising outlays and raised the price of condoms as part of an economy drive in 1975. The result was an immediate drop in sales by 45 percent to only 64 million condoms in 1975–76. Here the foreign assistance has been useful and effective, but the bureaucrats' distrust of the domestic private market system has consistently placed severe obstacles in the way of its effective utilization.

The pattern of methods used, shown in table 3.5, provides much information on India's family planning program. India's most distinctive successes in family planning have come with the use of male sterilization.[60] Sterilization of both males and females was provided in some state clinics and programs throughout the 1950s. By the end of the decade over 88,000 sterilizations had been performed, of which about 60 percent were female and 40 percent male. This in itself is quite remarkable, both for the large number and for the heavy proportion of male acceptors, all in the face of central government resistance to the method. Not until Sushila Nayar became minister for Health and Family Planning in 1962 was there top-level support for the use of sterilization. The initiative had been taken in the states, with Maharashtra, Kerala, Tamil Nadu, and Karnataka leading the way. During the 1960s, however, with the backing of the central government, male sterilizations grew very rapidly, overtaking female sterilizations, so that by the end of the decade more than a million vasectomies were being performed yearly, against less than 400,000 tubal ligations. It was at this point that the now famous "vasectomy camp" strategy was developed.

Late in the 1960s Dr. D. N. Pai opened a mass sterilization clinic at the Bombay Railway Station, which had over 200,000 travelers per day. The clinic was a considerable success and suggested a new tactic. In November-December 1970, Ernakulum District in Kerala State held a mass vasectomy camp in which all district offices were mobilized to recruit acceptors and to bring them to a central location where doctors performed operations in a setting that was a cross between a medieval fair and an automobile assembly line. Monetary incentives were given to both recruiters and acceptors. The camp was a considerable success, with 15,000 vasectomies performed in that one month, compared with just over 50,000 performed for the entire state in each of the two preceding years. This was especially encouraging, since it was precisely at this time that the IUD reverses were being experienced. Other states subsequently adopted the mass camp tactic.

In fiscal year 1971–1972, nine states organized vasectomy campaigns in 52 districts.[61] They recruited 761,138 acceptors, or 55.8 percent of all sterilization acceptors in those districts for the entire year. Efforts in-

TABLE 3.5
Number of Family Planning Program Acceptors by Method. All India, 1956–78

Year	Sterilizations			IUD Insertions	Conventional Users[a]	Total Acceptors
	Male	Female	Total			
1956	2,395	4,758	7,153			7,153
1957	4,152	9,584	13,736			13,736
1958	9,189	15,959	25,148			25,148
1959	17,633	24,669	42,302			42,302
1960	37,596	26,742	64,338			64,338
1961	63,880	40,705	104,585			104,585
1962	112,357	45,590	157,947			157,947
1963	114,621	55,625	170,246		298,000	468,246
1964	201,171	68,394	269,565		439,000	708,565
1965–3/66	576,609	94,214	670,823	812,713	582,000	2,065,536
1966/7	785,378	101,990	887,368	909,726	465,000	2,262,094
1967/8	1,648,152	191,659	1,839,811	668,979	475,000	2,983,790
1968/9	1,383,053	281,764	1,664,817	478,731	961,000	3,104,548
1969/70	1,055,860	366,258	1,422,118	458,726	1,509,000	3,389,844
1970/1	878,800	451,114	1,329,914	475,848	1,963,000	3,768,762
1971/2	1,620,076	567,260	2,187,336	488,368	2,354,000	5,029,704
1972/3	2,613,263	508,593	3,121,856	354,624	2,398,000	5,874,480
1973/4	403,107	539,295	942,402	371,594	3,010,000	4,323,996
1974/5	611,960	741,899	1,353,859	432,630	2,521,000	4,307,489
1975/6	1,438,337	1,230,417	2,668,754	606,638	3,528,000	6,803,392
1976/7	6,199,158	2,062,015	8,261,173	580,700	3,606,383	12,448,256
1977/8	187,609	761,160	948,769	325,680	3,692,000	4,966,449

Source: Government of India, Ministry of Health and Family Planning, *Family Welfare Planning Yearbook* (1980–81), tables D1–D4, pp. 59–62.
[a]Conventional contraceptives include condoms, diaphragms, foam tablets, and other spermicidals. Since about 1968 condoms have constituted the overwhelming majority of the count. The number of users is calculated in Indian documents by dividing the total item distribution by 72 for both condoms and foam tablets, 2 for diaphragms, and by 7 for spermicidal cream tubes. The condom count does not include condoms distributed free to sterilization acceptors.

creased in 1972–1973, when sixteen states organized campaigns in 210 districts and performed over 2 million vasectomies, which represented 82.7 percent of total annual vasectomy acceptors in those districts.

Success proved once again to be elusive, however. The campaigns were subject to abuse, especially as a consequence of the use of incentives. Ill-informed and overaged acceptors were brought in for the bounty, and the camps could not avoid the inevitable problems of infection, which even resulted in some deaths. Finally, the mobilization of all government offices meant that other services would be neglected, and acceptors often could not obtain adequate follow-up services after the campaign. Despite these problems, and the subsequent curtailment of the campaigns, vasectomies have continued to be the single most used contraceptive technique in India. In contrast, female sterilizations have had a less checkered career, showing a continuous, albeit gradual, rise to over 1 million in 1975–76.

Typical explanations for the extensive use of male sterilizations in India focus on advantages of the method: It is cheap and easy to use; it has few side effects and requires little follow-up; it is very effective; and it produces accurate statistics.[62] These are, to be sure, real advantages. It is important to note, however, that they are advantages primarily for the administrative system since they reduce the demands upon it. From the perspective of a client population, a more varied method mix would have far greater advantages. Sterilization is most useful for cessation of childbirth, but the reduction of a population's fertility also requires postponement of the first birth and greater intervals between births, both of which require more readily reversible contraceptive methods. By focusing on the method's advantages to the delivery system, observers are essentially noting the weakness of that system.

There is another critical point to be made concerning India's extensive use of male sterilization: It is distinctively Indian or South Asian. The advantages of vasectomy as a program method would easily apply to any family planning program, but the vasectomy is a major program method only in India. Of the roughly 1.5 billion people in thirty-seven high-fertility countries for which relatively good family planning data exist, excluding China, India's population constitutes only about 40 percent. Yet India has for years accounted for well over 90 percent of all vasectomies that were done under the auspices of public family planning programs.[63] Why India? Typical explanations for the nonuse of vasectomies in other programs focus on client rejection of a method often associated with castration or impotence, but field data in India also show that villagers often confuse vasectomy with castration and express some fear at least of "the operation."[64] If India did not use the vasectomy, extensively, these observations would usually be sufficient to explain its nonuse there as well.

We believe the explanation is to be found in cultural traditions and in elite rather than mass perceptions. Deep in Indian philosophy lies a diffuse perception of the human sperm as a life-giving force.[65] Retention of the sperm and sexual abstinence are common elements in classical music training, yoga postures, and religious tradition. In a sense, the physiology of Indian aesthetic life carries a significant fertility-limiting potential. Thus, the vasectomy offers an opportunity to retain the sperm and to conserve for the acceptor this life-giving force. It is at least plausible to argue that this cultural element made the vasectomy appear quite acceptable for extensive use in the national program.

The question to be asked is, acceptable to whom? We believe that here as in other aspects of national family planning programs, critical decisions are made, not by the masses of acceptors, but by the administrative elite; and it is in the upper socioeconomic groups, from which this elite is recruited, that these significant aesthetic traditions are carried. That is, they are elements of the high culture rather than of folk tradition, and their strength is thus positively related to socioeconomic position. Indeed, at least one survey in India has found a positive association between socio-economic status and the use of abstinence and other traditional fertility-limiting practices.[66] Admittedly, much of this is circumstantial and speculative. We really do not know why India has made such extensive use of the vasectomy when most other national public programs adopt it only haltingly. But the association of this sperm-retention value, its concentration in the high culture, and the use of vasectomy together does suggest a hypothesis that would be useful to pursue.

The Emergency and Family Planning

India is definitely a soft state, both by virtue of its poverty and for reasons of its political evolution as a pluralist parliamentary state. This has had a distinct impact on the organizational character of the system by which it is implementing its national fertility control decision. Compared with China, India's implementing system is more limited in scope and weaker in power.

In 1975, however, India underwent a profound change in which it attempted to become a strong state. In declaring the Emergency, Prime Minister Gandhi set aside the legal specifications that defined India's pluralism and attempted to mobilize the state for a bold new attack on the internal ill of poverty that did not vanish with the achievement of national independence.

Political opposition was proscribed and its voice silenced. Opposition leaders were jailed and the mass media were censored and controlled. To attack poverty, Mrs. Gandhi announced a twenty-point program for a second revolution. Family planning was not originally included in the twenty points, but new provisions were added in 1976 and a new sense of urgency was given to the program. The new provisions included a national law raising the minimum age of marriage to twenty-one years, freezing state allocations and legislative representation on the basis of the 1971 census, increasing monetary incentives for sterilization, providing 8 percent of central financial assistance to the states on the basis of their performance in family planning, and specifying an annual evaluation of that performance.

India was in effect attempting to mount a concerted program with strong top-level support and with many of the strong characteristics that are found in the Chinese program. To family planning enthusiasts these were welcome changes. A well-informed analysis by the Population Council in 1976 ended with a supportive and hopeful note.

> These measures could conceivably forestall the possibility of India's popula-
> tion reaching the one billion mark by the turn of the century, particularly if
> the rate of decline in mortality continues to be slower than projected. More
> importantly, vigorous action to lower fertility in the next few years will yield
> rich dividends to the generations to come, and *we hope the political leadership
> will continue to treat it as a top priority.* (emphasis added)[67]

Top political leadership did indeed continue to treat family planning as a top priority, but this only led to its overwhelming defeat at the polls.[68] In the election of March 1977, Congress received only 35 percent of the vote, against 43 percent in 1971. More important, its 352 seats in the Lok Sabha (lower house) were reduced to only 153. Throughout the northern states, Congress candidates were thrown out of office. Mrs. Gandhi lost her seat, as did many old line Congress representatives who had until then enjoyed strong popular support.[69] The reasons for this debacle are not difficult to discern, and they tell us a great deal about the sociopolitical organization of fertility control in modern India.

The family planning portion of the Emergency program did show considerable success. In 1973 and 1974 the program gained considerable momentum and recruited just over 4 million new acceptors. This rose to 7 million in 1975 and to 12.5 million in 1976. In 1975 all methods contributed substantially in generating the overall 59 percent increase. In 1976, however, the overall 77 percent increase came almost exclusively from sterilizations, and especially from vasectomies. IUD insertions were down by 10 percent, and new acceptors of "other" methods were also down slightly. Abortions rose by 28 percent, female sterilizations by 86 percent, and male sterilizations rose 336 percent, from 1.4 to 6.1 million. The total increase in new acceptors was about 5.4 million, of which male sterilizations alone accounted for 4.7 million. What began as a general push to increase all forms of contraceptive service ended in a mass vasectomy campaign and succeeded only in demonstrating the weakness of India's political-administrative system.

Mrs. Gandhi's son, Sanjay, took charge of the family planning program in 1976 to give it top level support. Although without formal political authority, Sanjay had become Mrs. Gandhi's most trusted advisor. With his close associate, the minister for defense, Bansi Lal, he developed an inner praetorian guard that took charge of development programs and gave special attention to population. The urgency attached to family planning was turned into action largely through coercive vasectomy campaigns. The center imposed ambitious targets, which were often made more ambitious by political leaders anxious to gain favor with Sanjay Gandhi.

From the growing literature of indictment, a few general examples can be used to illustrate how family planning worked under the Emergency.[70] First, the government imposed sterilization demands upon its own civil servants, making such things as promotions contingent upon certification of sterilization. This was subject to many local abuses and was in any event a measure limited to a small section of the urban middle class. Second, for the rural masses the states were permitted to develop their own programs. Uttar Pradesh, for example, instituted a plan whereby all eligible couples could receive a 50 percent rebate on land revenues upon documentation of sterilization. This might have been a popular measure, even though the sums involved were small, because of the importance of land, but the application of the rebate only to sterilization acceptors generated a great deal of popular hostility.

The most dramatic impact of the new urgency in family planning occurred in Delhi itself. Sanjay Gandhi had undertaken an urban renewal program that included razing of slums and relocation of the urban poor, with allocation of new house sites frequently requiring certification of sterilization. One major demolition program occurred in a Muslim neighborhood around the Turkman Gate and the Jama Mosque, where 150,000 structures were destroyed and an estimated 700,000 people made homeless. The residents resisted the demolition, and many lost all of their worldly possessions, and even their lives, in a bloody confrontation with the police and military. Other Muslim communities felt the brunt of this forced development and sterilization program, giving credence to rapidly spreading rumors that the program was directed primarily at Muslims. In effect, the family planning program was rapidly degenerating "into a terrifying program of forced sterilization."[71] As might be expected, the terror had its greatest impact on those least capable of resisting: the poor, the untouchables, and the Muslims.

Sanjay had demanded results. The administrative system was incapable of providing results through persuasion and effective service, but under the Emergency it did have the coercive capacity to give at least short-run success. The system that had evolved to provide votes for independence and indigenous leaders, precisely because of the character of that evolution, did not have the capacity to reach down to mobilize the poor.

INDIA AND CHINA   89

Long ago the Congress had opted to separate political from economic conflicts out of fear of the violence of class conflict that could erupt from linking the two. Thus, it came to rely on the rural landed elite to provide the votes it sought. Mobilization of the rural elite placed no radical new demands on the political-administrative system. The system's evolution did, however, give it the military and police power to maintain order. Under Sanjay's influence the weakness of the administrative system was ignored, and the only remaining instruments of power were used. With an almost childish naivete Sanjay mistook coercive power for effective political power and used it to gain results in family planning. Mrs. Gandhi had previously championed the interests of the poor. Through words, if not deeds, and in part through the sheer magic of her name, she did indeed gain a large following among the poor and the untouchables. The forced sterilization campaigns and the hostility generated by the terror undermined her credibility and were almost certain to be reflected in the polls if people were given the opportunity to vote. With apparent inevitability, the praetorian guard would give them that opportunity.

Governments in pluralist systems typically rely upon a high degree of popular support, upon the consent of the masses to permit the rulers to govern. Elections are typically ritualized processes by which that popularity and consent are demonstrated. They are not the only means of such demonstration, of course, though they tend to be the most accurate. This was also something that Sanjay and the praetorian guard did not understand.

To gain favor with this new, highly extraconstitutional leader, many political elites worked hard to provide other demonstrations of popular support. Everywhere Sanjay went he was met with crowds of supporters, apparently giving him a godlike image of himself. He found himself to be both powerful and popular. This, together with Mrs. Gandhi's strong, but by no means unambiguous, commitment to democratic procedures, led her to call elections in January 1977, which she expected would give her a mandate for her own brand of democracy-saving rule.

For the elections, opposition leaders were released from jail and the press was partly unfettered. The opposition united and took its case to the voters. Too late, the government recognized its double error—a heavy hand and the promise of free elections. Mass hostility generated by the forced sterilization program provided the opposition with powerful and ready-made issues, which it used with great success. India's attempt to use force rather than a deeply penetrating administrative system to build a strong state failed. The Congress Party lost the elections; the dissenting vote was especially heavy in the north where the excesses of the sterilization campaign had been most pronounced. The hoped-for "rich dividends for generations to come" proved illusory. The Emergency proved a severe setback, not only for the ruling Congress Party, but also for government credibility in general and for the family planning program in particular.

There is more than a little irony in the fact that Mrs. Gandhi was unseated by the excesses of the family planning program. In the past she had, according to some observers, shown deep political intuition in re-cognizing that family planning was not politically neutral and that it al-ways threatened to ignite the religious and communal differences that have lain close to the surface of India's tenuous national consensus for many generations.[72] It was this intuition that led the 1969 United Nations mission to tone down its recommendations for strong top political support for family planning. The Emergency apparently clouded Mrs. Gandhi's earlier intuition. With the opposition rendered powerless and voiceless, the rulers forgot the deliberately weak character of the administrative system they had created. In family planning they attempted to use the system for powerful action, much like that the Chinese government could more readily achieve. Both the attempt and the failure of that powerful fertility-limiting action exacted a high price for India's national political action.

Implementation: The States of India

Up to this point we have been talking about India as a single, more or less homogeneous, political and administrative system. This is both useful and accurate, but it is also incomplete. The states and union territories that make up India vary considerably in many ways. In population policy and fertility change, however, it is possible to argue that the states differ least in policy decisions. Here the center has had overwhelming impor-tance. States vary somewhat more in the implementation of national population policy, and they differ most in the impact the programs have had on fertility.

On state variance in policy decisions we need say very little. Family planning activity began in some states, or in some cities, as early as the 1920s. More recently some states decided upon the extensive use of steril-ization before it was an accepted method in the national program. Non-etheless, the broad policy decision that resulted in large and distinctive budgets for the large and distinctive family planning organizations was made by the central government.

More must be said, however, about the state differences in the implem-entation of the policy decisions. The differences lie not in the structure, but in what can be called the work that is put into the structure. All states have built roughly the same type of program structure; and, at least on paper, those structures are roughly the same size. The program calls for the creation of a fairly standard list of contact points at which it meets and delivers services to the population. Family planning clinics, mobile units, and family planning functions in established clinics have all been created in relatively routine fashion. By 1972–73 all India had created 40,369 of these contact points, or about 74 per million of the population. (See table 3.6 for all data on state-level implementation.) The states varied considerably in the actual number of contact points, but this is largely a function of the great differences in their size. For the twenty-two states, including the territory of Delhi, the correlation coefficient between the number of contact points and the total state population is .93. Apparently the states proceeded in normal bureaucratic fashion to create the structure whose blueprint was laid down by the central government.

This is true for the second bureaucratic step as well, the creation of personnel positions to staff the clinics. The central blueprint calls for the establishment of official positions for the doctors, nurses, midwives, field workers, clerks, drivers, and so on needed for actual service delivery. As shown in table 3.6, for all India 82,850 technical positions had been established by 1972–73 to staff the program's contact points. Again, the size of the state is the major determinant of the positions established. The tiny state of Manipur had established 197 technical positions, and the massive state of Uttar Pradesh had established 13,984. The correlation coefficient for state population and number of established positions was .99. The larger the state's population, the more technical family planning positions were established.

Creating both clinics and staff positions involves relatively uncomplicated bureaucratic procedures, however, requiring little more than following the instructions from the center and drafting the documents that establish a structure on paper. The next step is more difficult. It involves recruiting, training and placing staff in position, organizing their control and supervision, and providing them with the equipment and supplies they need to be of service to the population. This is, in fact, the real work put into the program structure. We can gain some insight into state differences in the capacity to implement a program by noting the proportion of established positions that are actually filled. In addition, we can examine these differences for both urban and rural clinics and staff. Given the acknowledged preference for urban postings and the resistance to rural positions, we can argue that it is much more difficult to staff rural than urban positions. Thus, the proportion of established positions actually filled in rural areas can be taken as a sensitive indicator of a state government's willingness and ability to move ahead vigorously with the implementation of its family planning program.

In 1972–73, approximately 57 percent of India's 75,703 rural family planning positions had actually been filled. This proportion varied from a low of 15 percent in Himachal Pradesh to highs of 81 percent in Kerala and 94 percent in Andhra Pradesh. Supporting the assumption that urban positions are easier to fill, we note that 65 percent of the 7,147 urban

TABLE 3.6
Indian States: Socioeconomic and Family Planning Program Data

| State | Population 1971 | | F.P. Outlets | | Family Planning Positions 1972–73. | | | | | |
| | Total (000) | % Urban | No. | No. per mill. pop. | Urban | | | Rural | | |
					No. Estab.	No. per mill. pop.	% filled	No. Estab.	No. per mill. pop.	% filled
Andra	43,503	19.3	3,986	91.6	668	80	96	6026	172	94
Assam	14,954	8.9	491	33.6	66	51	35	2,145	161	61
Bihar	56,353	10.0	3,551	63.0	401	71	74	8,594	169	35
Gujarat	26,698	28.1	2,229	83.5	569	76	20	3,425	179	63
Haryana	10,037	17.7	801	79.8	138	78	82	1,375	166	78
Himachal Pr.	3,460	7.0	335	96.8	132	545	15	756	235	15
Karnataka	29,299	24.3	1846	63.0	348	49	16	3,808	172	51
Jam/Kashmir	4,617	18.6	318	69.1	63	73	60	813	216	33
Kerala	21,347	16.2	3,088	144.7	174	50	48	3,287	184	81
Madhya Pr.	41,654	16.3	3,610	86.9	565	83	77	6,234	179	73
Maharashtra	50,412	31.2	2,333	46.3	252	16	43	5,798	167	47
Manipur	1,073	13.2	55	53.0	14	102	29	183	203	15
Meghalaya	1,012	14.6	65	64.2	18	122	39	215	254	16
Nagaland	516	10.0	0	0	0	0	0	0	0	0
Orissa	21,945	8.4	1,957	89.2	330	179	69	3,890	194	58
Punjab	13,551	23.7	1,048	77.3	174	54	76	1,799	174	66
Rajasthan	25,766	17.6	1,840	71.4	377	83	90	3,514	165	71
Tamil Nadu	41,199	30.3	3,603	87.5	631	51	52	5,152	179	62
Tripura	1,556	10.4	59	37.9	3	19	133	286	205	25
Uttar Pr.	88,341	14.0	6,938	78.5	1,139	92	69	12,845	169	51
West Bengal	44,132	24.8	1,797	40.6	702	64	59	5,316	156	44
Delhi	4,066	89.7	114	28.0	333	91	89	77	189	39
subtotal	545.675	19.7								
All India	547,950	19.9	40,369	73.6	7,147	66	65	75,703	173	57

State	F. P. Expenditure Ave. Ann. Rps./Pop		Promotion/manufacturing %		Female Literacy %	% Engible Couples (1974–75) Protected by:		
	1966–67	1971–73	Males	Females		Sterilization	IUD	Other
Andra	22	147	5	2	15.8	17.3	0.7	0.6
Assam	11	40	3	2	19.3	8.4	1.0	0.6
Bihar	8	58	3	1	8.7	5.9	0.7	0.2
Gujarat	20	170	10	3	24.8	18.3	1.1	2.2
Haryana	13	140	7	6	14.9	14.4	6.2	7.8
Himachal	0	88	2	0	20.2	7.6	1.4	0.5
Karnataka	26	146	6	4	21.0	11.0	1.0	1.0
Jam/Kashmir	10	96	3	1	9.3	6.2	1.6	0.2
Kerala	48	147	11	12	54.3	18.4	2.4	0.7
Madhya	13	138	4	1	10.9	11.4	1.5	0.9
Maharashtra	24	147	13	3	26.4	23.4	0.5	1.6
Manipur	0	49	2	1	19.5	1.7	2.4	0.5
Meghalaya	0	57	2	0	24.6	1.4	0.7	0.6
Nagaland	0	0	1	0	18.7	0.3	0	0
Orissa	28	140	2	2	13.9	14.6	2.5	0.5
Punjab	36	129	8	9	25.9	12.7	5.1	6.7
Rajasthan	20	117	3	1	8.5	5.8	1.1	0.8
Tamil Nadu	29	168	10	4	26.9	18.4	1.1	1.5
Tripura	0	32	2	2	21.2	5.7	0.2	0.5
Uttar Pr.	16	95	4	1	10.6	5.8	1.6	0.8
West Bengal	13	61	12	5	22.4	10.5	0.6	0.8
Delhi	45	75	22	11	47.7	11.1	3.8	22.9
All India	24	129	7	3	18.7	12.4	1.4	2.4

F. P. outlets include all rural FWP centers and subcenters, urban centers, and IUD/sterilization mobile units as of 9/72–6/73.

Technical positions include medical officers, extension education workers, lady home visitors, assistant nurse midwives, F. P. health assistants, F. P. welfare workers, and computers (statistical clerks). Data show number of established positions, established positions per million population, and percentage of established positions actually filled as of 30 June 1973.

Family planning expenditures are per 100 population, and for both periods are calculated on the base of the 1971 population. Expenditures for Delhi in 1966/67 include those for all Union territories. In this case, the denominator includes the population of Delhi (4,066,000) and that of all other Union territories (2,275,000). The total expenditure includes 23.7 million rupees in 1966/67 and an average of 517.3 million rupees for 1971–73 expended by the center and not attributed directly to any state. The central budget amounted to about 17.8 percent of the total expenditures in 1966/67 and about 7 percent of total expenditures in 1971–73.

Sources: Data in the following columns are taken from G.O.I., Ministry of Health and Family Planning, *Family Welfare Planning Yearbook 1972–73*: cols. 1 & 4, pp. 10–11; col. 5, p. 69; cols. 7, 9, 10, & 12, pp. 76–78; cols. 13 and 14 computed from data on p. 84; cols. 2, 3, 6, 8, & 11 are computed.

Data for labor force in manufacturing and for female literacy are taken from the 1971 census.

Protection rates are from Pravin Visaria and Anrudh Jain. *India, Country Profiles* (New York: Population Council, 1976), p. 38.

positions had actually been filled by 1972–73. This proportion also varied from 15 percent in Himachal Pradesh to 96 percent in Andhra Pradesh and 133 percent in Tripura (which, however, had only 3 established positions).

The implementation of public programs is also partly indicated by the amount of funds expended for them. We have already seen, however, that the expenditure of funds is partly a measure of program output and partly a measure of input and that it is difficult to separate the two. While we shall not use expenditures further in the more detailed analysis of state-level implementation, we can nonetheless show that they, too, varied considerably among the states.

In 1966–67 all India spent approximately 24 rupees per hundred persons on the national family planning program. States varied from a low of 8 rupees in Bihar to a high of 48 rupees in Kerala. By 1971–73, India was spending an annual average of 129 rupees per hundred persons on its national family planning program. The range in the states went from 32 rupees in Tripura to 170 rupees in Gujarat.

Aside from family planning, the states have varied considerably in the provision of other social services to their populations. One crude but nonetheless useful indicator of these differences lies in the literacy rates. Although these rates indicate the results of private as well as public service provision and are affected by many socioeconomic conditions, education is still primarily a government service. Thus, literacy rates may be taken as a rough indicator of the capacity of the state government to provide social services. Perhaps more important than the overall service provision, however, is its distribution, especially between males and females. It is common that women in developing countries receive less education than men, and that rises in female education come after rises in male education. It is not too great an inferential leap, then, to argue that societies that provide high levels of education or literacy to women show less inequality in the provision of services to males and females than societies with low levels of female literacy. In effect, female literacy can be used as a surrogate measure for the equality of social services provided to males and females. By 1971, 18.7 percent of females over ten years of age in India were literate, but this figure varied from a low of 8.5 percent in Rajasthan to a high of 54.3 percent in Kerala. Clearly some states are better than others in providing social services equally to men and women in their populations.

It is easy to sense, at least intuitively, the meaning of these differences across states for collective work in fertility limitation. Some states are clearly more effective than others in mobilizing resources to provide services in general, and family planning services in particular, to their populations. The more effective states do a better and more complete job of implementing the national population policy to limit fertility, and they should also show greater impact on fertility, a subject we shall address presently. Nonetheless, it is less easy to identify the causes of these differences. Some causes clearly lie in the levels of socioeconomic development in the state. States that are richer, more urbanized, or that already have a higher level of social services can logically be expected to be more effective in program implementation.

There is another cause of these differences, however, which is the overall quality of the states' political and administrative systems. Although we cannot yet say much about these differences for all the states of India, Maru provides important insights from his work in a few of the states.[73] He notes that the classical British model of public administration as a steel frame designed to serve any political leadership ignores an important exchange relationship between the polity and the bureaucracy. He also notes that this exchange relationship is differentiated in at least one important way—from a one-way flow to an exchange of mutual assistance. For example, in Uttar Pradesh he found that political leaders demanded that the family planning program hire their relatives and supporters and provide services to their favored constituents. The political leaders did not, however, return these favors with assistance to the program. The resource exchange flow was largely one way, from the program to the political leaders. This form of no-return political interference has also been extensively documented for Uttar Pradesh by Simmons, Simmons and Ashraf.[74]

In Gujarat and Maharashtra, in contrast, there was a clear two-way flow of resources. Political leaders demanded places and services for their favorites, but they also helped raise money for the program, helped to discipline the workers they placed in the program (or permitted program officials to fire their favorites for low performance), and helped to gain support of other local leaders for the family planning program. Most important, perhaps, was the fact that in these two states political leaders also demanded high performance of the program in general. There are no systematic measures for all of the states in the polity-bureaucracy exchange, but it is nonetheless easy to assume that the differences are real and that they have a major impact on the quality of family planning program implementation.

Impact: India

In the two decades from 1956 to 1976, the Indian family planning program performed 19.7 million vasectomies and 7.4 million female sterilizations, inserted 6.6 million IUDs, and distributed about 1.5 billion condoms.[75] It is estimated that by March 1977 the program was providing fertility protection to over 25 million couples, or just under 25 percent of those eligible.[76] Thus, the program's impact on contraceptive use has been real and significant. Especially given the levels of poverty and literacy, and the isolation of so much of the rural population, this level of impact must be considered substantial.

It is less easy to assess the direct impact of the program on fertility. The crude birth rate remained at quite high levels for almost two decades after independence. It is estimated to have been somewhat over forty births per thousand population from 1950 to 1965. Then it began to fall and in 1976 was estimated at thirty-six births per thousand population.[77] About half of this decline is attributed to the increased age of marriage. Some part of the decline is also attributable to the use of traditional fertility-limiting practices, such as withdrawal or abstinence. Survey data indicate that such practices may account for as much as 30 percent of overall contraceptive use, but they are not typically recorded in program statistics.[78] Some of this traditional practice may be attributable to changing socioeconomic conditions, but some is also undoubtedly related to the informational and motivational messages spread by the family planning program. All of this makes it virtually impossible to estimate the impact of the program on fertility decline with any precision. Nonetheless, there is considerable evidence for the judgment that the program has helped to depress fertility.

In a comprehensive survey of the Indian scene, Robert Cassen estimates that the family planning program has prevented at least one million births per year, especially since 1966–67 when sterilization began to be extensively used.[79] This represented about 5 percent of all births and about two points off the crude birth rate, or just under one-half of the overall decline observed between 1966–67 and 1972–73. Cassen also provides a crude but useful estimate of the program's cost-effectiveness. Using the most conservative estimates, he finds that the estimated one million births averted annually from 1966–67 to 1972–73, implies a per capita net national product 7 rupees higher than it would have been with those births. During this period, the family planning program spent roughly 435 million rupees per year. If those funds had been invested in the rest of the economy, rather than in family planning, the observed marginal capital output ratio would have provided an increase of only 2.5 rupees in per capita net national product. The estimates are rough, to be sure, but all of the assumptions have favored non-family planning activity. Even with these conservative assumptions, the family planning program appears to have a substantial and cost-effective impact on the national economy.

There is one other strategy that can give us further insight into the nature of the program's impact on Indian reproductive behavior. We noted above that the program's implementation differed considerably from state to state. As might be expected, this also appears to be the case with the program's impact. The data on fertility decline do not permit a confident assessment of the program's effect on fertility, but it is possible to examine the more immediate impact on contraceptive use in the states. For this the program statistics on the percentage of eligible couples protected, in total and by major contraceptive methods, provide useful measures.

The most recent data, as of March 1977, indicate that less than a quarter (23.9 percent) of all eligible couples in India were protected by program services. The range was from 0.3 percent in Nagaland, which did not have a family planning program, to a high of 51 percent in Delhi. The distribution was fairly even, with one-quarter of the states showing less than 14 percent protected, the median at 25 percent, and the upper quarter showing more than 30 percent protected. This general pattern of variation is roughly the same for all program methods, and for all states sterilization is by far the most used method.

The one exception to the dominance of sterilization reflects the impact of Sanjay Gandhi's forceful, if ill-advised, family planning push. In 1974–75, 37.7 percent of Delhi's eligible couples were protected by program services. At that time Delhi was the only area in which sterilization was not the most used method. It accounted for only 11.1 percent of eligible couples, while 22.9 percent used "other" methods, and 3.8 percent used the IUD. By March 1977 Delhi's overall use rate had climbed to 51 percent, and sterilization then was used, or claimed, by a third (32 percent) of eligible couples. The IUD and other methods together had dropped to only 19 percent. By implication, all new acceptors used sterilization, and many previous acceptors changed from the IUD or other methods to sterilization. The political conditions of the Emergency make it wise to discount the program data from March 1977, although it is not possible to estimate either the amount by which program figures should be discounted, or the statewise variance in the discount. Thus, for the attempt to use statewise variation to gain greater insights into program impact, it is preferable to use protection rates for the fiscal year 1974–75. These rates for states and methods are shown in table 3.6.

At this point we are interested in determining whether there is any relation between the implementation of the program and its impact on reproductive behavior. It is, of course, impossible to provide a definitive or precise answer to this question, but a useful strategy has recently been used to approximate an answer. A great deal of demographic analysis indicates that certain broad socioeconomic conditions of a population, the "modern" indicators (such as urban living, education or literacy, and employment in manufacturing), can be expected to have a negative impact on fertility. Further, virtually all high-fertility countries are now experiencing rapid changes in these conditions. The question then becomes one of determining the relative weight of these socioeconomic conditions and certain program conditions in explaining variance in contraceptive use or fertility across different areal units, such as states or nations. This question has been usefully addressed both for India and for a large number of high-fertility countries by employing multiple regression techniques.[80]

In following this strategy for India, we shall use contraceptive use rates by method as the dependent variable. Although this does not give us direct information on fertility, it is only one step away from fertility and it can give us more precise information about program impact, since we have seen that the program activity is heavily concentrated on the use of male sterilization. Given this concentration, we should expect that program characteristics will be more important in explaining sterilization use than in explaining the use of the IUD and other methods. Conversely, we should expect that socioeconomic conditions will be relatively more important than program conditions in explaining the use of the IUD and other methods. Finally, if our earlier argument is correct, that filling established rural positions is the most difficult part of program implementation and therefore gives us the most sensitive measure of a state's political-administrative capacity, we should expect that this will be the most powerful program measure for explaining the use of sterilization.

For the independent program measures we use the five implementing measures described above—the number of clinics per capita, and both number of established positions per capita and proportion of established positions filled for both urban and rural clinics. For the independent socioeconomic measures, we use five that are selected for the common observation of their impact on contraceptive use—male and female literacy and manufacturing employment rates and the proportion of the population living in urban areas. We also use the gross measure of population density for theoretical reasons.

Table 3.7 shows the results of our analysis. It presents the coefficients of determination, or R^2, which show the amount of variance among states in contraceptive use that is explained by socioeconomic conditions, by program conditions, and by the two sets of conditions acting together. The coefficients in panels A and B are from zero order correlations, and those in panel C are from multiple regression equations.

The coefficients in panel A only partly conform to our expectations. Socioeconomic conditions are positively associated with contraceptive use, but for the most part they are associated only with sterilization. It is only the specifically female socioeconomic conditions that are also associated with the methods that are not central program methods. Of course, these methods are more specifically for females. This is exclusively true of the IUD, but the "other" category contains a mix of female methods (pills and chemicals) and male methods (condoms).

The coefficients in panel B conform closely to our expectations. What we have called the most sensitive measure of implementing capacity,

TABLE 3.7
Coefficients of Determination (R^2) Showing the Impact of Socioeconomic and Program Conditions on Program-provided Contraceptive Use in the States of India

Independent Variables	Dependent Variables: Percentage of Couples Protected by:		
	Sterilization	IUD	Other
A. Socioeconomic measures (zero order corr.)			
Density	.17	.03	.03
Urbanization	.42[a]	.00	.11
Males in manuf.	.63[a]	.02	.12
Females in manuf.	.31[a]	.29[b]	.28[b]
Male literacy	.29[b]	.00	.01
Female literacy	.18	.00	.01
B. Program conditions (zero order corr.)			
Clinics per mill. pop.	.25[b]	.15	.03
Urban F.P. positions	.01	.00	.01[c]
Urban pos. % filled	.00	.03	.03
Rural F.P. positions	.01	.02	.00
Rural pos. % filled	.50[a]	.16	.17
C. Multiple regressions Males in manuf. (X_1) plus Rural pos. filled (X_2)[d]	.75[a]	.15	.19

[a]Indicates significance at 1 percent or less.
[b]Indicates significance at 5 percent or less.
[c]This is the only coefficient that was negative in the original correlation
[d] $Y = -.356 + .981X_1 + .102X_2$
(SE) =   (.161) (.230)   (.032)
F = 27.173
Sig. = .0000

percentage of rural family planning positions actually filled, is strongly related to sterilization use. It also affects IUD and other uses, but the coefficients are weak and statistically nonsignificant. It is also noteworthy that the sheer number of clinics per capita is also related to sterilization use. It follows rural positions filled quite closely, although the impact of this condition is considerably weaker. In effect, we can see the clinic as the physical presence through which services are delivered. The personnel are the resources that reflect the real amount of work put into that physical presence.

We see, then, that both socioeconomic conditions and program-implementing capacities affect reproductive behavior. How they affect such behavior when they are combined is shown in panel C. In this case, we have chosen the strongest socioeconomic condition (males in manufacturing) and the strongest program condition (proportion of rural positions filled) for the multiple regression equation. Selecting only one variable from each set avoids the problems of multi-colinearity. All of the socioeconomic measures are highly intercorrelated, as are the program measures. Including all measures will raise the R^2, or the amount of variance explained, but the results are more difficult to interpret because of the instability of the coefficients. For example, when more than one socioeconomic condition is included in the equation, the R^2 rises to .84, but only the males in manufacturing condition enters the equation with a positive sign. Other conditions are weakly *and negatively* related to contraceptive use. This is a common result of multi-colinearity. The use of only one variable for each set of conditions is thus more reasonable, but it also points to the need for special care in the interpretation. Each measure is only an indirect indicator of a broader and more complex set of conditions. The males in manufacturing condition is only an indirect measure of economic development or modernization. The percentage of rural positions filled is only an indirect measure of the broader complex of political and administrative capacities to implement public policies.

The results conform closely to expectations. When we combine socioeconomic and program conditions, we can explain a substantial 75 percent of the variance among states in sterilization use. (The full equation is shown below table 3.7.) It is important to note that this combination affects sterilization use only; it does not have a significant impact on the use of the methods that are not really central or universal to the program. By inference we can also say that the socioeconomic conditions alone explain a net 25 percent of the variance, program conditions explain a net 12 percent, and the overlapping or interactive effects of the two together explain 30 percent of the variance. The absolute size of these percentages should not be taken literally, but their rank orderings make a great deal of sense. Both socioeconomic and program conditions do have real and independent impacts on program outputs, but the socioeconomic effects are stronger. These sets of conditions are, however, interrelated, and that interrelated effect is stronger than either of the independent effects.

This analysis is admittedly crude. Aggregating measures at the state level masks much important variance within the state. All of the measures are subject to wide, and undetermined, error margins. The number of observations is too small to permit a full analysis of the myriad conditions that affect program-provided contraceptive use. Nonetheless, the analysis does provide some important insights into the Indian national fertility limitation program. That program does appear to have a substantial impact on reproductive behavior. Capacities to implement policies and the level of social and economic development vary considerably among the states. That variance is clearly reflected in variance in program output; that is, in the change of reproductive behavior that the program aims to produce: contraceptive use.

Implementation and Impact: China[81]

Compared with what we know about India from the masses of official publications, studies, and statistical data, we know almost nothing about China's fertility limitation work. From the beginning of the Great Leap Forward, which Li Chou-ming has called a "statistical fiasco,"[82] until the early 1970s, the entire statistical apparatus of China was very much in disarray. At a time when India and its legions of foreign observers were flooding the world with data, there was considerable debate among China watchers on whether or not a census was taken in 1964.[83]

Following the end of the Cultural Revolution, China has become more open and more conscious of the need for information. There is an increasing stream of visitors in both directions, and what by past performance can be called an explosion of official publications is now issuing from the Middle Kingdom. We can speak with some confidence about population and the fertility limitation activities, though we are still very far from knowing as much as we know about India's experience. Here we can provide only a rough outline of the implementing actions through the 1960s and 1970s and describe in more detail the structure of the program and some of its results as it appears in its highly politicized form over the past few years. Even this limited treatment, however, can prove illuminating, since it appears against the extensive background developed for the Indian program.

The fertility limitation program began to be implemented in a modest manner following the 1953 census. There was little infrastructure available, which dictated that the program be set within the Ministry of Health and primarily focused on the urban areas. Further, there was little in the way of an effective contraceptive technology available, which implied that massive propaganda and state directives would not be used. It was felt that such actions would only raise expectations beyond the ability of the system to deliver.[84] During the Great Leap Forward, when the tide of revolution flowed heavily, there was little mention at all of family planning. In the early 1960s the push for implementation increased, and again, it was the professional corps in the health ministry that took hold and had responsibility for the program. As we shall note below, at this time it was the reorganization of the health administration that probably had the greatest impact on the character of the program's structure. With the Cultural Revolution, not only family planning, but virtually the entire administrative structure, ground to a halt. Nothing was said about implementation, but it became apparent that service delivery was greatly curtailed, and there was some increase in the birth rate.

With the end of the Cultural Revolution and the renewed attention to central planning, there was once again a push to implement the family planning program. At this time there was also a sharp increase in the political emphasis on family planning. State Council Directive number 51 of 1970 or 1971 called for outstanding results in family planning and a reduction in the crude birth rate to ten in urban areas and fifteen in rural areas.[85] In 1973 the responsibility for family planning was removed from the Ministry of Health and placed within the State Council under the control of the reactivated Staff Office for Planned Births.[86] This did not change the major outline of the implementing structure, but it did greatly increase the political inputs into the program's implementation.

The planned birth program is today an integral part of the overall political-administrative structure of the state. We can describe this in its ideal form first, then consider evidence of how it works in actual practice.[87] In China the broad outline of this structure is characterized by the slogan "Politics takes command," but the political command of the administrative system is by no means unique to China.[88] As is common in revolutionary socialist states, the political party apparatus runs parallel to the functional administrative hierarchy. For each specialized function, technical direction comes from the next highest level, and political direction comes horizontally from the party office at the same level. Within party offices, the functional specialization reflects the specific priorities of the government at any time.

The administrative structure for rural areas in China runs from the center to the province, the commune, the brigade, and the production team, the lowest integral administrative unit. In urban areas, the levels are the municipal revolutionary committee, district and ward staff offices, and at the lowest level, residents' revolutionary committees, government offices, or state enterprises. The political structure parallels this hierarchy, with party offices and cadres at each level. Planned birth activities have typically been the responsibility of the health administration, and since 1973 at each level a party official is also specifically responsible for planned births.[89]

Below the lowest administrative levels, at least by design, virtually the entire population is organized into political study groups.[90] These exist at the residential block level for nonworking persons, in factories, offices, schools, agricultural production teams, the military, and even in prisons and other correctional institutions. They are a major organizational innovation of the Chinese revolution, reflecting in large part its Maoist peasant base.

The use of this pattern of total mobilization has been applied to the birth planning program in two ways. First, birth planning has been one of the topics for group discussion, especially since about 1970. The small group provides an important communication link by which central policies on birth control are diffused throughout the country down to the individual. Second, eligible couples are organized into planned birth groups for the process of establishing individual eligibility and allocating local quotas for individual births. In addition to its communication function, the small group also provides for the use of peer pressure to carry out the policies decided upon at the center.

The rural population is highly organized through the brigade and production teams, and the urban population through the neighborhood police station and resident revolutionary committees, supported by the beat police officers. These local units are involved in the distribution of rationed goods, the granting of marriage licenses and travel permits, and the surveillance of "suspicious" persons. It is at this level that we find the implementation of the first of the three pillars of the Chinese planned birth program: late marriage. Since marriage licenses are granted here, the permission to marry can easily be denied couples who are below the prescribed age. Both the highly political nature of the administrative structure and the highly public nature of marriage assure that there will be considerable surveillance of the age at marriage.

The second and third pillars of the planned birth program are long spacing between children and stopping at two births—or, more recently, one. Implementation of these two aims is through the free distribution of all forms of contraceptives and the provision of abortion, and through the organization of the planned birth groups. The fertility-limiting technology is distributed primarily through the public health network, though with close supervision from the planned birth cadres. In the rural areas, the barefoot doctors distribute contraceptive supplies along with other medical assistance at the level of the production team or brigade. Pills and condoms are distributed, and many of these paramedics have been trained in IUD insertion and vacuum abortion methods as well. Through the barefoot doctors, couples can be referred upward to brigade or commune health centers for sterilization or for abortion services not available at the production team level. The reorganization of China's health system, with its strong emphasis on preventive care, decentralization of control, assistance to rural areas, and the use of paramedical personnel has provided a highly effective structure for the distribution of contraceptives.[91]

The actual use of contraceptives and the limitation of birth also depends upon the action of the local planned birth groups. It is here that the national plans for slowing the population growth rate become translated into actual births. As might be expected, the linkage between the top and the bottom of this structure is highly politicized. Targets for the level of growth, for example, the aim to reach a crude birth rate of ten per thousand, are set at the national level and handed down to the provincial and metropolitan governments. These administrative units can calculate the number of actual births for the coming year prescribed by the growth target and can pass both absolute and growth rate targets to the next lower level, the commune or the urban district. The step to the brigade and the production team in the rural areas usually implies simply assigning targets in actual numbers of births expected for the coming year. In urban areas, birth targets are assigned to neighborhoods for nonworking residents, or to factories or other establishments employing married women. At the lowest levels, the targets from above are matched with conditions of the eligible couples in the planned birth group. (Eligible couples are not always organized into groups that meet periodically, but at least around the time of birth assignment, it appears that there is a great deal of group formation and discussion among these couples.) Here we find what must be considered a remarkable character of the Chinese planned birth program, community planning of individual births.

Community planning begins with the organization of all married and reproductive couples, plus those who plan to marry in time to be considered reproductive for the coming year. The community plan follows the pattern captured by the slogan "individual proposal and peer review," which is also used for other individual actions relevant for the entire group, such as setting work points for various tasks. Individuals submit their own birth plans to the group for review. Both the individuals and the group are to be guided by the three birth norms: late marriage, spacing of four years, and stopping at one or two children. If a couple desires a birth in the coming year and has observed late marriage and the long spacing norms, they can be considered eligible for a birth. It usually happens, however, that the target for births given from above is less than the number of eligible couples who wish to have a child. In this case the group decides on the allocation of birth targets. At this stage local conditions of the individual couples can be taken into account. For example, a childless couple with older parents may be given priority over a childless couple with no parents, both to provide the comfort of achievement for the grandparents and to allocate a birth where there are older family members to assist in child care. Adjustments can also be made by trading quotas between couples, using the quota of a couple who has been unable to conceive for a couple that accidentally conceived. But the peer structure of community birth planning is not only useful for making these positive adjustments, it is also used to reinforce group acceptance of the target. Couples who are not eligible, or who have not been given a quota for the coming year, are expected to use contraceptives, or to abort if they experience a contraceptive failure. Couples with two living children are under strong peer pressure to accept sterilization.

To facilitate contraceptive use, acceptors are compensated for time and effort lost in accepting contraceptives. Days of leave are given for IUD insertions, sterilizations, or abortions. These are defined not as incentives for acceptance, but as compensation, which is especially important for poor people, to defray the real costs of contraception. Compensation rates have been set by the state for state employees. Rural workers obtain compensation decided upon locally, although the government encourages a standard rate for all units. An early 1970 schedule cited by Chen gives the following prescription of days of leave with pay for various methods: induced abortion, fourteen, tubal ligation, ten, IUD insertion or removal, two to three, and post-partum tubal ligation seven days in addition to the prescribed fifty-six days of paid maternity leave.[92] Chen also notes that "generally speaking peasant women are provided with the equivalent number of days or work points as women in the cities and state-owned non-agricultural enterprises and service units."[93] To further acceptance, all contraceptives are distributed free of charge.

This process of implementation bears the unmistakable marks of a totalitarian regime. At the upper level the state assumes the right and the necessity of extensive intervention in human affairs. Inequality and human misery are seen to be deeply embedded in age-old social structures, and only a radical attack on those structures can produce a more just and equitable society. "Politics takes command" is an apt slogan. In the revolutionary situation, everything becomes political, and political direction is needed to carry the revolution through to its fulfillment.

Despite this authoritarianism, the Chinese revolution was in some respects unique in that it was a peasant revolution. The Chinese accomplished what Marx considered an impossible feat—the mobilization of the peasantry. To do this the Chinese had to build a form of organization that penetrated deeply into and ultimately rested upon the peasant masses. Thus, in addition to authoritarianism from on high, the revolution developed a strategy of adaptation to and mobilization of the rural masses.

The "mass-line" orientation states this strategy in its broadest forms. In birth control the comparable slogan speaks of *state guidance with voluntarism of the people*.[94] The state will set guidelines for human reproduction that will be translated at the local level to bring about voluntary acceptance by the masses. Voluntarism is engineered in the local planned birth groups, using peer pressure mobilized and directed by the cadres.

Peer pressure and community norms are not left to themselves, however, and voluntarism does not mean letting people do as they please. The will to direct is strong, as it is in any revolution, but the emphasis on local mobilization through persuasion is also strong. As a 1977 statement, *Population Theory*, explained, "State guidance is not to be equated with issuing administrative orders, which we have always opposed. And people's voluntarism is decidedly not laissez-faire, letting them do what they want."[95]

The impact of this program of massive mobilization can be assessed through an examination of age of marriage and of various contraception and reproduction rates. All show impressive movement toward drastic reduction in fertility.

Parish and Whyte summarize data on age of marriage and add their own observations from their limited but carefully considered samples of refugees in Hong Kong.[96] Average age at first marriage for women is variously shown between 17 and 18.5 for the pre–1940 period; for men, the figures are 20.4 and 21.5. By 1973–74 the figures stand at 21.4 for women and 25.3 for men. This represents a substantial gain, even though it does not match the aim of a combined age of 50 for the two partners. In urban areas, the average ages are higher than for the overall sample, implying slightly lower than average rates for the rural areas. Urban female age at first marriage increased from 20.5 in the pre–1949 period to 24.6 between 1971 and 1978. Comparable average ages for males increased from 23.6 to 27.8. Lyle's data for Tientsin in 1978 show even greater compliance with the late marriage norm.[97] Of all marriages in that year, 95 percent of men and women were above 25, and only 5 percent were below 20. (Since these are individual rather than couples data, it is still possible that all marriages were above the norm of a combined age of 50.) She also reports that the marriages conforming to the norm were 96.6 percent in the urban area, 94.9 percent in the suburban area, and 93.2 percent in the county.[98] Age at first marriage appears to have increased substantially in China and, at least in the urban areas, compliance with the specific late marriage norm is near complete. Urban rural differentials are similar to those experienced in most countries, with younger ages at marriage in the countryside. For the moment we shall postpone the question of the source of this change.

Comparable data for India show far less movement.[99] Age at marriage of males stood at about 20.2 between 1901 and 1910 and declined to 18.4 over the next two decades. From that time it rose to 22.2 between 1961 and 1970, with the 1971 census showing it at 22.5. For females the respective figures are 13.2 for the first decade of this century, declining to 12.6 in two decades, then rising to 17.2 between 1961 and 1970. The overall mean age of marriage for females stood at 17.1 in the 1971 census.

The data are somewhat misleading, however, since marriages often occur among minors, but are not consummated until some time later. Thus it is customary to consider age at effective marriage, which is defined as the time at which cohabitation begins. Data for effective marriage age are, of course, not available on the systematic and comprehensive basis for which we have age at legal marriage. Various legal attempts have been made over the past century to increase the age of marriage, but these have proved singularly unpopular and ineffective. In short, the laws have not been, and probably cannot be, enforced.

Rural-urban differentials in marriage ages are similar to those in China, with higher urban ages. Differences by state are more extreme and are extensively documented. For example, the overall proportion married for rural India was 70 percent for the 15– to 19–year-old group in 1969. The state range was from a high of 86 percent in Rajasthan to a low of 30 percent in Kerala. For the 20– to 24–year-old group, the all-India figure stood at 93 percent, with a high of 97 to 98 percent in Rajasthan and the Punjab and a low of 72 percent, again in Kerala. All states show a peak of above 90 percent for the age group 25 to 29, except for Kerala, which only reaches 85 percent. From age 30, all state rates decline, as does that for all India, reaching a low of 71 percent for the 45 to 49 age group. Age of marriage thus appears to have been lower in India than in China before 1950. In both countries age of marriage has increased, but far more dramatically in China than in India.

Prevalence rates, or the proportion of eligible couples practicing contraception, are also apparently much higher in China than in India. Chen reports "birth limitation rates" ranging from 70 percent in Guangxi to 85 percent in Shanghai city proper.[100] (No date is given but it is presumably for 1978.) For Tientsin, Lyle reports 73 percent for the county, 76 percent for suburban areas, and 89 percent for the urban areas.[101] Here again we see data that are spotty and far from comprehensive, but all reports are quite consistent in showing very high rates of contraceptive practice.

All birth control methods are used in China, including abortion. Abortion aside, the IUD appears to be the most used method, with Chen reporting the all-China rate at 50 percent (presumably of all contraceptors). Pills may be next, with heavy use characteristic of the urban areas. Lyle shows 32 percent of all contraceptors using the pill in Tientsin proper, 28 percent in the suburbs, and 15 percent in the county. Xian municipality has a rate of 22 percent, and the other rural or provincial rates reported by Chen stand at 5 to 7 percent. Tubal ligation varies from a low of 4 percent in Hengxien rural county to a high of 40 percent in Shanghai. Lyle's Tientsin data show 21, 17, and 19 percent respectively for the city proper, the suburbs, and the county. Male sterilizations are highest in Guandung, with 20 percent of all contraceptors, and lowest, with 1 percent, in Hengxien rural county. There are no vasectomies in Lyle's Tientsin data.

Abortion is extensively used for fertility limitation, but its use also varies dramatically by area. Chen summarized abortion rates per thousand live births for selected areas. In 1978 Guandung had a rate of only 277, while Tianjian (Tientsin) had 651. Two municipalities, Xian and Chengdu, had much higher rates: 1,213 and 1,200, respectively, but two had more moderate rates: 818 for Changsha and 333 for Nanjing. Two rural county rates, 288 for Xinhui in Guangdong and 279 for Taoyuan in Hunan, permit the hardly surprising inference that urban rates are much higher than rural rates.

Finally, the impact on the crude birth rate of this extensive fertility-limiting activity has been dramatic, even if it is overstated in official statistics. Estimates and data from different sources vary, but there is general agreement on the overall trend.[102] Birth rates were in the high 30s or about 40 per thousand, and the population increase was probably above 2 percent per year through 1970. Since that date there has been a dramatic decline in fertility and growth rates. Chen reports an overall crude birth rate of 18, but Banister estimates that with corrections for underreporting, the crude birth rate was probably about 24. As Banister notes, the crude birth rate decline must have slowed after 1975 due to the increasingly unfavorable age structure, and the decline of from 26 to 24 between 1975 and 1979 was mild despite the continuing decline in total fertility. Chen's data show variance among municipalities and provinces from 7 to 20, with most rates hovering around 15. Banister cautions against accepting figures that demonstrate complete conversion of a province from a noncontracepting one to one with below replacement levels of fertility in such a short period, especially when strong political pressures are exerted for fertility limitation, but even her more cautious estimates allow for a dramatic decrease in fertility and population growth.

In the decline of fertility, however, we can also see some limitations of the program's impact. In Chen's data, 30 percent of all births in the late 1970s were to women in the third or higher birth order. These are clearly outside the norm of 2 births, or the more recent norm of 1 birth per family. The variance is from 5 percent in Changsha (1977) to 40 percent in Guangdong (1978).[103] Lyle reports that of the roughly 108,000 births in Tientsin in 1978, 1 percent occurred to couples who did not follow the late marriage norm, 12 percent to couples who did not conform to the long spacing norm, and 17 percent to couples who did not stop at two children.[104] Thus, 30.3 percent of the births occurred outside of the three reproductive norms. Recognition of this fact led the municipal planned birth committee to resolve to step up its educational and propaganda campaigns for the three norms.

On all of these rates, China has experienced far greater change than has India. Contraceptive prevalence rates for all India stand at about 22 percent, although they vary by state from 10 percent to about 36 percent.[105] The government program gives heavy, almost exclusive, emphasis to male sterilization, with female sterilization second in importance.[106] The IUD is used sparingly, largely in the urban areas, and the pill is virtually unused. Abortion is far less used in India than in China. Thus, China's much higher prevalence rate is achieved at least in part through the use of a much wider range of methods than we find in India. Crude birth rates are also higher in India than in China and have shown far less dramatic declines. The overall rate in India is currently about 35, having declined from previous levels of about 40 to 45. The overall growth rate still stands above 2 percent per year, and it may have risen slightly in some parts of the past quarter-century through the more rapid decline in mortality.

For China, then, we are left with two strong impressions. First, there are a number of powerful socioeconomic changes and political-adminis- trative pressures working to reduce fertility. Second, there is statistical evidence of a very dramatic reduction in fertility, but this is balanced by a recognition of serious gaps in the evidence itself. Incomplete coverage, weak technical competence, and high politicization of data collection and analysis imply that the change has almost certainly been overstated. Non- etheless, even the more conservative estimates do show rapid declines in fertility, especially over the past decade.

Thus, although we can believe that there has been a decline in the population growth rate, we are uncertain about the causes. How much of the decline is due to broad social and economic changes, and how much can be directly attributed to the programed planned birth effort? Ob- servers differ in their estimates. Parish tends to attribute more of the decline to broad social and economic changes,[107] and Reimert Ravenholt is more impressed with the programmatic efforts of the planned birth drive.[108] The truth may lie somewhere in between. We cannot undertake for China the kind of regional analysis that for India permitted some assessment of the weight of the two sets of factors. We can, however, review some of the broad evidence on both sides.

The planned birth program stands out as one of the most extensive programs to be found in the world of planned fertility limitation. It now has strong top-level political support, which reaches down to each village and urban resident through a mobilizing structure that impresses even the most skeptical observers. There is both political pressure and organiza- tional power to raise the age of marriage, and it is almost certain that age of marriage has increased. In addition to the strong programed efforts, however, there are also important socioeconomic changes that work in the same direction. The drive toward female liberation, while by no means as successful as the stated aims of the regime, is impressive, and among other things, this gives women real alternatives to marriage and reproduction. Typical of centrally planned socialist economies, however, are other diffuse pressures against marriage. Long periods of apprentice- ship, low wages, housing shortages, and the scarcity and high cost of consumer goods all work to discourage early unions. In addition to strong political and economic pressures for fertility reduction, the free distribu- tion of a wide range of contraceptives and the extensive use of abortion permit the planned birth program to have a marked negative impact on marital fertility.

The extensive mobilization of the population through the planned birth committees provides an organizational mechanism by which the regime's fertility reduction aims can be implemented, but the reality of this mobil- ization is almost certainly overstated. Chen's observation that planned birth committees were in place in all brigades by the late 1970s can be read in two ways.[109] Although this degree of mobilization is impressive, if indeed it is true, it must be balanced by the observation that it took almost a decade to achieve. It must also be balanced by other direct evidence. That 30 percent of births occurred to women with two children or more, that even in a major urban center, Tientsin, 30 percent of all births occurred outside of the three birth norms, and the recent reports of widespread resistance to the new sterilization drives all indicate that the mobilization is far short of what the regime desires.

Indirect evidence increases the advisability of some skepticism in accepting the claims of mass mobilization. Parish notes that it is achieved through the use of local cadres, who are an integral part of the village.[110] They are unable to press government demands for unpopular programs, and their frequent resignation when forced to do so indicates that they are often unwilling as well. The bride price has been officially proscribed, but it continues to be a strong element of rural marriage processes, usually with the collusion of the cadres. Women have been liberated, but they still do not enjoy complete equality with men. Although divorce remains rare; it is increasing, but when it occurs, women do not have the full rights to property and children that equality would indicate. The mobilization is impressive, but it is neither as widespread nor as popularly accepted as its enthusiastic supporters seem to believe.

More diffuse social and economic changes also play a role in fertility reduction. The transformation of peasants into agricultural wage laborers, with women and men taking part in paid productive work, brings pressures for lowered fertility. Rapid urbanization and the even more rapid growth of the female nonagricultural labor force work against continued high fertility in two ways. First, women are provided with real alternatives to reproduction and childraising. In addition, women are brought into situations that are more easily and directly controlled by the regime. For the industrial work force, the control of housing and all maternity benefits, as well as the close scrutiny factory work makes possible, give the regime greater direct powers to control the population and thus to achieve its reproductive aims.

China's planned birth program does appear impressive, but it is only one element of a more complex set of changes that work toward increasing the age of marriage and reducing overall fertility. In addition to this political-administrative change is the social and economic change that leads independently to reduced fertility. At present we cannot even begin to weigh the relative impact of the two sets of changes.

CONCLUSION

This is a long story, even though told in the highly abbreviated fashion used here. It is also a useful one, however, for it provides some of the detail needed to specify the forms of human organization that will affect the character of the political-ecological adjustment. Both India and China are poor and economically far too underdeveloped to lead to the expectation of a decline in fertility comparable to that by which the demographic transition was completed in the West. Yet both are now showing unmistakable signs of a spread of contraceptive use and a modest to rapid decline in fertility. It is quite clear that in both cases identifiable political and administrative actions have played a large role, though not by any means the only one, in bringing about this change in the populations' reproductive behavior. Both countries made formal and unambiguous, though often ambivalent, decisions for policies to limit fertility. In both cases these formal decisions were followed by deliberate and rational actions to create specific administrative instruments to implement the policy decisions. And both have experienced some positive impact of these policy decisions and implementing actions. In India and China today we can see powerful and identifiable political-administrative systems playing a large part in the current processes of fertility decline.

We have also seen that these political-administrative systems differ considerably in their character. The differences appear as the outcomes of long-term historical processes, at least some of which can be readily identified. They also appear to have identifiable consequences for the ecological adjustment that is reflected in fertility decline. In the most general terms we can speak of the differences in strength of the political-administrative systems. The broad judgment is that China has had a stronger political-administrative system than has India, and that this is in large part responsible for the more complete implementation of the antinatalist policy decision and the more powerful impact of that decision on reproductive behavior in China than in India.

It is also possible, however, to use the details of these two histories to specify some of the critical elements that make up the political-administrative system. For the purposes of understanding the political-ecological adjustment, three elements can be identified from the experiences of India and China. These are the strength of central political rule, the strength of the commitment to economic development, and the capacity of the administrative system to monitor social and economic changes in the population at large. All three gradually emerged in the complex historical processes of imperialism, colonialism, and the struggle for national wealth and independence. In both countries strength or capacity of these elements was associated with the broad movement to a political-ecological adjustment. Between the two countries, the greater strength of some of the elements is related to the more powerful pattern of adjustment in China than in India.

The British began their conquest of India from three centers: Madras, Bengal, and Bombay. From this they built a patchwork of territorial units tied with varying strength to a political-administrative center, located first in Calcutta and later in Delhi. The long-term trend in this system was toward greater and greater centralization of administrative control, though pockets of local autonomy, such as the princely states, consistently resisted incorporation into the larger unit. Independent India continued this process, but with greater fervor, ultimately drawing the territory into a single union of states in which the central authority has considerable power to determine the course of events in the states. The centralization was sufficient for the Union government to begin formulating long-term goals for the entire territory and then to move with increasing vigor toward the achievement of those goals.

At the same time, this centralization of power was mitigated by a commitment to parliamentary forms of government, in which individual and group autonomy were protected against the encroachments of the state. It was also moderated by a deliberate political strategy that eschewed class struggle, worked primarily to mobilize voters, and in the end gave substantial power to established economic interest groups.

With independence there also emerged a strong commitment to economic development. It is important, however, that this term be seen in its precise and rather narrow sense, one implying increases in real per capita output generated by state-directed capital formation and minimal institutional change. Industrialization has for some time, even before independence, been seen as the major institutional change that would produce development. In effect, the emphasis has been on development rather than on revolution. And the perception of development has been heavily influenced by Western economic ideologies of state planning to create the physical infrastructure and plant for a primarily industrial society. We have seen how this specific emphasis on development, measured by the single term per capita output, played a major role in producing the Indian antinatalist policy decision and also in increasing the sense of national urgency behind efforts to implement the decision.

Finally we have seen that the increasingly centralized political system created specific organizational capacities to monitor social and economic changes. The most notable, but far from the only one of these, was the national population census. The census increased in coverage, accuracy, and complexity, and it was joined by capacities in national income accounting and a wide array of national statistical surveys. These provided the political organizations at the center with increased ability to perceive the pressure of population that came with rapid growth, and this too provided a major push toward both an antinatalist policy decision and increasingly energetic efforts to implement that decision in a national family planning program.

A parallel process ensued in China. From the political fragmentation produced by warlordism and Western penetration through the Treaty

Ports to liberal and then to radical nationalist movements, China moved toward greater political centralization as it moved toward greater political independence. The processes that produced a revolution in China legitimized a much more powerful central political control there than did the more evolutionary processes in India. As India was led to an ideological commitment to protect the autonomy of individuals and groups, China was led to an ideological commitment to a dictatorship—of the proletariat, to be sure, but a dictatorship nonetheless. Political centralization was stronger in China than in India.

China's revolutionary commitment led it to emphasize economic development, but not without important reservations. The implications for fertility control programing were powerful and visible. The commitment to development led, as in India, to an antinatalist policy decision; and the greater strength of political centralization led China to a more vigorous pattern of implementation. Despite this, the ambivalence over revolution and development also had an impact on population policy. When the commitment to revolution was stronger, antinatalism was weakened; when the commitment to development dominated, antinatalist activities were pursued with greater vigor.

In China, as in India, the increased capacity to monitor social and economic change, and especially the growth of the population census, increased the state's commitment to antinatalist activity.

There is much historical diversity, both within and between the two countries, that is neglected, if not violated, in this set of generalizations. Nonetheless, it is possible to trace in both of these massive pioneers in the modern political-ecological adjustment an identifiable, and in some respects rational, process of change. In tracing this process, we can specify the three critical elements of organizational change that constitute the political aspect of the modern political-ecological adjustment. Thus, we can conceive the general strength of the political-administrative system to be composed of varying strengths or capacities in political centralization, development commitment, and administrative capacity to monitor change. In the next chapter we shall attempt to apply this paradigm of system characteristics and ecological adjustment to a larger number of countries in Asia.

4

Asia: State and Region in the Ecological Adjustment

THE STATES AS ACTORS

Asia's massive population is currently arranged in forty-five statelike units, giving us the possibility of using a systematic cross-national analysis to explore the political-ecological adjustment. The differences among the units are so vast and profound, however, that it is unwise to treat all of them together in one analysis. At one end of a continuum are the populous giants, China and India, and the economic giant, Japan. Each calls for a separate treatment. At the other end of this continuum are twenty-one states whose small size and questionable political integrity, or whose cultural separateness (Australia and New Zealand are in Asia, but scarcely a part of it), caution against treating them together with the more substantial states of the region.

Between these extremes, however, are another twenty-one units that reasonably fit the image of modern nation states with populations organized by the type of authoritative institutions and administrative systems we have come to associate with the state. These twenty-one are not, and for our purposes need not be, identical in their political and administrative systems. They can nonetheless be recognized as states, with a wide range of justifiable expectations that they do such things as control their boundaries and organize their populations for substantial forms of concerted action.

These twenty-one states contain about 650 million people, more than all of Latin America (342 million) or Africa (431 million), and almost larger than both together. In short, this is not an inconsequential sample of states and populations for an examination of the political-ecological adjustment.

There is among these states much variation in the historical processes we argue are associated with the Third World's current ecological adjustment. As in India and China, eighteenth- and nineteenth-century Western imperialist penetration and twentieth-century indigenous reaction to that penetration differed greatly. Hong Kong and Singapore, for example, were built from virtually empty lands into the great city states they are today. Thailand, Nepal, and Iran, in contrast, are old societies that retained their territorial integrity when their neighbors fell to the epidemic land-grab of capitalist colonialism; but their territorial integrity also demanded that they accept some of the profound influence of the Western world. Afghanistan, or at least its central city, was subdued more than once, but never effectively ruled by an outside power. Taiwan and Korea were insulated from Western penetration, but succumbed to the onslaught of the new Asian colonial power, Japan. The others, from Pakistan and Sri Lanka to Vietnam, the Philippines, and Fiji, today fit with ease the category of new states that were conquered and ruled for a time by an external power.

Nationalism too has varied greatly in these twenty-one states. Some of its roots are ancient, with Vietnam showing two thousand years of anticolonial struggles directed primarily against the Chinese. Even with the mushrooming of modern nationalism in the twentieth century, there are considerable differences. The Philippines can lay claim to the first of the modern Asian nationalist uprisings at the close of the nineteenth century. After that bloody insurrection and its betrayal and even bloodier suppression by the Americans, however, Philippine nationalism has been vocal and organized, but scarcely militant. It was also posed against a metropolitan power that readily acceded to demands for self-government. Burmese nationalism was also vocal and assertive, and under Japanese stimulus militantly anti-British, but ultimately it found its old metropolitan ruler ready to grant full independence. Militant Vietnamese and Indonesian nationalist movements did not fare so well; they were often brutally suppressed by colonial rulers, and ultimately they required armed struggle to gain independence. Malaysia, Singapore, Laos, and Cambodia had far weaker nationalist movements, but nonetheless these states gained independence in the post-World War II period when the entire overseas imperial system came apart.

Despite these differences in the region, the modern nationalist movements were alike in that they aimed not to destroy but to take over and use for themselves the foreign-built administrative structures. From Burma eastward, Japan gave great support to these aims by destroying the military presence of the West. Japan, however, was also a modern bureaucratic state, and thus only helped to dislodge the foreign masters while leaving their ruling structures largely intact.

The defeat of Japan in 1945 moved all of these Asian states closer to full political independence and also to an explicit commitment to modern economic development. The commitment was not, and has not been, equal in all of the states. In some there has been a strong and unambiguous drive for development. In others isolationist tendencies are more evident, interlaced with greater concern for identity than for development. And in still others there is vacillation from development in the world economy to isolation from it.

In effect, not only are these twenty-one Asian states a substantial sample of both demographic and political numbers, they are also a sample rich in relevant variation. The differences in their political and administrative histories have produced wide differences in the ecological processes by which the states are currently adjusting to rapid population growth. It is from this rich variation that we can gain greater insight into the political-ecological adjustment process itself.

A systematic examination of this variation presents a number of analytical problems. The first concerns the period and units to be used. We have seen that the period of greatest activity in adopting antinatalist policies was the decade of the 1960s; thus, we must begin here with the political units as they were then defined. Since there will normally be a time lag between the political decision for an antinatalist policy and both the implementation and the impact of that policy, we shall use the period from roughly 1965 to 1975 to assess both implementation and impact. This means, of course, that we shall do some violence to the definition of the political units whose boundaries we currently acknowledge. During the 1960s Vietnam was two states, and Pakistan one. Today these situations are reversed, but it is still useful and necessary for us to use the definitions of the 1960s. Tables 4.1 and 4.2 show the states of Asia, distinguishing the twenty-one to be used in this analysis, together with their estimated populations in 1970 and 1977. Figure 4.1 shows the location of these twenty-one states on the map of Asia.

From the perspective developed in the first three chapters, the following general model of the political-ecological adjustment process can be proposed. A strong political-administrative system will perceive population pressures arising from rapid growth early and will move relatively quickly to a collective decision for an antinatalist policy. This will in turn lead to implementation through a strong fertility limitation program, which will produce extensive contraceptive use and rapid fertility decline. In path analytic form, this model can be represented as follows.

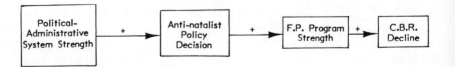

TABLE 4.1
Estimated Population of 21 Asian States, 1970 and 1977 (000)

Country	1970	1977
Afghanistan	10,059	14,967
Burma	27,078	31,958
Fiji	526	600
Hong Kong	3,959	4,514
Indonesia	121,717	141,462
Iran	30,129	37,121
Kampuchea[a]	7,060	7,895
Korea, North	14,185	17,571
Korea, South	32,976	38,195
Laos	2,962	3,462
Malaysia	10,835	13,004
Mongolia	1,248	1,537
Nepal	11,311	13,341
Pakistan	130,818	158,983
(W. Pakistan)	(61,091)	(75,472)
(Bangladesh)	(69,727)	(83,511)
Philippines	37,537	44,863
Singapore	2,075	2,308
Sri Lanka	12,532	14,068
Taiwan	14,598	16,793
Thailand	37,091	44,284
(Vietnam)[b]	(42,984)	(49,984)
Vietnam, North	23,641	27,471
Vietnam, South	19,343	22,477
Subtotal	553,680	658,454
Less developed world	2,634,239	3,103,216
More developed world	1,087,279	1,154,430
World Total	3,721,518	4,257,655

[a]Given the recent genocidal forces in Kampuchea it is tragically inappropriate, and yet necessary, to include that country in our analysis.

[b]The source gives the total population for Vietnam. We have divided the total using recent estimates that showed the North with about 55 percent and the South with about 45 percent of the total population.

Two other sets of variables can be added to this exclusively political-administrative model in order that we may include both socioeconomic and ecological conditions. Socioeconomic conditions imply the level of a population's wealth or productivity, its physical vigor, and its social communication. Ecological conditions imply the level of population density, or the sheer pressure of people on the land. For the purposes of this analysis, we need not specify the relationship between density, socioeconomic development, and the strength of the political-administrative system. All three will be used as independent variables, which will operate in different ways on the three stages of the adjustment process.

First, we have already seen a positive relationship between population density and the adoption of an antinatalist policy. Other things being

TABLE 4.2
Twenty-four Remaining States in the Asian Region, with
Estimates of 1977 Populations (000)

Country	Est. Population 1977
China	982,531
India	643,040
Japan	113,860
Australia	14,062
New Zealand	3,153
American Samoa	31
Bhutan	1,235
Brunei	182
Cook Islands	61
French Polynesia	138
Gilbert Islands	61
Tuvalu	61
Guam	96
Macao	279
Maldives	138
Nauru	7
New Caledonia	137
New Hebrides	100
Papua New Guinea	2,908
Pacific Islands	129
Samoa	153
Solomon Islands	206
Tonga	90
Wallis and Fortuna	10

Source: U.S. Bureau of the Census, World Population
1977 (Washington, D.C., 1978).

equal, a strong political-administrative system is more likely to perceive
population growth as an obstacle to other national goals if density is high
than if it is low. There is no reason, however, to propose a relationship
between socioeconomic development and a specific population policy.[1]

Second, the strength of the policy implementation, or the national fertility
limitation program, will be determined by the timing of the policy decision
and by the level of socioeconomic development. The longer a policy is in
force, the more we can expect that its implementing agencies will address the
range of daily problems posed by implementation. Further, the longer a
policy is in force, the greater the opportunity of the agency to learn from the
examples of similar agencies in other states. Finally, the quality of implementation is also affected by the level of socioeconomic development.
Wealthier societies will have more financial resources to put into action
programs. Healthier and more literate societies will have more abundant
and higher quality human resources for public programs.

Third, the policy impact, or the rate of decline in fertility, should be
positively affected by density, implementation strength, and socioeconomic development. The stronger the fertility limitation program, the

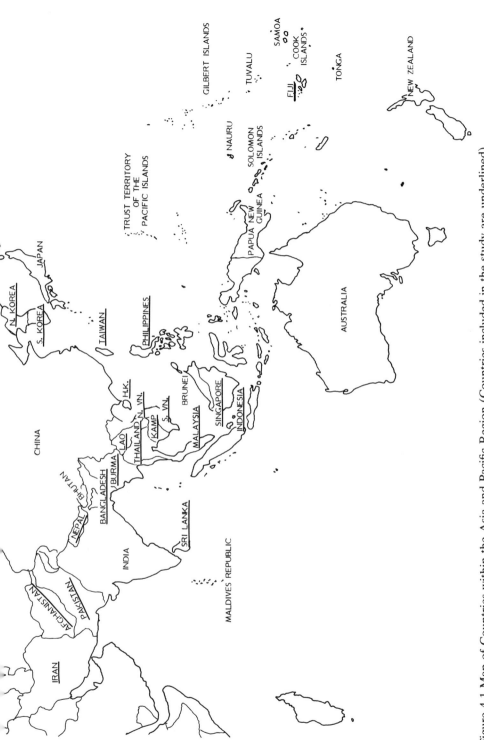

Figure 4.1 Map of Countries within the Asia and Pacific Region (Countries included in the study are underlined)

Figure 4.2 A Path Model of the Political-Ecological Adjustment

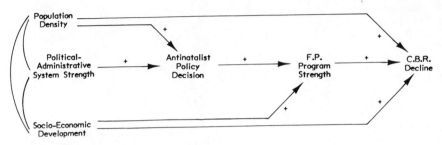

more effective it will be in distributing and gaining acceptance of the modern contraceptive technology. Since density alone, at least at very high levels, appears to be negatively related to fertility, we can propose that density is positively related to the rate of fertility decline.[2] Finally, extensive demographic analysis has documented on both aggregate and individual levels the negative relationship between wealth, health, and education on the one hand and fertility on the other. Thus, we can also propose a positive relationship between the level of socioeconomic development and the rate of fertility decline. With the addition of these variables, a slightly more complicated model of the political-ecological adjustment process can be described as follows:

Testing this model with our twenty-one Asian countries presents us first with a problem of analytical strategies. There are too many countries to permit the detailed historical narrative analysis used in the examination of India and China, and too few for a rigorous statistical analysis.[3] Thus, we must develop a middle ground in which we combine the statistical and narrative styles. We shall first examine the statistical relationships predicted in the model, and then supplement these with discussions of the inferred causal relations illustrated with cases that fit and cases that deviate from the predicted relationships. In effect, we shall be moving back and forth between path coefficients for all the twenty-one countries and historical discussions of action programs of individual countries.

Our first measurement problem is to develop a quantitative indicator of the strength of the political-administrative system. From the preceding analysis[4], we have identified three dimensions of variance that are relevant for the ecological adjustment. A strong political-administrative system is one that has (a) a strong center of political decision making, (b) an administrative capacity to monitor social and economic change in the population at large, and (c) a strong commitment to goals of modern social and economic development. We have operationalized each of these three variables by developing a narrative description of five different levels of strength for each and then assigning each country to one of the five levels for each variable.

TABLE 4.3
Political Centralization, 1960–70

Score	Character	Countries
5	strong ruling party or group in effective control of government and territory throughout the decade	Singapore, Taiwan, South Korea, North Korea, North Vietnam, Mongolia
4	strong ruling party or group in control of territory and government throughout most of the decade; some factions resisting central rule; some reverses in electoral losses or riots	Malaysia, Iran, Nepal, Thailand, Hong Kong
3	major reverses during decade from strong to weak or weak to strong governing group, *or* one group or party in control with major resistance; or group turnovers	Indonesia, Pakistan, Sri Lanka, Fiji, Burma, Afghanistan
2	weak ruling party or group with major factions and persons in resistance: control primarily in capital	(Bangladesh), Kampuchea, Philippines
1	little or no effective control by local political parties, groups, or persons	South Vietnam, Laos

Two strategies were used to assign countries to different levels on each variable. First, we undertook our own assignment from a general reading of the political and economic histories of the countries during the period 1960–70. Second, we selected a panel of judges knowledgeable about the countries and asked them to code the countries independently on each of the three dimensions of system strength. We shall first show the results of our own coding, then discuss the judges' reactions in appendix 1.

We first assumed that a strong political center implies a ruling group or party in effective control of the territory for the full decade. Effective control also implies that the ruling group itself be capable of making collective decisions, establishing priorities, and disciplining its members. It further implies an administrative apparatus by which the ruling group maintains order, mobilizes and allocates resources, and communicates with the local elements of the apparatus. We attempted to capture this sense of strength with the ranked statements shown in table 4.3. For each statement we show the countries we assigned to that level.

For administrative effectiveness in monitoring, we concentrated primarily on the capacity to carry out a national population census and to undertake various national sample surveys for socioeconomic data. We have noted the impact of the long development of an effective census in India and the more recent census in China on these countries' population policy decisions. We have also observed the impact of such monitoring

TABLE 4.4
Administrative Monitoring Effectiveness, 1960–70

Score	Character	Countries
5	series of censuses, socioeconomic surveys, extensive accurate data	Singapore, South Korea, Taiway
4	censuses, surveys, extensive registration, but with data gaps or resistance to specific measurements	Malaysia, Hong Kong, Fiji, Sri Lanka, Philippines, North Korea, North Vietnam
3	censuses and some survey work, data of questionable validity	Thailand, Iran, Pakistan, Indonesia, Mongolia
2	census, very little survey data, questionable validity	Afghanistan, Nepal, South Vietnam, (Bangladesh), Kampuchea
1	virtually no census or survey data, little more than trade data available	Burma, Laos

capacity on Malaysian population policy.[5] Finally, our theoretical perspective identifies the collective monitoring capacity as a critical variable in determining the character of a population's response to any specific condition. Since all of these countries have been involved in some way in the colonial export system, developed especially since about the middle of the last century, they tend to have at the minimum some external trade data. The five statements in table 4.4 show how we rank countries on this administrative monitoring capacity.

The commitment to modern economic development can be noted in a series of observations of behavior in the sphere of planning. From our own previous observations of planning in the region we identified three conditions as effective indicators. First, high commitment is indicated by a sequence of development plans. When plans occur in orderly sequence we typically find that they exhibit increasing scope, size, and sophistication, which indicate an increasing capacity to perceive national conditions and to prepare long-term programs to deal with those conditions. Second, we find development commitment to be indicated by a strong planning unit. Again, a sequence of plans typically indicates an increasing size and technical capacity of the planning unit itself. Finally, we ask whether the planning unit has effective links to the cabinet, such that the plans are annually translated into national fiscal and economic policy. Thus, the scale is built on the observation of a series of structural and behavioral conditions. The ranked statements and country assignments for development commitment are shown in table 4.5.

To obtain a summary score of the political-administrative system, we

TABLE 4.5
Development Commitment, 1960–70

Score	Character	Countries
5	successive development plans, strong planning unit, effective links to cabinet, plans strongly affect economic policy	Singapore, Taiwan, South Korea, Mongolia, North Korea, North Vietnam
4	successive development plans, effective planning unit, good links to cabinet, but some conflict and resistance over priorities	Malaysia, Iran, Fiji, Sri Lanka
3	plans and planning units, moderate links to cabinet, heavy reliance on external financial and technical planning assistance, or major reverses from weak to strong or strong to weak planning	Thailand, Pakistan, Indonesia, Afghanistan, Nepal
2	plans, but weak planning unit and weak links to cabinet, weak concept of plans and planning	(Bangladesh), Philippines, South Vietnam, Hong Kong, Burma
1	no effective development plans, no effective planning unit, and no use of planning in cabinet processes	Laos, Kampuchea

TABLE 4.6
Political-Administrative System Strength Scores, 1960–70

Score	Countries	Score	Countries
15	S. Korea, Singapore, Taiwan	9	Indonesia, Nepal, Pakistan
14	N. Korea, N. Vietnam	8	Afghanistan, Philippines
13	Mongolia	7	Burma
12	Malaysia	6	(Bangladesh)
11	Sri Lanka, Fiji, Iran	5	Kampuchea, S. Vietnam
10	Hong Kong, Thailand	3	Laos

simply summed the scores of each of the three variables. Thus, the range was from three to fifteen. The twenty-one countries in this analysis and their total political-administrative system scores are shown in table 4.6.

Knowledgeable observers of any set of countries are invited to disagree with this ranking. The panel of judges whose assistance we requested in assessing political-administrative system strength generally agreed with our rankings. For the measure of political centralization the Pearsonian correlation coefficient between our scores and those of the judges was .903; for administrative monitoring effectiveness the correlation was .863; and for development commitment the correlation was .648. The judges' combined score for political-administrative strength correlated .853 with our overall score. (All of these coefficients are significant at the one percent level.) Where the panel of judges disagreed with our evaluation, we used ours. A note in appendix 1 to this chapter examines cases of agreement and disagreement and makes one test for our own bias.

The other two independent variables—population density and socio-economic development—are rather standard measures in cross-national analysis. In appendix 2 to this chapter, we show how these two variables are constructed and examine their adequacy. Here we need only describe them briefly. For population density we have used the log of total density for Hong Kong and Singapore and the log of agricultural density for the other states. Although agricultural and total density are highly correlated across nations, the former is theoretically more acceptable for our analysis. For Singapore and Hong Kong, however, the figure is virtually meaningless, and the total density figure is theoretically more adequate.

To assess the level of socioeconomic development, we have used an ordinal scale combining measures of the infant mortality rate, per capita gross domestic product, and proportion of school-aged females enrolled in school. In appendix 2 we show that this measure is highly correlated with other single- and multi-measure indices of development. The specific measures that were used in this index were selected on the basis of our judgment of their sensitivity to major dimensions of development. They include indicators of human productivity measured in modern market terms, human physical welfare, and human communication. For the latter we preferred to use female rather than male school enrollment figures, because we feel these are more sensitive to differences in communication that are relevant for fertility. In effect, our socioeconomic development index measures the extent to which a country is healthy, wealthy, and wise.

As in the analysis of India and China, we conceive of the political-ecological adjustment as three analytically separable sets of actions, which follow in a logical sequence. First, there is a decision for a policy. Second, this leads to the construction of a program for action, which finally leads to a specifiable impact. Operationalizing these variables is, at least on the surface, not very complicated. Let us look first at the surface of each variable, and then examine some of the difficulties that lie underneath.

Since our theory holds that the stronger the political-administrative system, the earlier will be the antinatalist policy decision, we measure the policy decision by the date it was officially taken. If we express this date as the number of years that a policy had existed up to 1975, we have a positive interval variable that can be used in a rather uncomplicated form. There is not much difficulty in assigning to most programs either dates or the number of years the policy had existed. Pakistan adopted an antinatalist policy in 1960, and thus had an official policy for fifteen years at our cutoff point. We have taken the dates of policy formation for the most part from the Population Council's *Factbooks* for various years; only a few minor adjustments were required. Hong Kong adopted an official antinatalist policy only in 1973–74, but it had provided official support to a private family planning program since 1956. In this case we divided the total years by two, essentially counting each year of support as half the weight of a year of official policy. We also counted the Taiwan decision from 1964, when in effect the entire island came under the government family planning program, though the official antinatalist policy was not announced until 1968. In effect, 1964 was the date when Taiwan province, rather than China as a fictional whole governed by the Kuomintang, made the official decision for antinatalism.

For the character of strength of implementation we have used the Lapham-Mauldin quantitative index of Family Planning Program Strength, which was developed in 1972 and updated by Freedman and Berelson in 1976. Although that index is not based on systematic and observable program behavior, it is generally accepted as a valid measure of program strength. It uses the judgments of informed observers, who answer a series of relevant questions with a "Yes, Qualified, No" response, which can then be weighted and summed for all questions to give a quantitative score.

Finally, for program impact we use the percentage of crude birth rate decline over the period 1965–75. The data are taken from the Population Council publications that have also used these rates of decline to measure program impact. Specific measures for all variables and all countries are shown in appendix 2 to this chapter.

We can now examine these twenty-one Asian nations to see to what extent they fit our model of the political-ecological adjustment. In anticipation, we can say that the path coefficients fit quite well, and we could simply stop there. That would, however, be neither prudent nor interesting. The small number of cases, the error margins in the data, and the questionable independence of some of the measures suggest that it will be useful to look very closely at the specific countries whose measures produce these well-fitting coefficients. This will permit knowledgeable observers of those countries to judge more fully the adequacy of our perspective and interpretation. It will also provide a more interesting story.

We shall follow a standard format in examining the three stages of the adjustment process. First, we shall present a simple scattergram of the independent political variable with the dependent variable in each stage of the adjustment process. This will help to illustrate both the overall character of the relationship and its deviant cases. Then we present a path-analytic model that shows all of the independent variables that together determine the stages of the adjustment process. From this multivariate analysis we can identify deviant cases, or multivariate outliers,

Figure 4.3 Scattergram of Political-Administrative System Strength and Years of Antinatalist Policy

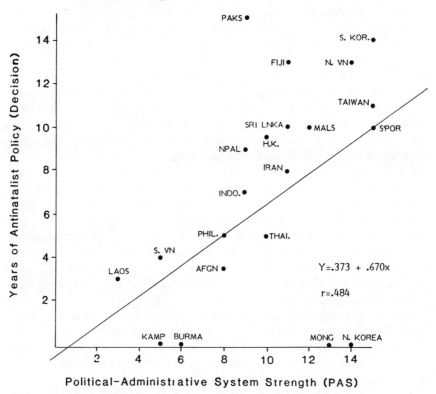

Political-Administrative System Strength (PAS)

that require more extended narrative discussion. Paths are shown when the regression coefficient is substantially greater than its standard error. In all but two cases the significance level of the coefficients is better than 10 percent. Deviant cases are identified as those that lie two or more standard deviations from the mean of the residuals.

Stage 1: The Antinatalist Policy Decision

The first official act in the political-ecological adjustment is the adoption of an antinatalist policy. Our theory holds that the stronger the political-administrative system, the earlier such a policy is adopted, or the longer a country will have had an antinatalist policy. Figure 4.3 shows a scattergram of countries arranged by the strength of the political-administrative system and the years of antinatalist policy. There is a clear positive relationship, with only a few deviant cases. For the most part the strong systems made early decisions, the weak systems made very recent, or no, decisions.

At the upper right is Taiwan, with a strong central political organization and serious and effective economic planning dating back to 1953. It was, in fact, an economic-administrative elite, working in organizations such as the Joint Commission for Rural Reconstruction, who saw the problems of rapid population growth very early in their vigorous and effective efforts to promote modern economic development. Taiwan is also a country of exceptionally well developed social statistics, with accurate census and other survey data supplemented by the national population register. All of these conditions were part of the actual process that led to the antinatalist policy decision. Much the same can be said for South Korea, Singapore, and North Vietnam, which also occupy the upper right corner of the scattergram.

At the lower left is Burma, whose government has not been effective outside of the central river valleys since independence, whose drive for a distinctive Burmese socialism has proved singularly ineffective, and which has not had a complete and accurate census since 1940. Kampuchea, Laos, and South Vietnam also share the lower left with Burma. For these, the tragic events of a larger regional struggle and an international intrusion into civil wars essentially deprived them of any real semblance of autonomous and effective government.

The deviant cases in figure 4.3 are Pakistan, Mongolia, and North Korea. Pakistan has a much older decision than predicted by the strength of its political-administrative system, and the lack of a decision in Mongolia and North Korea is inconsistent with their strong systems. Examination of these deviant cases can help to make the process of the adjustment more understandable. Before discussing the deviant cases, however, we must put together the two variables that our theory proposes determine the date of the policy decision. Figure 4.4 shows the first step in the path diagram, indicating that political-administrative system strength and population density together determine the date of the policy decision. The two path coefficients shown are strong, their error terms are modest, and the overall amount of variance explained is considerable.

Deviant cases can be identified here just as they were in the two-variable scattergram. They are the cases whose decisions are either much older or much younger than predicted by system strength and population density together. Using this multivariate definition, only Pakistan and North Korea appear as deviant cases, or multivariate outliers.[6] Mongolia's very low population density removes it from the statistical definition of a deviant case. That this is more than a statistical definition is clear from the fact that Mongolia explicitly identifies its own low population density as an obstacle to more rapid agricultural development.

Pakistan and North Korea are cases whose statistical deviance can be explained by political conditions. Pakistan made its antinatalist decision in 1960, shortly after Ayub Khan came to power. His accession marked a move toward pronounced strengthening of both the political center and

Figure 4.4 Path Diagram of the Determinants of Population Policy Decisions

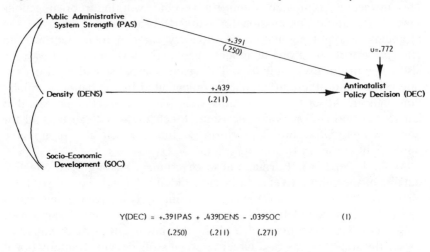

$$Y(DEC) = +.391PAS + .439DENS - .039SOC \qquad (1)$$
$$ (.250) \qquad (.211) \qquad (.271)$$

$$F=3.8358 \ Sig.=.0289 \ R^2=.404$$

the commitment to modern economic development. It appears to have been precisely in the activity of planning that population growth gained its specific identification as an obstacle to development. Subsequently, of course, the strength of the political center proved more illusory than real. The commitment to development turned into an import substitution industrialization policy, paid for and very much resented by East Pakistan. The strength of the political center was much in doubt by 1968, as resistance in both West and East Pakistan mounted. The dissolution of the system and the emergence of Bangladesh followed, and neither country has since been able to rebuild an effective form of national government. Nonetheless, the decision was made in 1960 and however ineffective the implementation, it still stands as an official act.

From its strong, revolutionary and development-committed political character in combination with its high population density, North Korea should have adopted an antinatalist policy long ago, according to our theory. It has, however, continued to resist this policy. This resistance can be explained on a number of political grounds, but two are probably the most important. One is the strong Marxist ideology, which can lead to a rejection of antinatalism as a reactionary Malthusian ideology. Probably more important, however, is North Korea's military stance toward the South. One need only recall the 1950 invasion of the South and the continued maintenance of a massive military force to support this interpretation. In addition, with its roughly seventeen million people, compared with the South's thirty-eight million, the North has little difficulty in perceiving its numerical inferiority. The combination of its revolutionary ideology and its military orientation gives North Korea a perspective on population that is much that of older traditional governments: people are power, power for production and power for warfare. Under these conditions, one would not expect the adoption of an antinatalist policy.

All of these cases permit us to restate this portion of the theory. A strong political-administrative system will quickly adopt an official anti-natalist policy *when that appears to be an appropriate instrument for advancing its national development goals.* For most of the countries of Asia, but not for all, the instrument has been considered highly appropriate.

Stage 2: Creating a Strong Family Planning Program

The next step in the process involves the creation of an effective national family planning program to implement the antinatalist policy. We expect that strong systems with early decisions and with high levels of socioeco-nomic development will produce strong family planning programs. Figure 4.5 shows a scattergram of the number of years of the antinatalist policy and the strength of the family planning program. Again, there appears to be a strong positive relationship. In the upper right of the diagram are South Korea, Fiji, Hong Kong, Taiwan, and Malaysia, whose program strength scores are commensurate with their earlier antinatalist decisions. At the lower left are Afghanistan, Laos, and South Vietnam, whose weak programs are associated with their late antinatalist decisions. In this fi-gure, deviant cases appear to be Pakistan, North Vietnam, and possibly Nepal, all with weaker programs than would be predicted by the timing of their antinatalist decisions. No programs appear substantially stronger than predicted in this bivariate distribution. Again, however, before we discuss deviant cases it will be necessary to put together all the indepen-dent variables our theory proposes as the determinants of program strength—policy decision and socioeconomic development. Figure 4.6 shows the path diagram for this stage of the analysis. Again, the two coefficients directly affecting program strength are large, their error terms are small, and the overall amount of variance explained is considerable. Neither population density nor political-administrative system strength have a significant direct impact on program strength.

From the multivariate analysis, Indonesia and North Vietnam emerge as the deviant cases. Note that adding the socioeconomic development level removed Pakistan and Nepal from the statistical definition of devi-ance, since their levels of development are so low that one would not expect them to have strong programs. North Vietnam is deviant in having far less program strength than expected (2.9 standard deviations below the mean of the residuals). This is explained, however, by the lack of any score at all for North Vietnam. The analyses done by Lapham and Maul-din essentially omitted North Vietnam because no data were available to

Figure 4.5 Scattergram of Years of Antinatalist Policy and Family Planning Program Strength

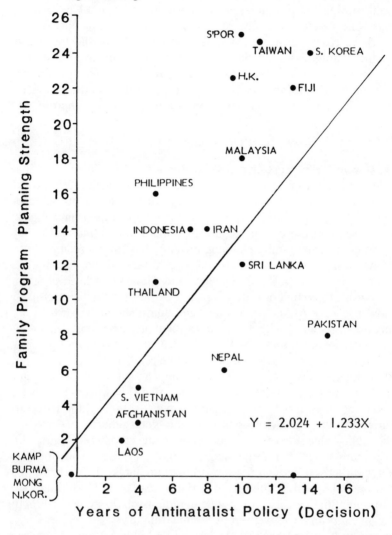

permit the evaluation of their program strength. Other reports from the few population-oriented missions that have visited Vietnam since 1975 indicate that the program functions fairly well, at least in the North. Thus it is our data rather than the program itself that appear deficient.

Indonesia provides a more interesting case whose appearance as a multivariate outlier is especially illuminating when considered in comparison with Pakistan. Pakistan has the older policy decision, 1960 as against 1968 for Indonesia, and both countries are very low in their socioeconomic

Figure 4.6 Path Diagram of the Determinants of Family Planning Program Strength

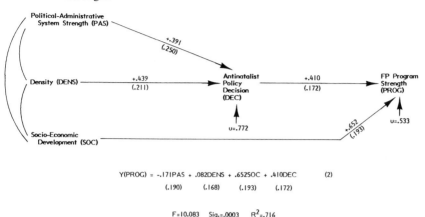

$$Y(PROG) = -.171PAS + .082DENS + .652SOC + .410DEC \quad (2)$$
$$(.190) \quad (.168) \quad (.193) \quad (.172)$$

$$F=10.083 \quad Sig.=.0003 \quad R^2=.716$$

development levels. Yet Indonesia has a relatively high score, fourteen compared with Pakistan's eight, on its program strength measure. Recent evidence would also suggest that this score itself may be an underestimate, for Indonesia has emerged as one of the clear and remarkable success stories in modern family planning programing.[7] It has generated a vigorous approach through a village-based system of supply depots, supported by volunteer workers and women's clubs. From strong beginnings in East Java and Bali, this energetic program is now well established throughout Java and is rapidly moving to provide service in the outer islands.

At this point the major explanation for the radical difference between Pakistan and Indonesia lies in the direction of political dynamics over the past decade. Pakistan appeared politically strong in the early 1960s and then deteriorated. Indonesia began the decade of the 1960s with a weak government and an even weaker commitment to economic development. The fall of Sukarno in 1965–66 and the rise of the Suharto government signaled the return of a strong commitment to development and an equally impressive reorganization of the administrative services to make them an effective instrument of central government policy. Family planning was an integral part of that new development orientation and administrative reorganization. Thus, it appears that political commitment can make up for a considerable amount of development-level weakness in creating a strong family planning program.

In this analysis, we find no direct impact of the political-administrative system on the strength of the family planning program. Whatever impact there is comes through the policy decision rather than directly on the implementing process. These statistical findings are not in accord with our own experience in the field. We have impressions of strong governing systems, whose strength is directly translated into effective programmatic action. There are two issues raised by this experiential and statistical disagreement. First, our statistics require further refinement. We do not believe that we have a full and accurate reflection of either the political system or the strength of the program. It is possible that more accurate indicators would indeed show what we believe is the case: a direct impact of government strength on programmatic action. Second, we are not convinced that we fully understand how government programs work, or that we can identify the detailed organic connections between the governing system and any specific program. Both the statistical refinement and the theoretical development are problems that must await further research.

Stage 3: Policy Impact: Crude Birth Rate Decline

The final step in the political-ecological adjustment links the strength of the family planning program to the decline of fertility. We expect that fertility will decline more rapidly where there is a stronger family planning program, but also where there are higher levels of socioeconomic development and higher levels of population density. The simple scattergram of family planning program strength and crude birth rate decline in figure 4.7 again shows a strong positive relationship. The path diagram in figure 4.8 shows, however, that although program strength and development level do determine the rate of fertility decline, the level of population density is not a significant determinant. Population density apparently works on fertility decline in these cases only through the medium of political decisions and their subsequent impact on programmatic implementation. For the other determinants, however, the coefficients are strong, their error terms small, and the overall variance explained is substantial.

Figure 4.7 clearly shows that stronger programs are associated with more rapid declines in fertility. The two major deviant cases in this scattergram are Iran and North Vietnam. In the multivariate analysis Iran is an outlier, with an actual fertility decline 2 standard deviations below the residuals' mean. North Vietnam is less an outlier, with an actual fertility decline about 1.5 deviations above the residuals' mean. We have already seen that the lack of data on the family planning program is in part responsible for what is in effect an invalid score for North Vietnam's family planning program strength. The zero score on program strength would naturally predict a very low fertility decline. The actual rate of decline, however, has been substantial and thus well above the predicted level. In this case, however, it is merely the lack of good data, rather than a program or political condition, that explains the country's deviant position. The deviance is statistical rather than substantive. We have retained Vietnam as it is in the statistical analysis to provide a more conservative construction of the data, or to stack the cards against a supportive outcome.

Figure 4.7 Scattergram of Percent CBR Decline and Family Planning Program
Strength

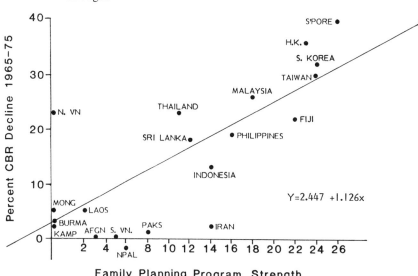

Family Planning Program Strength

Iran's unexpectedly low position in fertility decline is, at least on the
surface, not easy to explain. It is the wealthiest of all the twenty-one
nations in this analysis, with the exception of Singapore. It is more urbanized than all except, of course, Hong Kong and Singapore, and it made
vigorous attempts to transform itself into a modern industrial state over
the two decades preceding 1976. By the Population Council's usually
well-informed evaluation, Iran had a fairly strong family planning program, well endowed with financial and human resources. The program
made use of young women, trained for national service in the Women's
Corps, to bring family planning information and services to the rural
areas. Finally, the program appears to have had a great deal of governmental support, with many organizations led by national elites involved in
some form of fertility limitation activity.[8]

Beneath this surface of vigorous national development activity, however, there were critical weaknesses in the pattern of social development
and in the character of the family planning program. The weakness in
social development consisted in the low levels of female literacy and
educational achievement. In the family planning program, it is our con-
tention that the program score greatly overestimated its real strength.
The position on social development can be made clear by examining
indicators of the six countries with roughly comparable scores (between
ten and twenty) on program strength. These data are shown in table 4.7.

Despite its considerable wealth, Iran had the lowest level of female

Figure 4.8 Path Diagram of the Determinants of Crude Birth Rate Decline

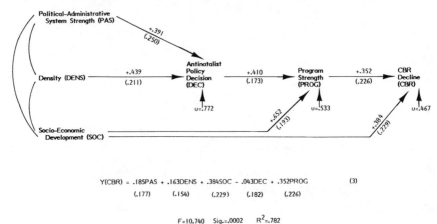

$$Y(CBR) = .185PAS + .163DENS + .384SOC - .043DEC + .352PROG \qquad (3)$$
$$ (.177) \quad (.154) \quad (.229) \quad (.182) \quad (.226)$$

$$F=10.740 \quad Sig.=.0002 \quad R^2=.782$$

school enrollment and the second highest level of infant mortality. Data on infant mortality were probably not very reliable and were infrequently reported. It is probable, however, that the rank ordering is about correct. Iran had a slightly lower infant mortality rate than Indonesia during this time period, a slightly higher rate than the Philippines, and a substantially higher rate than the others. The impact of infant mortality on fertility limitation is being hotly debated, with child survival and child replacement hypotheses being both stoutly defended and criticized. It is argued that people will not willingly limit their fertility unless they perceive real increases in the chances for the survival of existing children, or that people have high fertility to replace lost children. Both are plausible hypotheses, but the data fail to support the second and are mixed on the first. There is a general correlation between infant mortality rates and crude birth rates, but it is also apparent that the causal direction is not by any means certain.

The substantial fertility decline in Indonesia in the face of higher infant mortality rates already makes this clear. Further, the Indonesian data understate the extent of contraceptive acceptance and fertility decline that is occurring in areas served by the family planning program. East Java and Bali, for example, where the program has been especially vigorous, showed roughly 30 percent and 50 percent contraceptive use rates in the 1976 World Fertility Survey, along with declines in the total fertility rate of 15 percent and 35 percent from the late 1960s to 1976; all of this despite estimated infant mortality rates of 134 and 132, respectively. Apparently an effective program can change individual fertility under many different levels of infant mortality.[9]

Data on female school enrollment are probably more accurate and are reported more frequently. In this area, Iran had made very rapid progress, but was still behind its poorer Muslim cousin, Indonesia. Table 4.8

TABLE 4.7
Selected Characteristics of Iran and Five Countries with Comparable Levels of Family
Planning Program Strength

Country	Program Strength	IMR	Socioeconomic Development				
			% Fem. Sch. Enr.	GDP/Cap US$	% Urban	% CBR Decline
Thailand	11	62	52	185	15	23
Sri Lanka	12	53	72	170	24	18
Indonesia	14	137	37	105	19	13
Iran	14	120	32	385	44	2
Philippines	16	97	86	285	16	23
Malaysia	18	41	56	320	30	26

Source: Appendix 3, table 4.19 for program strength and CBR decline; remaining figures
from The World Bank. *World Development Report, 1978.*

Table 4.8
Primary School Enrollment by Gender in Indonesia and Iran, 1960–76

Primary School Enrollment (% eligible population)	Indonesia		Iran	
	1960	1976	1960	1976
Males	61	81	41	90
Females	55	75	27	67

Source: The World Bank, *World Development Report, 1978.*

shows relevant data on school enrollment for 1960–76. As early as 1960,
Indonesia's female school enrollment rate was 90 percent of the male rate
(males 61 percent and females 55 percent), and it climbed another three
points in the next fifteen years. This indicates substantial equality between males and females in both the provision and the utilization of
modern social services. Although Iran had made great progress and had
almost all of its primary school-aged boys in school by 1976, the female
enrollment was still only 74 percent of the male rate (males 90 percent
and females 67 percent). Female seclusion has typically been more strict
in Iran than in Indonesia, regardless of the at least nominal religious
similarities.[10] Although Iran experienced rapid change in this area over
the two decades prior to 1976, it had further to go and it remains significantly less developed than Indonesia.

Many studies have shown that education, literacy, and opportunity for
movement for females is powerfully related to fertility limitation. To put
this another way, low levels of female education indicate a pattern of
isolation in which women are deeply influenced by traditional norms and
relationships supportive of high fertility. These conditions are in some
respects similar in their programmatic demands to the condition of high
infant mortality. Both indicate a level of isolation that requires strong

extension efforts in all social services, and especially in family planning programs, in order to lower fertility. Indonesia's experience amply demonstrates that a program strongly oriented to providing high quality services to the rural areas can be very effective in overcoming the isolation that is indicated by poverty and by physical or social distance. Iran's low rate of fertility decline thus raises the question of how strong the program was, and especially how strong was its orientation to delivery of services to the rural areas.

The program's impact on rural areas in Iran does not appear to have been very pronounced. Commonly reported figures for about 1975 indicate that between 12 and 15 percent of eligible couples were practicing contraception, and that program acceptors constituted about 10 percent of married women of reproductive age. These are not encouraging prevalence levels, especially after almost a decade of well-financed programing. Further, the figures are typically not broken down by rural and urban residence, permitting the inference that most of the acceptance was in urban areas and that rural acceptance rates must have been very low indeed. One bit of evidence in this direction comes from a 1971 report indicating that the roughly one thousand government clinics were recruiting about 70 percent of the acceptors. The more rural-oriented Women's Corps members were recruiting only 5 percent. The remaining acceptors came from the ten or more predominantly urban-based organizations that provided part of the upper-level structure of the program. Finally, a series of small studies from Isfahan and Kava indicate that special attention to the villages could have greatly increased acceptance there.[11] Such studies must be treated with caution, of course, but they nonetheless support the interpretation that at least as late as 1975, the Iranian program was not having much impact on the villages because it had not developed a strong orientation to village outreach. This is especially clear in contrast with Indonesia's program, where a strong village orientation has brought higher program acceptance rates in the rural areas than in the cities.

There is one other comparison with Indonesia that can provide important insights into the weaknesses of the Iranian program. Both countries developed high-level boards, one of the major responsibilities of which was to coordinate the family planning activities of all other government agencies and private groups. The boards were originally not designated as operating agencies; family planning services would be provided for the most part by the Ministry of Health, especially through the rural health programs.

The actual evolution of services in the two countries was quite different, however. The Indonesian coordinating board has taken on a large measure of direct operations. This has been especially evident in the move beyond the clinic to the village-based distribution system. The village family planning strategy was designed and is controlled by the board, which pays field staff directly for the program. It is also a strategy that was opposed by the Ministry of Health, but which has been put into practice nonetheless. In effect the coordinating board in Indonesia has demonstrated considerable power not only to coordinate, but also to override objections of the health ministry and to move itself to direct operations. Perhaps more fundamentally, effective coordination requires power to direct coordinated units. The Indonesian coordinating board has obviously had such power, and the exercise of this power was a critical ingredient in moving the program to its strong orientation toward the rural areas.

Almost the opposite pattern of development can be seen in Iran. The Ministry of Health retained major responsibility for direct services. The public and private organizations involved in family planning in Iran, however, proved too powerful to be coordinated by the central board. Lack of coordinating power in this case was closely associated with the weak rural orientation of the program. The lack of central coordination in Iran has been commented upon privately, but not publicly, in a number of external evaluations of the program. It appears that this lack of public discussion reflected the political conditions that were responsible for the lack of coordination. The more important public and private organizations responsible for family planning in Iran—the Red Lion Society, The Women's Organization, and others—were in part reflections of the personal power and influence of patrons in or close to the royal family. This organizational patronage system, typical of a modernizing patrimonial regime, ensured certain organizations of resources for themselves, but it also rendered the entire structure impervious to central planning and coordination. It also appears to have strengthened the orientation toward urban at the expense of rural services. When a strong patrimonial center can make critical decisions about resource allocation, especially to favored organizations or projects, it is important for organizational elites to remain in close touch with the center. Visible, proximate urban services thus receive more attention than the more remote, less visible rural service programs.

The Iranian family planning program appeared strong to external observers. It received high marks on the check-list of attributes considered, not incorrectly, critical indicators of program strength. Nevertheless, beneath this fine veneer of a modern and extremely wealthy family planning program, there was an organizational network oriented primarily upward to its patrimonial source of wealth, rather than downward to the mass need for service. The Iranian program had the financial and human resources to be a strong program, but it lacked the larger political-administrative system that could turn those resources into effective services for the masses of rural poor.

THE ESCAP REGION

Although the actual processes of policy decision making and implementation proceeded within, and were profoundly affected by conditions of, the individual states in the region, neither the states nor their policy processes operated in a vacuum. They were part of a larger development of both a regional and a world community, which intruded upon and helped to shape the decisions and the actions of the state governments. Here we shall examine two aspects of that external influence.

Perhaps the most important of these was the development of the regional community, which can be seen clearly, if not always precisely, in the work of the UN's regional economic commission. Formed in 1947, this organization was initially called the Economic Commission for Asia and the Far East, ECAFE. In 1974 the name was changed to the Economic and Social Commission for Asia and the Pacific, ESCAP, a change whose significance we shall consider below. It was in the commission that the states found increasing technical and normative support for their own political-ecological adjustment. In addition, the larger world community provided a form of support that can best be seen in the financial assistance offered for population work. Since this support can be rather precisely quantified, we shall be able to assess its weight and influence with the same statistical analysis used above to account for the character of the political-ecological adjustment process within each of the individual states.

The two forms of analysis are complementary, each providing different advantages and disadvantages. Since we can quantify the flow of external funds into the states, we can construct a theory of state and world community interactions in the political-ecological adjustment and can test that theory with precisely measured variables. The precision is, however, more apparent than real. Accounting procedures are by no means standardized and the high complexity of funding—its schedules, motivations, and actual usage—cannot be fully captured by the simple observation of money flows. Nonetheless, the statistics can be generated, we can have some confidence in their relative magnitudes, and since they vary by state, they can be used to provide a rough approximation of both size and character of the external influence.

From the narrative history of the regional commission, however, we can learn much more about the flow of that influence, the emergence of a sense of distinctive regional identity that gave important meaning to it, and the manner in which that influence worked on each of the states. Here we lose precision and comprehensiveness, for the actions cannot readily be quantified, and too much is happening at the same time to include all forces in the interpretation of the influence flow. The data do not yet permit us to see the variance in states' participation in the emerging community. In effect, a narrative history can only begin to scratch the surface of this complex regional development. Its full story has not yet been told, though the data are there, awaiting only a serious research attempt. The ESCAP files are filled with records of the flow of persons, the meetings and conferences, and the research and writing that could be used for an analysis of the emerging network that is the regional community. Here we shall only trace some of the outlines of that network, while hoping others will take up the task of developing the details and testing our interpretations.

Two brief observations can be made here to indicate the character and impact of the regional development. Surveying the ECAFE scene in 1962, David Wightman observed that given the dramatic proportions of the Asian population problem, "ECAFE was surprisingly slow off the mark in analyzing its economic implications."[12] We believe this judgment is incorrect, since it does not take account of the other directly relevant developments within the region, or of the intense conflicts over population issues then raging within the UN as a whole. We shall attempt to show how the same observation Wightman made in 1962 can be given a different interpretation from a different perspective on both regional and world community developments.

Late in 1969, just after winning an unprecedented second term in office, the Philippines' President Marcos announced that the country would have a formal policy to limit fertility. This was late by regional standards, of course, but it is important to note that in this decision the Philippines became the first Roman Catholic country to establish a formal and explicit fertility-limitation policy. The late development derives from internal political-administrative conditions in the Philippines; the more advanced position derives from its regional environment. By contrast, with a stronger political-administrative system, Chile established a fertility limiting program as early as 1965. It was, however, a program of state support for contraceptive distribution through, and hidden in, the maternal and child health network. The program was there, but there was no explicit policy decision for fertility limitation. Our perspective leads us to argue—speculatively, to be sure—that had Chile been located in the ECAFE region, its program decision in 1965 would have been an explicit policy decision. That is, the developments in the region itself had a substantial impact on the individual countries of the region.

Development of a Regional Community

In March 1947 the United Nations Economic and Social Council formally created both the Economic Commission for Europe and the Economic Commission for Asia and the Far East.[13] This represented a substantial victory for Asia in that it gave explicit recognition to Asian problems and it created the organizational instrument by which Asian interests and identities could be advanced. European members had argued for a quick formation of a European commission to pay attention to the immediate and pressing needs of reconstructing that war-devastated region. They proposed delaying creation of a commission in Asia because there were insufficient data to identify clearly the needs of that region and the tasks that should be taken on by a regional commission. Led by the Chinese delegation, Asians successfully argued that their problems were no less pressing and that regional attention to those problems represented one of the most important moves the United Nations could make in the postwar era. Lest it be thought that the North-South debate is only of recent origin, it is well to recall that the early debates over issues of regional commissions saw Asia and Latin America ranged on opposite sides from Europe and North America. Against Western resistance, Chile supported Asia's bid for a regional commission, and later China supported the same request from Latin America.

The Asians were less successful in the choice of a name for the commission, however. P. C. Chang, leader of the Chinese delegation resisted the use of the term "the Far East," since China had always considered itself the center of the universe. The Indians also resisted this clear Europocentric perception of the world, but the debate was not successfully carried by them at that time. The composition of the commission helps to account for the name and also reflects European dominance in the world organization at that time. There were four Asian members—China, India, the Philippines, and Thailand—and six non-Asian members—Australia, France, the Netherlands, the United Kingdom, the Soviet Union, and the United States.

Despite European perspectives and resistance, however, the formation of a regional economic commission gave the Asians the organizational forum they needed to forge their own sense of regional identity, to identify their own interests, and to work toward the promotion of those interests.

By 1974 most Asian nations and a number of Pacific islands had become independent and had gained UN and commission membership. Asia was now a legitimate region in its own right. It was not the center of the universe, but neither was it simply a place far from Europe. It was one of the major regions in an emerging world community. Also by this time the Asians had recognized that their problems were as much social as economic. Thus, the name was changed to the Economic and Social Commission for Asia and the Pacific, or ESCAP.

Through the 1950s and 1960s, ECAFE exerted a substantial influence that led the region to a broad-based political-ecological adjustment. It could do little to promote the development of strong political centers, other than to support and recognize the independence movements that were a necessary, if not sufficient, condition of such development.[14] The commission's more important influence lay in the promotion of a strong commitment to economic development, the creation of an organizational capacity to give life to that commitment, and the building of the necessary organizational capacity to monitor social and economic change. That is, its major influence lay in developing information that would focus the communities of the region on the tasks of increasing human productivity and welfare.

Population planning flowed naturally and inevitably, if not immediately, from this work of information mobilization. We can trace the outlines of this work through the major publication of the ECAFE, the *Economic Bulletin for Asia and the Far East,* published quarterly, with its fourth number each year issued as the more far-ranging *Economic Survey for Asia and the Far East.*

The first two *Surveys*, for 1948 and 1949, were concerned with identifying the needs for economic reconstruction following the war, and were summarized in the first article of the *Bulletin,* in January-March 1950. These discussions covered five major topics, which were to be the core topics for the next quarter-century: production (including agriculture and manufacturing), foreign trade, transportation, currency and banking, and prices. More than half the discussion and the data in these first two years were on foreign trade, reflecting the continuation of the export character of the economies that the colonial powers had produced. There was also, however, in the first issue of the *Bulletin* an article on the mobilization of domestic finances for economic development. The new emphasis on development began in a modest way, but it would grow rapidly throughout the first decade. The third number of the first volume carried an article on budget classification, which was concerned with technical instructions for using the government budget as a tool of development, rather than as a tool of fiscal conservatism.

Over the next two years, other technical articles appeared on the diversification of production, the use of taxation for development, and the analysis of specific needs, such as for chemical fertilizers in agricultural development. In 1953 the first number of the *Bulletin* carried an article on the aspects of urbanization, noting the problems of rapid urbanization and the need for standard classification of populations by locations. The *Survey* for that year expanded the five standard topics to include a discussion of development problems and policies in the region.

A more substantial leap into development, monitoring, and population issues was made in the next two years. The 1954 issues carried discussions of deficit financing for development, which represented a radical change from conservative colonial economic policy. No longer would the annual balanced budget of the colonial finance secretary be the major goal of government economic policy. Deficit financing was legitimized on grounds of promoting increases in productivity.[15] The review continued its discussion of development by making a survey of development plans and programs in the region. Further, in 1954 the statistical reports included new tables on population and area and on employment and wages.

The population statistics show rather clearly why, if that is a correct judgment, ECAFE was "slow off the mark" in its discussion of population problems. By 1954 no country had yet had two postwar censuses, and many had not had even one. India (1951) and China (1953) each had their first postwar census. Of the twenty-one countries in our statistical analysis, only eight had had one postwar census (Sri Lanka, 1953; Malaysia and Singapore, 1947; Nepal, 1952–54; Pakistan, 1951; the Philippines, 1948; South Korea, 1947; and Thailand, 1947). As in India in the 1950s, the magnitude of the population growth problem was suspected by some demographers, but could be conclusively demonstrated by none. This lack of information was shown again in the next year, when only limited surveys and estimates were available to show that mortality had rapidly declined without concomitant reductions in fertility. It was noted that the mortality declines came from modern medical technology and not from increases in the standard of living, and there was a pessimistic speculation that increasing pressures would not reduce fertility in the near future. A problem loomed on the horizon, but its magnitude and full implications could not yet be fully assessed.

Reports of the Bandung Population Conference held in 1955 were not reported in the *Bulletin* until 1956, but the conference did provide important information on population. Again, the prospects for rapid population growth were accurately predicted, though not precisely known. More important, discussion at that conference showed in considerable detail the high costs of rapid population growth in many fields from employment and capital requirements to increasing pressure on educational and public health services. Nonetheless, the tone of the conference was one in which solutions to the pending problem were sought in development and the expansion of output, rather than in the curtailment of fertility.

Development planning also received more emphasis in 1955, as a working party on development and development planning was created and began a series of important technical discussions on all aspects of planning. Reports of this working party were published annually for the remainder of the decade and on into the next. They presented full discussions of a wide range of planning issues, from sectoral analyses and capital formation problems to forecasting, administration, and social planning. Further, in the statistical reports for the second number of the 1955 volume, national income data appeared for the first time.

The first number of the *Bulletin* in 1956 carried an article on population and food supply in the region. The prognosis was pessimistic, since the increases in production and yields experienced in the late 1940s had fallen off, and some declines were found. Per capita production and yields clearly provided a negative outlook for the future. Here again, however, the solution to the problem was seen to lie in increased production and in the capital and new technology that would bring these increases. That year also saw the Fourth Regional Conference of Statisticians, specifically convened to consider problems of carrying out the round of censuses that the United Nations was promoting for 1960. The conference recommended that it be organized into an ongoing Conference of Asian Statisticians, which was to regularize the development of social and economic monitoring in the region.

Over the next three years there was extensive coverage of development problems, with case studies of planning and development in a private market economy (Japan), a mixed economy (India), and a centrally planned economy (China). There was technical discussion of taxation and development, the use of growth models, and the problems of industrial development. In the first number of volume 10, for 1959, a lengthy article discussed population trends and related problems of development in the region. Like the Bandung Conference it presented a full review of mortality declines and high fertility, with an extensive discussion of implications for capital formation, employment, age structure, education, housing, and food supply and demand.

By 1961, at the beginning of the UN's First Development Decade, ECAFE could show considerable advancement in the mobilization of information on economic development. A regional review, volume 12, number 3, showed that India was into its third five-year plan and China near the end of its second. In addition, fourteen of the twenty-one countries in our statistical analysis had at least begun a five-year development plan. Many of these were to be stillborn, of course, but for at least seven (Afghanistan, Taiwan, Malaysia, Iran, Nepal, Singapore, and Thailand) this was the beginning of a sustained and organized effort to stimulate national economic development.

The review also noted achievements in population monitoring. The 1961 statistical survey showed that India and another seven countries in the region had now had their second postwar census. (The seven were Malaysia, Nepal, Pakistan, the Philippines, South Korea, Singapore, and Thailand.) Seven more had had at least their first postwar census. In the following year, the *Survey* could unequivocally state that population growth was more rapid than previously estimated, and that it threatened the growth targets of the UN's Second Development Decade.

During the 1960s the publications show much discussion of development planning, with issues being covered in an increasingly sophisticated and detailed manner. There was, however, relatively little on population planning. In large part this was because significant developments were taking place that would produce a specialized forum for the discussion of population issues. Over the objections of some members of the UN's Population Commission, ECAFE convened the First Asian Population Conference in New Delhi in 1963.[16] This was just one element in the larger debate within the United Nations over technical assistance to population work, and especially to fertility limitation. As we saw in chapter 1, India, Ceylon, and the Scandinavian countries led the argument for, and the United States and the European Roman Catholic countries led the argument against, technical assistance for fertility limitation. The institutional autonomy of ECAFE proved useful in this case, for the Asians could move ahead of the world body, at least with open discussion of the implications of population growth and the feasibility of fertility limitation programs.

The New Delhi Conference was the second setting for what can now be seen as an evolution of thinking through three regional population conferences. The first Conference was held in Bandung, Indonesia in 1955. The second, titled the First Asian Population Conference, was held in New Delhi, and the third was the Second Asian Population Conference, held in Tokyo in 1972. The size, scope, technical preparation, and recommendations of these three conferences show a clear and powerful pattern of growth in regional population thinking.

The Bandung Conference was attended by 103 participants, including 37 official representatives from thirteen countries in the region. Forty-five technical papers were prepared, including eight country statements. The agenda included four major items: the demographic situation, demographic aspects of economic planning, demographic research needed, and the organization of demographic research and training. A sixty-seven-page report was published in 1957. Family planning was conspicuous in its absence as a distinctive topic for discussion.

The New Delhi Conference was attended by 201 participants, including 71 representatives from twenty-two countries. One hundred twelve technical papers were distributed, plus eighteen country statements. Six major agenda items were listed, including one on policies designed to affect population trends. Under this item, family planning programs received close attention. India, Pakistan, Taiwan, Korea, and Ceylon were noted as countries with experience in various types of family planning programing. Much attention was given to the experience of Japan in reducing fertility, both through the use of abortion and through the more extensive use of family planning services, which helped to cut down the abortion rate.

The Bandung Conference had called for more extensive research on demographic issues and had noted the special need for Asian research to reduce the dependence on Western research and experience. The research recommendations of 1963 were less concerned with regional identity—that was an issue already resolved—and more with the specific micro- and macro-level studies on a wide range of topics relevant to population in development planning. The conference also called for the regularization of the Asian Population Conference, which should be held every ten years, hence the Tokyo conference in 1972. It also recommended that ECAFE play a central role in building greater international cooperation in both population research and action programs.

The Second Asian Population Conference, held in Tokyo in 1972, was attended by more than 300 representatives and experts. Scores of background papers were circulated and a 450–page report was issued less than a year after the conference. Eleven major agenda items were listed, including one on family planning programs. There were seventy-nine specific recommendations, with fourteen on various aspects of family planning research and action programs.

One of the most noteworthy observations of this conference was the high degree of consensus generated in the region on the nature of the population problem and its solution. There was no doubt that rapid population growth was detrimental both to national developmental goals and to individual human welfare. There was full agreement that family planning programing—direct public intervention into reproductive behavior—was legitimate, necessary, and useful. There was also, however, a clear statement that family planning programs alone would not solve the problem. These should be integral parts of overall development programs, which could only succeed if they were aimed at creating equality and social justice along with increased human productivity. In contrast with the highly ideological and often poorly informed debates at Bucharest in 1974, the Tokyo Conference demonstrated that the Asian region had indeed come a long way in generating a rational and humane attack on its problem of rapid population growth.

Out of the New Delhi Conference in 1963 came a series of actions that show further development of perceptive capacities in the region and also help to explain the lack of extended discussion of population issues in the *Bulletin*. A series of recommendations led first to a working party on ECAFE's role in population affairs, and then to the creation of a Population Division in ECAFE in 1969.

Even before the establishment of a division, however, ECAFE had appointed four regional demographers and had begun the publication of a special series, the Asian Population Studies Series. The first number in the series was a technical monograph on the administration of family planning programs, issued in 1966. Over the next twelve years forty-three technical papers were published in the series, together with a special set of country monographs begun in 1975. Of the technical papers, twenty-one were specifically on family planning programing. Titles covered a wide range of problems, from administration and target-setting to service statistics, cost-benefit analyses, evaluation of impacts, training of field workers, and evaluation of educational materials.

ECAFE had come a long way in the little more than three decades since its inception. It began with what now appears modest ambitions to bring attention to Asian needs in reconstruction and to mobilize Asian nations for individual and collective efforts at improvement. In its first decade it moved vigorously to identify the problems of economic backwardness and the activities that could produce development. It created a regional environment in which individual countries were surrounded by the work of economic planning and social and economic monitoring. In a relatively short time this work showed increasing elaboration and sophistication. Concepts, tools of measurement, and even the goals themselves were differentiated and made more precise. In the process it became increasingly evident that the fabric of social and economic life was woven of many strands that were joined together in complex but understandable ways. As perceptions of the different strands and their interconnections became clearer, development goals became more complex, involving many different aspects of human behavior. One of these aspects was population growth and human reproduction. In just a few decades this aspect was transformed from an exogenous, given condition into one that could be programed. Population growth was no longer something to be accepted, but something that could and should be the object of public policy and programs.

In summary, then, we can see that ECAFE began with aims of reconstruction, quickly moved to aims of heavy industrialization, and then advanced to aims of national social and economic development, in which fertility limitation ultimately became an integral and altogether feasible programable element. We believe that population planning in the region in part grew out of the emergence of a regional community in which states influenced each other toward this end. This is, of course, only our interpretation, or a hypothesis that is supported by the observation of the sequence of public writings and public discussions. It is not confirmed by this observation. It would require more detailed analysis to determine just how much this emerging external regional community actually did influence individual countries, but it is at least useful to identify this as part of the research agenda.

External Financial Assistance

Between 1965 and 1975, great amounts of financial resources were mobilized for population assistance. The figures do not, of course, begin to match those for military expenditures or for total foreign economic assistance. Nonetheless growth was rapid, and by 1975 the magnitude was substantial. Various estimates of total world resources for external assistance to population programing during that decade run from US$1.054 to US$1.402 billion.[17] In 1965 there was almost no financial support for population programs, except for small amounts from private foundations and associations. By 1975 some US$300 million was being put together annually by various donors for population programs in the high-fertility countries.

Estimates and accounts of foreign financial aid for population programs vary considerably. As yet we have no standardized procedures for classifying assistance to population planning. In some cases, donors count only funds going directly to specific population programs, such as family planning programs. Since the formation of specific population assistance programs, there has been a tendency to count other funds as well; for example, funds for national population censuses. This tendency inflates the growth rate of population funds. Further, as is the case with all foreign aid, much is used to subsidize exports or other activities of the donor countries.[18] US AID, for example, has provided much financial support for contraceptive supplies and technical assistance to population programs abroad, but it has also provided substantial aid to institutional development in the United States for research on population problems. This includes support for biological research on reproduction and contraceptives, as well as for social science research in demography and other relevant disciplines. Here the recent tendency has been to narrow the distribution rather than to broaden it, since there is increasing pressure to allocate population funds directly to high-fertility countries instead of for institutional development in the United States.

Political considerations in the countries also impose problems in accounting for population program support. If countries have made explicit antinatalist policy decisions, funds are allocated to specialized population agencies and present little problem in accounting. In other cases, however, funds can only be granted to such things as maternal and child health, nutrition, education, and rural development programs that have real, if not always explicitly visible, fertility limitation components.

All of these considerations make it difficult to be certain about the magnitude and distribution of population assistance. The figures we present here represent our best estimate of funds that have gone to the twenty-one high-fertility countries of the ESCAP region for population programs. Where there has been a choice between narrow and more inclusive definitions, we have used the more inclusive. Thus, for example, between 1965 and 1975 the Hong Kong family planning program received about US$1,170,000 in foreign assistance.[19] In the same period, however, almost US$3 million was allocated to various educational and health projects directly related to population affairs.[20] In this case, we have used the more inclusive figure in an attempt to obtain a more comparable figure for all countries. This still strikes some discordant notes of noncomparability, of course. Hong Kong has never received support for its population censuses. For Laos, on the other hand, almost all the funds allocated for population assistance have been for the census. This is also true of the recent support to Burma, and, of course, a great deal of the current assistance to Africa is in the form of census assistance.

These problems will always plague attempts to analyze the role and impact of foreign assistance, but we believe the figures we have accumulated here provide a good estimate of the external assistance for population programing as we know it in the high-fertility countries. In any event, we shall attempt to be clear about our figures so that others can examine the bases for our conclusions and can then go on to provide better estimates.

We saw in chapter 2 that Asia has received the largest share of the resources of the United Nations Fund for Population Activities. Our estimates here show that the twenty-one ESCAP countries together received over US$200 million from all sources between 1965 and 1975. Table 4.9 shows the distribution of the funds by three major categories of donors and by the two halves of the decade.

The table shows two major developments through the decade. One is a large increase in external assistance, the other is an increasing diversification of the source of funding. Almost 90 percent of all funds were given in the second half of the decade, with all donors showing a substantial increase in the period. In the first half of the decade, virtually all of the funds came from the United States. By the end of the decade, the United Nations had achieved a position of greater importance. In the first half of the decade, the "Other" category was dominated by the International Planned Parenthood Federation; by the end of the decade a number of other bilateral donors, including the Northern European countries, Japan, and The World Bank, were substantial components of the group.[21]

To understand the role of this external assistance in the political-ecological adjustment, we must understand what determines the level of assistance and what impact that assistance has on the three steps of the adjustment process—policy decision, program implementation, and impact on fertility. For these questions there is little theory to use in developing propositions or a testable model. If foreign assistance is seen as a rational process of capital and technology transfer for economic development, then the identified need and the absorptive capacity of the recipient would determine the flow. If foreign aid is seen as an extension of the foreign policy of the donor nation, then its national interests, broadly stated, would determine the flow. If one's unit of analysis is the entire world system rather than individual nations, then the flow would be determined by more complex network interactions that can be defined by a wide range of perspectives, from sustained dependency to world development. That is, there are many broad perspectives from which to choose, and little in the way of codified theory from which one could develop testable propositions.

Table 4.9
External Financial Assistance for Population Programs Received by the 21 ESCAP Nations,
1965–75 (US$000)

| Years | Major Donors | | | Total |
	US AID	UN	Other	
1965–70	25,969	264	448	26,721
	97%	1%	2%	100%
	19%	1%	1%	12%
1971–75	110,634	34,518	48,274	193,426
	57%	18%	25%	100%
	81%	99%	99%	88%
Total	136,606	34,782	48,722	220,110
	62%	16%	22%	100%
	100%	100%	100%	100%

Source: Appendix 3, table 4.18.

For our purposes, it will be useful to return to the original observations of population planning in Asia, and from there to construct a reasonable scenario that keeps us as close as possible to the national and international dynamics of the region. In comparing the Philippines and Malaysia,[22] we noted that with its stronger political-administrative system, Malaysia made a population policy decision largely from its own internal decision-making processes. Further, it went on to mobilize its own financial and human resources for the program. In the Philippines, in contrast, it appeared that external assistance was an incentive to making the policy decision, which the weaker political-administrative system was unable to generate by itself. Further, the Philippines mobilized few internal resources for its program and relied heavily on external support for its policy implementation. From these observations we can propose that the level of external support is determined negatively by the strength of the political-administrative system. From this perspective, a dependency model appears more plausible than a model of international assistance for the development of sovereign states in explaining the relation between external assistance and policy decisions.

We have also observed, however, that a policy decision is a critical element in determining the flow of funds. When a policy decision is made for a fertility limitation program, the internal bureaucratic and legal situation facilitates the flow of assistance from the outside. If a policy and program exist, administrators from domestic and foreign agencies can identify legitimate tasks and can both ask for and allocate resources to those specific tasks. This leads us to propose that the age of the policy decision positively determines the level of external assistance, a proposition that derives from or implies a rational model of international development assistance to sovereign states.

For the character of the impact of external assistance on program strength and fertility decline, a number of scenarios can be supported from observations of Asian programs. For strong political-administrative systems, external assistance can simply make more resources available for the program, and thus will increase its strength and fertility impact. If a government knows what it wants to do and is capable of mobilizing its administration for that task, then external assistance can provide the contraceptives, equipment, and even personnel to help get those tasks done. Whatever level of external assistance is provided, it will be used effectively for program ends. This seems to characterize the programs in Singapore, South Korea, Taiwan, Malaysia, and more recently Thailand and Indonesia.

Under the condition of a weak political-administrative system, two different possibilities exist. On the one hand, external assistance can make up for some system weakness. In this case the external resources bring support to those individuals and groups within the country who wish to see fertility limitation programs work well. External assistance thus brings resources and political support that would not otherwise be available. If this condition obtains widely, we should expect strong positive paths from the level of external support to both program strength and fertility decline, and weaker paths through the internal stages of decision making to program strength to fertility decline. This scenario appears to describe some of the conditions found in Thailand and Indonesia.[23]

On the other hand, under weak political-administrative conditions, it is possible that external assistance will simply be drawn in for the personal benefit of system leaders and will not have a positive impact on program strength. This may appear a not unreasonable description of the programs in the Philippines or Pakistan.[24] The implication of this scenario is the absence of a significant path from external assistance to program strength. The impact on fertility decline is more problematic, since external assistance may include funds to nongovernmental groups within the country. The programmatic impact of these groups is not measured in our model, since our program strength measure includes only the government program. External funds to private groups may increase their effectiveness and lead to a decline in fertility. Thus, we could propose no path from external assistance to program strength, and either none or a positive path from external assistance to fertility decline. If external assistance works in this way, we should also see a weakening of the internal paths from program strength to fertility decline.

Before testing these complex and contradictory propositions with the available data, it will be useful to examine the specific levels of assistance to the twenty-one countries in our list. Table 4.10 shows four measures of external assistance for all the countries. First, the countries are ranked by the level of total funds per capita for the period 1965–75. In the next

Table 4.10
Per Capita and Absolute Levels of External Assistance for Population Programs to 21
ESCAP Nations, 1965–75

Country	1965–75 Per Capita Funds (US ¢)	Absolute Funds (US$000)		
		1965–70	1971–75	1965–75
Laos	189.7	2,110	3,508	5,618
Philippines	152.4	7,881	48,286	54,167
Hong Kong	105.8	389	3,779	4,188
South Korea	74.6	3,730	20,864	24,614
Fiji	68.4	0	360	360
Singapore	62.5	100	1,198	1,298
Malaysia	59.9	183	6,306	6,489
Thailand	59.2	3,268	18,627	21,940
Sri Lanka	55.0	89	6,808	6,897
Afghanistan	53.2	243	6,176	6,419
Pakistan	43.2	5,538	23,939	29,477
Indonesia	34.8	3,707	38,671	42,378
Nepal	33.8	941	3,823	4,764
N. Vietnam	21.8	0	5,145	5,145
S. Vietnam	17.7	280	3,137	3,417
Iran	12.8	143	3,716	3,859
Burma	5.0	0	1,345	1,345
Kampuchea	1.0	0	73	73
Taiwan	0.8	120	0	120
Mongolia	0	0	0	0
North Korea	0	0	0	0

Source: Appendix 3, table 4.18.

three columns, we show the absolute level of funding for the first and second halves of the decade, and then for the total period.

As might be expected, the larger countries tend to receive more funds, while smaller countries receive less in absolute amounts. In fact, the simple zero-order correlation between population size and absolute levels of external funds is .642 for the period 1965–70, .692 for 1971–75, and .702 for the entire decade. There is also a positive, but slightly weaker, relationship between the amount of external assistance and the country's level of population growth ($r = .543$ for the total period, .585 for 1965–70, and .562 for 1971–75). Thus, there is some tendency for the funds to go to countries where they are needed most: where there are more people and where the numbers are growing most rapidly. Lest we conclude too rapidly that the aid distribution system is a neat and rational one, however, it is useful to make a few other observations.

Population growth rates may not accurately reflect need, since they can be low either from low fertility and mortality rates or from high fertility and mortality rates. The former would not indicate a need for assistance, but the latter certainly would. Further, if population size is a major determinant of external assistance, it is useful to correct for this by using per capita levels of assistance, and then to ask what besides sheer size determines assistance levels.

If table 4.10 shows that size is a major determinant of external assistance, it also shows some interesting anomalies. The most dramatic of these is the Philippines. It received the largest amount of assistance, even in the period before it announced a formal antinatalist policy. Following this it again received more funds than any other single country in the region (except, of course, India, which is not included in this analysis). The special relationship that has marked American-Philippines relations for so long appears to carry over into population planning as well, and also reflects the dominant role of the United States in assistance to the region.

The other large recipients also show signs of American dominance in population assistance. Following the Philippines, Indonesia, Pakistan, South Korea, and Thailand take up the overwhelming bulk of the funds to the region, receiving $173 million, or 78% of all the region's external population funds. Although these countries also make up the bulk of the total population, their share of the whole is only 66 percent, or less than their share of funds. These are also countries that have been central to much of American foreign policy interest in the region for the past decade or more.

There is, however, more than simply American foreign policy interest at work in the allocation of population funds. Hong Kong, Singapore, Malaysia, and Fiji all show higher than average per capita levels, reflecting the spread of private family planning associations from the United Kingdom through the Commonwealth network. For Malaysia The World Bank has also been a major donor. This cannot be attributed to the Bank's success and rationality in population work, however,[25] but to its eagerness to lend money to a political-economic system that is quite certain to repay. Malaysia is a low-risk country, and its massive and successful land development program has drawn heavily on The World Bank for financing. Since that land development program has shown internal rates of return of between 12 and 14 percent, the Bank is by no means a reluctant lender, and its powerful review and planning procedures have easily carried family planning loans along with the more substantial land development loans.[26]

As might be expected, then, the region shows no simple character with regard to external influence in population affairs. The regional and world communities have been active, as have been individual donor countries with their highly specific national interests. There is a proliferation of bilateral assistance relations, as well as growth in financial assistance for population programing provided by the United Nations and various private foundations and associations. We can possibly shed more light on the role of external financial assistance if we ask what its impact has been on the internal processes of policy decision, program implementation, and fertility impact. For this we can return to the path analytic models used above and simply add the level of external funding per capita as an additional variable.

Decision. In equation 1 (fig. 4.4) we saw that the strength of the political-administrative system and population density together had significant impact on the timing of the antinatalist policy decision. The level of socioeconomic development did not have a significant impact, however. If we wish to add the level of external funding to this equation, we must use only that funding that came in the period 1965–70; that is, before all of the countries had made their decisions. Equation 4 shows the results of the estimation. Note that the variance explained does not rise significantly, and the external funding variable has no significant impact on the decision.

$$Y(DEC) = .391PAS + .439DENS - .039SOC \tag{1}$$
$$(se) = (.250) \quad (.211) \quad (.271)$$
$$F = 3.836$$
$$Sig. = .0289$$

$$R^2 = .404$$

$$Y(DEC) = .460PAS + .385DENS - .045SOC + .177Ext\$ \tag{4}$$
$$(se) = (.265) \quad (.222) \quad (.273) \quad (.208)$$
$$F = 3.011$$
$$Sig = .0498$$

$$R^2 = .429$$

These data support the interpretation of a rational transfer of technology and capital for population planning. Countries appear to be making their policy decisions on the basis of their own internal conditions, and not in response to the offer of external funds.

The next step in this rational model proposes that the timing of the decision will have a positive impact on the flow of external funds. Figure 4.9 and equation 5 show the results of this estimation.

Here we note that the political-administrative system plays something of a contradictory role. The stronger the system, the earlier an antinatalist decision is made, and thus the larger will be the external funds for population planning. At the same time, the stronger the system, the less need it has for external funds and the greater is its independent capacity to mobilize its own resources for population planning. Weaker systems get more external support than do stronger systems. Specific cases can easily illustrate this relationship. Mongolia and North Korea have been judged to have strong political-administrative systems, but their ideologi-

Figure 4.9 Path Diagram of the Determinants of the Level of Per Capita External
Assistance for Population Programming, 1965–1975

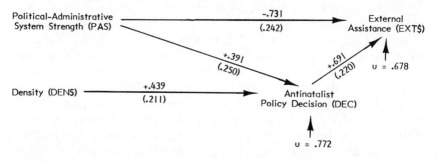

$$Y(EXT\$) = -.731PAS + .076DENS + .057SOC + .691DEC \qquad (5)$$
$$(.042) \qquad (.214) \qquad (.246) \qquad (.220)$$

$$F = 4.6944 \quad Sig. = .0107 \quad R^2 = .540$$

cal commitments and the specific subset of nations with which they are
closely aligned in the larger regional and world community place them
outside of the network of active international population assistance. They
therefore receive no support. At the other extreme, the Philippines and
Laos are judged weak systems, but have received large amounts of foreign assistance; the former because of its special relationship with the
United States, and the latter in part because it is a very small country,
and even the limited support given to a national population census appears as a large per capita level of assistance.

The complex set of relationships shown here appears to fit quite well
with our earlier perspective on Asia and the political-ecological adjustment. Asia led the way for the world community as a whole. Thus, its
own internal conditions are powerful determinants of its policy decisions.
Since Asia led the way, however, it was also in a good position to receive
substantial external support once the donor agencies decided to make
contributions to population planning.

Program implementation. What role has external assistance played in
determining the strength of the family planning program? Our analysis,
shown in figure 4.10 and equation 6, shows no significant impact. The
level of socioeconomic development appears as the strongest determining
condition. External funding has no significant impact, but the addition of
this variable has reduced the strength of the policy decision impact. For
the path from policy decision to program strength, the coefficient is still

Figure 4.10 Path Diagram of the Determinants of Family Planning Program
Strength

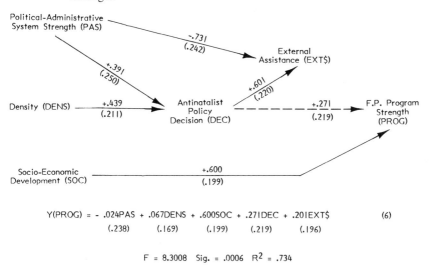

$$Y(PROG) = -.024PAS + .067DENS + .600SOC + .271DEC + .201EXT\$ \qquad (6)$$
$$\quad\quad\quad (.238) \quad\quad (.169) \quad\quad (.199) \quad\quad (.219) \quad\quad (.196)$$

$$F = 8.3008 \quad Sig. = .0006 \quad R^2 = .734$$

larger than its standard error, but the level of significance has now
dropped to about .236. (We show the path as a broken line to indicate its
reduced strength.)

With this small number of cases, there is too much variance in the
character of external funding to permit a generalization about its impact
on program strength. High external inputs in Laos and the Philippines
have not had an appreciable impact on the program, nor do low inputs
into such programs as that in Taiwan appear to have had a debilitating
effect. Taiwan is quite interesting in this regard because, although it has
not had much external financial support, it has enjoyed a very high quality of assistance, especially from the Population Council and the University of Michigan's Center for Population Studies.[27] These external
agencies have worked with progressive groups in Taiwan to produce what
is certainly one of the finest examples of the use of social science in public
program engineering. Unfortunately, our data do not permit an assessment of the quality of external assistance, merely of its quantity.[28] Assessing the quality is an important item that must be placed on the research
agenda.

There are other cases, however, in which it appears that the level of
external assistance has had a positive impact on program strength. Indonesia is the clearest example of such a relationship. Funds from US AID
helped greatly to move the Indonesian program out beyond the clinic into
village groups for both motivation and contraceptive supply. That AID
was willing and able to provide large amounts of grants rather than loans,

that the funds were quickly made available, and that AID developed a process for moving funds rapidly from the center to the provinces certainly contributed a great deal to the strength of the program. These are conclusions of an evaluation of AID inputs into the Indonesian family planning program, and they are supported at least indirectly by our calculations.[29]

By adding the external funds variable, we weaken the path from policy decision to program strength. That is, the external funds may be making up for weakness in the internal processes, making it less critical that a country have an early policy decision in order to have a strong program. In addition, when we examine the deviant cases, or the multivariate outliers, at this stage, we find an important change from the analysis of countries as independent units. When external funding was not included, Indonesia emerged as a deviant case, with a stronger family planning program than was predicted given its rather late policy decision and very weak level of socioeconomic development. Now when we add the external funds, although the overall equation remains much the same, Indonesia is not identified as a deviant case. That is, it has a predictable level of program strength, in large part because the external funds play a role in the explanation.

At this point we are not in a position to determine which general perspective on foreign assistance for population planning is more powerful. To explain the decision-making process, the rational technology-capital transfer appears to work best. It also appears that external funds can help to make up for some of the weakness of a political-administrative system in translating policy decisions into programmatic action, but the data do not permit us to be certain of this. Whatever impact external funding has on program implementation, our data are not sufficiently detailed or sensitive to identify that impact or its character very clearly.

Impact on Fertility. When we add external funds to the equation explaining the rate of decline in fertility, the original model, displayed in figure 4.8 and equation 3, changes somewhat. The level of socioeconomic development remains a strong determinant of fertility decline. This at least fits with most demographic theory and observation. As in figure 4.8, program strength continues to have some impact, but the level of significance drops considerably. Although external assistance did not have an impact on program strength, it does have a direct and positive impact on fertility decline. Finally, with the addition of the external funds variable, the strength of the political-administrative system now has a direct and powerful positive impact as well. Its influence on fertility decline is no longer felt only through the policy decision and the program implementation. When the multivariate outliers are identified in this equation, they remain as before: Iran had a much lower fertility decline than predicted (two standard deviations below that predicted), and North Korea joined

Figure 4.11 Path Diagram of the Determinants of Crude Birth Rate Decline 1965–1975

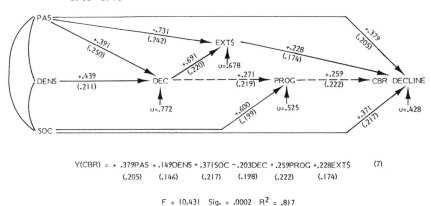

$$Y(CBR) = + .379PAS + .149DENS + .371SOC - .203DEC + .259PROG + .228EXT\$ \qquad (7)$$
$$(.205) \quad (.146) \quad (.217) \quad (.198) \quad (.222) \quad (.174)$$

$$F = 10.431 \quad Sig. = .0002 \quad R^2 = .817$$

Iran in being below the predicted level. The path diagram and equations for this estimation, shown in figure 4.11, are as follows.

These path diagrams permit us to make a general assessment of the role of external financial assistance in the political-ecological processes in the Asian region. First, we can see more independence than dependence in the processes by which nations came to perceive rapid population growth as a problem and then move to a decision for a fertility-limiting policy. At least in Asia it was internal political processes that led to these decisions, rather than the mere promise of external funding. The external developments within the region, in areas of technical assistance for development planning and information gathering, were of considerable importance, as was the increasing legitimacy given to population planning through cumulating public discussions. The funding, however, came in large part after, rather than before, the deeper decision-making processes were under way.

Funding came afterwards in the causal chain as well. When a nation had made an antinatalist policy decision, the legal bureaucratic processes opened the organizational network and facilitated the flow of funds to the country. External funding to the states of Asia for population planning grew rapidly during the decade of 1965–75. Those funds went most rapidly to the states that had made an antinatalist decision, but they also went more to the weaker than to the stronger states of the region. This suggests that external funding can provide an alternate path from the political-ecological conditions to the decline of fertility. For the strong states, that path leads through internal decision making and organizational implementing conditions. For the weaker states, external funding permits the implementing path to be weaker, and leads from decision making through external assistance to fertility decline.

From our data we cannot be sure just how this happens, but it is possible to suggest a plausible explanation. Some of the external funding goes to the private sector family planning associations as well as to the public sector programs. We have no measure of the former here, which may account for the lack of any discernible impact of external funding on the strength of the family planning program itself. Assistance to the private sector can well have an impact on fertility decline without a commensurate impact on the public family planning program.

This line of reasoning can give comfort to foreign aid agencies. One of the fundamental justifications for foreign assistance lies in the argument that there is only a weak institutional structure in the receiving nation. That weakness implies an incapacity to take initiative and to sustain action in a whole range of development activities. In this situation, assistance can come from those societies with stronger institutional bases and richer human and material resources. The assistance can help to increase human welfare and productivity, temporarily making up for internal institutional weakness by generating needed results, and in the process increasing institutional strength for local initiative.

Whether external assistance ultimately helps to build such strength is, of course, a critical issue. Results, such as fertility decline, can be achieved with external assistance without increasing a society's capacity for local initiative. When this happens, as it so often does in foreign assistance, dependence rather than independence is increased, and the more altruistic aims of foreign assistance are subverted. At this point, we cannot tell from our data what has really happened in the business of foreign assistance for population planning.

Our impression from observations in the region is twofold. First, foreign assistance has, as our path diagrams suggest, provided an alternate line of activity that can give some assistance to people in the absence of strong governmental implementing capacities. Second, it has not changed very much the capacities of governments to implement their policies. The strong states have gone ahead with good programs, and probably would have done so without a great deal of foreign assistance. The weaker states have absorbed a great deal of assistance and have not significantly changed their own capacities for implementation. None has been made either weaker or stronger in any appreciable way through foreign assistance. One or two exceptions may stand out. Indonesia may well have been helped in its public program, and Thailand may well have been assisted in its public and private programs in rather substantial ways. Most states, however, have simply become more like themselves, either because of or despite foreign assistance.

These are, it must be emphasized, only our own impressions. To understand more clearly the role of foreign assistance we need much more detailed information over a longer period of time. For example, if we knew year by year how much financial assistance came from what sources and for what kinds of activities, it would be possible to disaggregate external assistance in ways that would permit testing a series of hypotheses on its role in local institutional development as well as in fertility decline. If we knew more about the qualitative differences in foreign assistance and about the mechanisms by which it is organized, dispersed, and monitored, it would be possible to speak with greater confidence of its precise role in the political-ecological adjustment. That foreign assistance has played a role in the political-ecological adjustment process in Asia seems quite certain. A fuller understanding of what that role has been will require more research, which is at least a common, if not always welcome, concluding statement in such analyses.

APPENDIX 1: POLITICAL-ADMINISTRATIVE SYSTEM CODING

For the three dimensions of the political-administrative system, the coding of the panel of independent judges was very close to our own coding. Agreement was strongest for the degree of political centralization (r=.925), next for administrative monitoring capacity (r=.863), and weakest for the degree of development commitment (r=.648). The following shows for each of the three dimensions the patterns of agreement and disagreement. Numbers in parentheses show the panel score followed by our score where there is disagreement on the scoring.

Political Centralization
  Agreement: N=16:
    Burma, Afghanistan, Indonesia, Pakistan, Nepal, Hong Kong, Thailand, Sri Lanka, Iran, Malaysia, Mongolia, North Korea, North Vietnam, South Korea, Singapore, Taiwan
  Panel Higher: N=5:
    Laos (2–1); Philippines, Kampuchea (3–2); Fiji (4–3); South Vietnam (3–1)

Administrative Monitoring Capacity
  Agreement: N=14:
    Laos, Kampuchea, Afghanistan, Philippines, Indonesia, Nepal, Thailand, Sri Lanka, Iran, Malaysia, Mongolia, North Korea, North Vietnam, Singapore
  Panel Higher: N=5:
    Burma (2–1); South Vietnam (3–2); Pakistan (4–3); Fiji, Hong Kong (5–4)
  Panel Lower: N=2:
    South Korea, Taiwan (4–5)

Development Commitment
  Agreement: N=10:
    Kampuchea, Burma, Indonesia, Thailand, Fiji, Malaysia, Singapore, Taiwan, North Korea, North Vietnam
  Panel Higher: N=5:
    Laos (2–1); Philippines, South Vietnam (3–2); Pakistan (4–3); Hong Kong (4–2)
  Panel Lower: N=6:
    Afghanistan, Nepal (2–3); Iran, Sri Lanka (3–4); South Korea, Mongolia (4–5)

Out of sixty-three pairs of observations, there was complete agreement on the scoring in forty. Of the twenty-three cases of disagreement, the differences are only one level in twenty cases, and two levels in the remaining three cases. Note, however, a possibly important difference in the direction of disagreements. The panel scores were higher than ours in fourteen cases, and our scores were higher in only nine.

There is one important type of bias that can creep into this form of coding, and our disagreements help us to provide one limited test of that bias. In all cases we are making subjective judgments of the strength of the political-administrative system. To be valid, these must be independent of judgments on the dependent variables. While we can attempt to base our judgment on, for example, the degree of political centralization, there is no way we can erase from our memories our own knowledge of a country's population policy decisions, its family planning program strength, or the rate of decline in its crude birth rate. Thus, our judgments on the political strength may be contaminated if we are influenced by knowledge of the final results. Our panel of judges was not informed, however, of the specific intent of this scoring process. For the most part we can therefore assume that they did not prejudge the results, although it is quite possible that their own observations of strength or weakness in fertility control may have contributed to their judgments of political strength or development commitment.

One possible test of our own biases is available from examining the differences in the dependent variable scores when the panel's political system scores were higher than ours and when they were lower than ours. A bias in our scoring would be indicated if scores on the dependent variables are higher for those cases in which we give higher scores on the political variables and lower when the panel gives higher scores. The following table shows the means and standard deviations for each of the three dependent variables when the panel's scores are higher and when our scores are higher.

Table 4.11
Means and Standard Deviations of Dependent Variable Scores

		Dependent Variable Scores		
		Policy Decision	Program Strength	CBR Decline
A. PC + AE + DO				
Cases where panel scores are higher				
N = 14	Mean	7.1	10.9	11.5
	S.D.	5.3	9.1	13.1
Cases where our scores are higher				
N = 9	Mean	8.2	12.4	13.6
	S.D.	4.8	9.6	14.6
B. PAS Total				
Cases where panel scores are higher				
N = 8	Mean	6.2	9.5	11.0
	S.D.	5.7	9.6	13.2
Cases where our scores are higher				
N = 7	Mean	8.0	11.9	12.9
	S.D.	4.7	9.6	14.0

In all cases the small number of observations and the large standard deviations render the differences between the means statistically not significant. Nonetheless, there is the suspicion of a bias in our judgments. In all categories, when our judgments of the country's political-administrative scores are higher than the panel's, the means of the dependent variables are larger than when the panel's political scores are higher. Given this suspicious pattern, we have estimated the model using the panel's PAS score rather than our own, even though on substantive grounds we trust our own judgment more than that of the panel. The results of the new estimation are as follows.

The use of the panel's PAS score increases the strength of the determination of the system on the policy decision and on the program strength. In the determination of CBR decline, all coefficients are weakened, and the program strength coefficient is the only one for which the standard error is substantially smaller than the coefficient. Still, the model is not radically different from that using our political scores. Further, the deviant cases identified in this model are the same as those that emerged from our model. Overall, then, there does not appear to be a significant bias in the estimation of political-administrative system scores.

Figure 4.12 Path Diagram of the Determinants of the Political-Ecological Adjustment Using Panel Scores

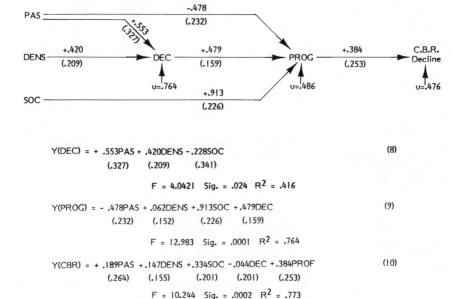

Y(DEC) = + .553PAS + .420DENS - .228SOC   (8)
         (.327)   (.209)   (.341)

         F = 4.0421   Sig. = .024 R^2 = .416

Y(PROG) = - .478PAS + .062DENS +.913SOC +.479DEC   (9)
          (.232)   (.152)   (.226)   (.159)

          F = 12.983   Sig. = .0001 R^2 = .764

Y(CBR) = + .189PAS +.147DENS +.334SOC -.044DEC +.384PROF   (10)
         (.264)   (.155)   (.201)   (.201)   (.253)

         F = 10.244   Sig. = .0002 R^2 = .773

APPENDIX 2: MEASURES OF SOCIAL AND ECONOMIC DEVELOPMENT

Our measure of socioeconomic development is based on that used by Berelson and Freedman in their 1976 assessment of family planning programs, which combined GDP per capita, infant mortality rates, and female school enrollment. These three measures appear to us most intuitively acceptable as fundamental dimensions of human productivity and welfare. The problem, of course, is that measures are not available for all countries, and the error margins in the measures are both substantial and variant. With data gaps it is necessary to estimate specific levels where the data do not exist. With the known and suspected error margins, the use of exact figures and the imputation of firm meaning to exact intervals do not seem justified. To deal with these twin problems, we constructed a special ranked score of socioeconomic development.

First, we ranked each of the three variable measures for those countries for which data were readily available. For this primary ranking we used the measures provided by Berelson and Freedman. Next, we used natural breaks in the ranked scores to establish five broad levels for each variable. Finally, for countries for which no data were available, we estimated their position in the five-part ranking. This procedure provided us

Table 4.12
Per Capita GDP Scores

Countries with Given Data	US$	Assigned Score	Countries Estimated
Singapore	965	5	
Hong Kong	780		
Fiji	423	4	
Iran	385		
Taiwan	330		
Malaysia	320		
Philippines	285	3	N. Korea
S. Korea	265		
Thailand	185	2	Mongolia
Ceylon	170		S. Vietnam
(W) Pakistan	145		
Kampuchea	129		
Indonesia	105	1	Pakistan
Nepal	85		Afghanistan
Burma	82		Laos
Bangladesh	80		

Table 4.13
Infant Mortality Rate Scores

Countries with Given Data	IMR	Assigned Score	Countries Estimated
Fiji	19	5	
Hong Kong	20		
Singapore	21		
Taiwan	40	4	
S. Korea	41		
Malaysia	41		N. Korea
Sri Lanka	53		
Thailand	62	3	N. Vietnam
Philippines	97		S. Vietnam
			Mongolia
Iran	120	2	Burma
Nepal	125		Pakistan
(W) Pakistan	128		
Indonesia	137		
Bangladesh	150	1	Kampuchea
Afghanistan	150		Laos

Table 4.14
Female School Enrollment Scores

Countries with Given Data	%	Assigned Score	Countries Estimated
Philippines	86	5	
Hong Kong	82		
Singapore	77		
Taiwan	73		
Sri Lanka	72		
S. Korea	69		
Malaysia	57	4	N. Korea
Fiji	55		S. Vietnam
Thailand	52		N. Vietnam
			Burma
Indonesia	37	3	Mongolia
Iran	32		
(W) Pakistan	15	2	Pakistan
Bangladesh	15		
Nepal	7	1	Kampuchea
Afghanistan	3		Laos

Table 4.15
Total Score of Socioeconomic Development for All
Countries in This Analysis

Country	Score	Country	Score
Afghanistan	1	S. Korea	7
Sri Lanka	6	Singapore	9
Fiji	8	S. Vietnam	5
Hong Kong	9	Thailand	5
Indonesia	2	Taiwan	8
Iran	5	Burma	3
Laos	1	Kampuchea	1
Malaysia	7	Mongolia	4
Nepal	1	N. Korea	6
Pakistan	2	N. Vietnam	5
Philippines	6		

with measures for all countries on each of the variables, but it did not force us to make precise estimates for any missing data. For example, we estimated that North Korea's per capita GDP put it in level 3, along with the Philippines and South Korea. In effect, our estimate is that it lies somewhere between about US$200 and US$300. We feel more comfortable with this range for the estimate than we would with a precise figure. To arrive at a total score on socioeconomic development for each coun-

Figure 4.13 Scattergram of Socioeconomic Development Level and Physical Quality of Life Index for 18 Asian Countries

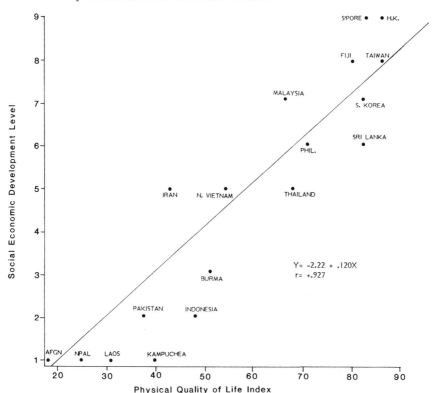

try, we simply summed the score for the three variables and then transformed this total into its ordinal ranking, which provides nine levels, giving identical scores for ties. Tables 4.12, 4.13, and 4.14 show the transformation from raw scores to ranked levels for each of the variables. The final ordinal score for each country is shown in table 4.15 and in appendix 3, together with all statistical data used in this chapter.

We compared our socioeconomic development score with two other composite scores for these countries. Our first comparison is with the Physical Quality of Life Index (PQLI) developed by Morris D. Morris.[30] This index is available for eighteen of our countries, all except Mongolia, North Korea, and South Vietnam. The correlation coefficient for the PQLI and our score is +.927. Figure 4.13 shows a scattergram of the countries with these two scores. In addition, we constructed an index of per capita GDP comparable to the indices Morris used in his PQLI and added this to his index. This adds a measure of human productivity to his

Figure 4.14 Scattergram of Socioeconomic Development Level and Combined Indices of Physical Quality of Life Plus Per Capita GDP for 18 Asian Countries

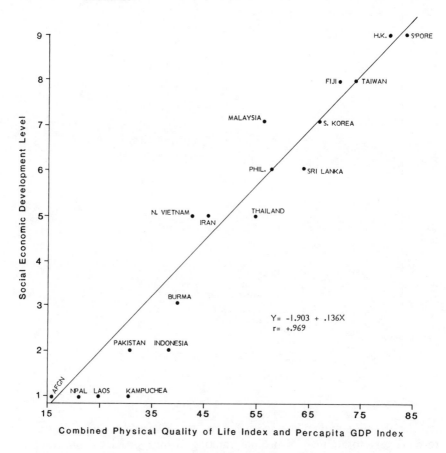

measures of human welfare. The correlation coefficient of these two indices for the eighteen countries for which data are available was found to be .972. The correlation coefficient between the new PQLI plus productivity (PQLY) and our socioeconomic development score was .969. Figure 4.14 shows a scattergram of the eighteen countries for which data are available on these two measures.

It is apparent that there is a very close relationship between these three different measures of socioeconomic development. We conclude from this that our measure has some validity, and that we can have some confidence that it is not seriously biased in any direction. It should be noted, or course, that some portion of the high agreement derives from the common data base that is used in all efforts to quantify development. The

UN and The World Bank are probably the two most frequently used sources; and with most observers going to the same data sources for the construction of indices, we should expect much agreement, even when we suspect high error margins in the data.

APPENDIX 3: COUNTRY DATA

The following tables show the raw data and indices used for the analyses in this chapter.

Table 4.16
Population (1970), Agricultural Density, and Two Measures of Socioeconomic Development

Country	POP70	AGDENS[a]	PQLI[a]	PQLY[a]
Afghanistan	10.060	137	18	15
Sri Lanka	12.530	584	82	63
Fiji	.530	172	80	70
Hong Kong	3.960	4,043	86	80
Indonesia	121.720	690	48	38
Iran	30.960	94	43	45
Laos	2.960	90	31	24
Malaysia	10.840	320	66	56
Nepal	11.310	266	25	20
Pakistan	130.820	373	38	30
Philippines	37.540	288	71	57
S. Korea	32.980	1,235	82	66
Singapore	2.080	3,869	83	83
S. Vietnam	12.340	248	na	na
Thailand	37.090	269	68	54
Taiwan	14,600	1,378	86	73
Burma	27.080	153	51	39
Kampuchea	7.060	174	40	30
Mongolia	1.250	1	na	na
N. Korea	14.190	637	na	na
N. Vietnam	23.640	950	54	42

[a]Agricultural density, AGDENS, is the population per square kilometer of arable land. For Hong Kong and Singapore, however, total density is used. The PQLI, or Physical Quality of Life Index is from Morris D. Morris, *Measuring the Condition of the World's Poor* (1979). The PQLY is constructed by adding an index of per capita GDP to the PQLI measure.

TABLE 4.17
Group (GRP) and Ness-Ando (NA) Scores for Political Centralization (PC), Development Commitment (DO), Administrative Monitoring Efficiency (AE), and Total Political-Administrative System Strengh (PAS)

Country	GRPPC	GRPDO	GRPAD	GRPPAS	NAPC	NADO	NAAE	NAPAS
Afghanistan	3	2	2	7	3	3	2	8
Sri Lanka	3	3	4	10	3	4	4	11
Fiji	4	4	5	13	3	4	4	11
Hong Kong	4	4	5	13	4	2	4	10
Indonesia	3	3	3	9	3	3	3	9
Iran	4	3	3	10	4	4	3	11
Laos	2	2	1	5	1	1	1	3
Malaysia	4	4	4	12	4	4	4	12
Nepal	4	2	2	8	4	3	2	9
Pakistan	3	4	4	11	3	3	3	9
Philippines	3	3	4	10	2	2	4	8
S. Korea	5	4	4	13	5	5	5	15
Singapore	5	5	5	15	5	5	5	15
S. Vietnam	3	3	3	9	1	2	2	5
Thailand	4	3	3	10	4	3	3	10
Taiwan	5	5	4	14	5	5	5	15
Burma	3	2	2	7	3	2	1	6
Kampuchea	3	1	2	6	2	1	2	5
Mongolia	5	4	3	12	5	5	3	13
N. Korea	5	5	4	14	5	5	4	14
N. Vietnam	5	5	4	14	5	5	4	14

TABLE 4.18
External Expenditures (US$000) for Population Programs by Source and Period

Country	AID	UN	Other	Total	Per Cap (US ¢)
			1965–1970		
Afghanistan	227	16	0	243	2
Sri Lanka	0	89	0	89	.7
Fiji	0	0	0	0	0
Hong Kong	0	0	388.6	388.6	9.8
Indonesia	2,200	1,507	0	3707	3
Iran	0	143	0	143	.5
Laos	2,110	0	0	2,110	71.2
Malaysia	0	183	0	183	1.7
Nepal	934	7	0	941	8.3
Pakistan	5,538	0	0	5,538	4.2
Philippines	7,682	199	0	7,881	22.2
S. Korea	3,730	0	0	3,730	11.4
Singapore	0	0	99.7	99.7	4.8
S. Vietnam	280	0	0	280	1.4
Thailand	3,268	0	0	3,268	8.8
Taiwan	0	120	0	120	.8
Burma	0	0	0	0	0
Kampuchea	0	0	0	0	0
Mongolia	0	0	0	0	0
N. Korea	0	0	0	0	0
N. Vietnam	0	0	0	0	0
			1971–1975		
Afghanistan	5,155	492	529	6,176	51.2
Sri Lanka	0	4,500	2,308	6,808	54.3
Fiji	179	108	73	360	68.4
Hong Kong	0	0	3,799	3,799	96
Indonesia	26,507	5,657	6,507	38,671	31.8
Iran	0	2,073	1,643	3,716	12.3
Laos	2,939	569	0	3,508	118.4
Malaysia	0	2,274	4,032	6,306	58.2
Nepal	3,294	126	403	3,823	25.5
Pakistan	13,594	5,992	4,353	23,939	39.2
Philippines	36,923	4,429	4,934	48,286	130.2
S. Korea	8,200	2,940	9,724	20,864	63.2
Singapore	0	919	279	1,198	57.8
S. Vietnam	2,988	149	0	3,137	16.2
Thailand	10,855	3,272	4,545	18,627	50.3
Taiwan	0	0	0	0	0
Burma	0	1,345	0	1,345	5
Kampuchea	0	73	0	73	1
Mongolia	0	0	0	0	0
N. Korea	0	0	0	0	0
N. Vietnam	0	0	5,145	5,145	21.8

TABLE 4.18—*Continued*

	1965–1975	
Country	Total	Per Cap (US ¢)
Afghanistan	6,419	53.2
Sri Lanka	6,897	55
Fiji	360	68.4
Hong Kong	4,187.6	105.8
Indonesia	42,378	34.8
Iran	3,859	12.8
Laos	5,618	189.7
Malaysia	6,489	59.9
Nepal	4,764	33.8
Pakistan	29,477	43.2
Philippines	54,167	152.4
S. Korea	24,614	74.6
Singapore	1,297.7	62.5
S. Vietnam	3,417	17.7
Thailand	21,940	59.2
Taiwan	120	.8
Burma	1,345	5
Kampuchea	73	1
Mongolia	0	0
N. Korea	0	0
N. Vietnam	5,145	21.8

TABLE 4.19
Summary of Data Used in Path Analyses

Country	Pol.-Ad. Sys. Str. Score	Soc-Ec. Devel. Score	Yrs. Antinat. Policy	F.P. Str.	CBR Dec.
Afghanistan	8	1	4	3	0
Sri Lanka	11	6	10	2	18
Fiji	11	8	13	2	22
Hong Kong	10	9	9.5	23	36
Indonesia	9	2	7	14	13
Iran	11	5	8	14	2
Laos	3	1	3	2	5
Malaysia	12	7	10	18	26
Nepal	9	1	9	6	−1
Pakistan	9	2	15	8	1
Philippines	8	6	5	16	19
S. Korea	15	7	14	24	32
Singapore	15	9	19	26	40
S. Vietnam	5	5	4	5	0
Thailand	10	5	5	11	23
Taiwan	15	8	11	24	30
Burma	6	3	0	0	3
Kampuchea	5	1	0	0	2
Mongolia	13	4	0	0	9
N. Korea	14	6	0	0	5
N. Vietnam	14	5	13	0	23

5

The Political-Ecological Perspective: Implications and Controversies

THE ARGUMENT RECAPITULATED

Our central argument has been constructed to deal with the observation of two integrally linked phenomena of our time: rapid population growth and the antinatalist policy revolution. Each would be important in itself, but it is the two together that give our era its truly distinctive political-ecological character.

Rapid population growth is best seen in the long-tailed exponential growth curve that abounds in popular and scientific analyses of our times.[1] For most of the past eight thousand years or so, the growth of the human population has been less than 0.1 percent per year. For the past three centuries, the rate of growth has been increasing, until now world population growth is about 2 percent per year. It is common to note that this rate of growth cannot continue for long without radical changes in the human environment. For example, a 2 percent growth for the next three centuries would give us a world population of about 1500 billion, compared with the approximately 4 billion who exist today. Further, if this growth continued into the future for a span equal to that of the Christian era, there would be sufficient human beings to cover every bit of matter known in the entire universe. This, of course, is nothing more than the logic of compound interest, or the frightening prospect of an exponential growth curve extending indefinitely into the future.

Interesting as is this growth curve for the world as a whole, it becomes even more enlightening when it is disaggregated by the world's high- and low-fertility regions. If the world still shows a curve of exponential growth, the two groups of countries show somewhat different curves. The industrial world went through a period of exponential growth from about 1700 to about 1900. The nonindustrial world entered the process of rapid

171

growth later, generally in the latter part of the ninteenth century. The industrial world ended its rapid growth in the late nineteenth and early twentieth centuries, and the nonindustrial world is still in the process of rapid growth. Another way to put this is to say that the industrial world passed through a demographic transition, from high natural fertility and rapid growth to controlled low fertility and low growth. The nonindustrial world has entered the demographic transition with its declining mortality, but remains marked by high fertility.

Given this situation, it is not the world's population, but the nonindustrial world's population that will people all the known matter in the universe over the next two thousand years.

The antinatalist policy revolution is an equally dramatic condition of our time. Most governments for most of human history have been pronatalist. People have usually been seen as a resource for governments to mobilize: They can be taxed, worked, and sent to war. It is not surprising, then, that governments have historically been pronatalist. This pronatalism, however, is now only a thing of the past.

In the nonindustrial world, rapid population growth has produced serious ecological imbalances, which in the words of our East Javanese poor make it difficult to breathe. In the industrial world's past, rapid growth had also made breathing difficult, but for the poor and the rising middle classes, not necessarily for governments. Individuals used a variety of means to limit their fertility, often against the stated interests of governments.[2] In the nonindustrial world today breathing has become difficult for the people and for governments alike. For the first time, governments in large numbers have moved to adopt deliberate policies to reduce fertility. This constitutes a policy change of revolutionary proportions. We have shown that this policy revolution is not spread evenly throughout the high-fertility world. It came earlier, has been more unambiguous, and is more pervasive in Asia than in Latin America, Africa, or the Islamic Mediterranean World.

We have shown that this policy revolution is also linked to major programmatic changes: the creation of national-level programs to distribute modern contraceptive information, supplies, and services. And finally, we have seen some decline in fertility and the possibility that politics and policies have played some role in that decline. This represents a major ecological adjustment in which political organizations and their activities have played a key role.

The political component of these changes consists of three major conditions. One is the government's capacity to make effective policy decisions for the population and to maintain control of programs that grow out of these decisions. The second is a commitment to the achievement of modern economic development and the creation of a series of structures both to mobilize resources and to allocate those resources in such a way as to

achieve the development goals. The third condition is a capacity to monitor social and economic changes in the population under the control of
government. When these political capacities are well developed, and
when they are associated with high population density and high levels of
social and economic development, they produce early antinatalist policy
decisions, which are translated into strong programmatic actions, which
then have a marked impact on fertility. It is this capacity of political
organizations to play an important, and possibly decisive, role in fertility
reduction that makes the current ecological adjustment a distinctively
political-ecological adjustment.

At this point we have mapped only the broad contours of this adjustment. The systematic variance we have been able to observe between
Asia and the other high-fertility regions, and the variance within Asia
itself, lead us to believe that our mapping is accurate. If we are right, two
types of comments can be made from this perspective. First, we can
identify some of the many details that remain to be worked out. This
constitutes something of a research agenda, which, if carried out, should
shed more light on the processes of population change in the high-fertility
world. Second, from this perspective we can make a number of observations on the major controversies that continue to rage over issues of
population programing, and especially over the current conditions of
family planning or fertility limitation programs.

IMPLIED QUESTIONS

Our model of the political-ecological adjustment includes hypotheses
about the relations between political conditions, population density, socioeconomic development, population policies, family planning programs,
and fertility decline. Any subset of these interrelations requires more
extensive investigation. Some, such as the relation between socioeconomic development and fertility, have already been the subject of massive investigation, which continues to raise more problems than it solves.
We cannot begin to identify all of the issues that require further investigation. It will, however, be useful to focus on the political aspects of our
model, since these appear to have been the most neglected in past population research, and to use this portion of our model to identify further
questions that should be addressed. Here we confine ourselves to five
major sets of questions. We believe that attention to these questions will
provide useful insights both for policy makers and for observers of the
process of modern population change.

1.   Our conception of the political-administrative system is specifically
focused on what we found to be important for population planning. We
observed that in many countries of Asia the thrust for fertility limitation

policies came largely from economic planning units and was especially linked to the goals such units establish and the monitoring capacities they developed. Thus, our coding system was designed to obtain systematic judgments of the strength of planning activities and monitoring capacities. We believe that our measures are valid in their general outlines and that we have indeed tapped critical components of the strength of both the political and administrative systems. A question now arises of the generalizability of such system strength. Is our conception of political-administrative system strength critical for a wide range of public policies, or is it specific to population planning policies? Is the same type of system strength important for such problems as agricultural and industrial development, health and educational development, and housing policies?

We can advance two conflicting observations that support contradictory answers to this question. On the one hand we can observe some generalizability of a political-administrative system's strength. It is often noted, for example, that among the states of India, some do almost everything well, while others do almost nothing well. Kerala, the Punjab, Gujarat, and Tamil Nadu show effective public programs in a wide variety of areas. These are also states with generally higher levels of socioeconomic development. Uttar Pradesh, Bihar, West Bengal, and Rajasthan have few public programs or development activities that gain recognition for efficiency or effectiveness.

The same question of generalizability applies to the countries of the region. South Korea, Taiwan, Singapore, and Malaysia stand out as usually effective governing systems that have produced a broad-based pattern of modern economic development. Nepal, Bangladesh, Iran, and the Philippines have more detractors than admirers in the realm of development promotion. Note that the latter list includes the very poor, the relatively wealthy, and the not-so-badly-off, indicating that whatever the source of weakness in development activities, it is not simply that of financial resources.

These observations are current among observers of development in Asia, but they are nonetheless only impressions, and they are not usually sustained by rigorous and systematic evaluations. Nonetheless, they support the hypothesis that the political-administrative system is a generalized beast, whose strength or weakness affects all forms of public activities, including population planning and fertility limitation.

Another set of observations suggests that system strength may be multifaceted, with different types of strength needed for different types of development programs. A brief comparison of Malaysia and South Korea can illustrate this point.[3] One set of detailed observations showed that the family planning program in Korea had increased its output to input ratio over a period of more than a decade. Costs per acceptor showed a secular decline, and acceptors per staff input showed a secular increase. By contrast, the cost per acceptor in Malaysia has shown a steady increase and the acceptors per staff input a steady decrease over time. Needless to say, these measurements leave much to be desired, but they nonetheless show distinct differences that we believe would be supported by the impressions of knowledgeable observers. More important, however, is the observation that another government agency, the Malaysian Federal Land Development Authority, has shown a stable or slightly increasing trend of the output to input ratio over its more than two decades of operation.[4] Thus the rising costs, or the declining cost-effectiveness seen in the family planning program are not necessarily common to all government programs.

Both Malaysia and South Korea score high on our measures of political-administrative system strength, and common impressions tend to support this measurement. What appears critical in explaining the difference in family planning cost-effectiveness is the homogeneity of the population. Korea has a highly homogeneous population. Malaysia's population is divided by powerful ethnic differences, especially between the Malays and the Chinese. It is not unusual to find that population policies in ethnically divided populations raise delicate political issues. In countries as different as Sri Lanka, India, and the United States, public fertility limitation policies raise fears of radical changes in ethnic balances, or at worst, fears of genocide.

It is clear from our observations that the Malaysian national family planning program is constrained by the ethnic cleavages in the country. The land development program, on the other hand, is a government program aimed primarily at the rural Malays. It raises some envy or resentment among non-Malays, but it gains considerable political support precisely because it is a program for Malays. That is, in this generally effective Malaysian political-administrative system, programs with the support of strong political interest groups are more efficient than those that raise political tensions. This observation indicates that population policies may need very different kinds of political and administrative capacities than do other development programs.

It may well be that the capacity of a political system and its administrative apparatus is a generalized capacity, but it is also quite likely that different types of development programs make different demands on those capacities. Identifying the demands of different development programs thus remains a critical issue both for policy makers and for analysts of the process of modern social change.

2. We have found that a political capacity conceived of as centralized power—to make decisions, establish priorities, and mobilize action around those priorities—is important for the political-ecological process. We have not dealt with the issues of popular participation or political decentralization. Yet many observations indicate that participation and decentralization are important for success in fertility limitation programs.

For example, the move to village programing in Indonesia appears to have been important for increasing fertility-limiting behavior. When village women's clubs and village volunteers were recruited for the family planning program, they apparently helped to increase the numbers of program users and the rate of fertility decline. There are similar observations around the strategy of "community based" family planning programs that have attracted attention throughout the world over the past decade. A recent ESCAP seminar on "Integration and Local Participation in Family Planning" reviewed much of the evidence and found the argument for local participation a compelling one.[5]

There is undoubtedly some political fashion in this argument, as well as some long standing political commitment to voluntarism and participation. Nonetheless the question remains of the importance of local participation for fertility limitation. Important questions also remain on the meaning of local participation. Is it contradictory to or complementary with a high degree of centralized political power? A recent argument set forth by Arthur Stinchcombe has it that the strength of a central regime is enhanced by local participation, and that such strength is contraindicated by the extent to which the regime uses coercion. Weak governments need force to shore them up; strong governments are rooted in popular acceptance, which springs in part from local participation.[6] The issue is, to say the least, unresolved.

3.   We have found that development planning itself has an important impact on the political-ecological adjustment, but we have only begun to identify some of the linkages that are involved. It is relatively easy to see that defining the goals of development planning as, in part, increased growth of per capita output itself implies a definition of population growth as an obstacle to goal achievement. Further, we have seen that the act of planning dramatically illuminates the financial pressures implied by population increases. Larger numbers mean immediate increases in the demand for funds for education and health, and less immediately for housing and employment. It is also apparent from the comparison of India and China that economic planning represents a commitment to a kind of technical activity that insulates against, or runs counter to, more revolutionary political ideologies.

We may also follow Myrdal, who pointed out that planning as we know it is itself an ideological commitment.[7] Thus, economic planning and revolution may constitute competing ideologies, which have quite different implications for population planning. This is, of course, a frequently discussed issue, although much of the discussion tends to be more heated than enlightening.[8] In any event, knowing more about the ideology and technology of planning, and how these are linked to specific public policies and programs, will certainly enhance our understanding of the modern process of population change in the high-fertility countries.

4. The capacity to monitor social and economic changes has been shown to have a significant impact on the process of population change, both in connection with development planning and directly on population policy. There are also other linkages, however, which our experience in Asia suggests, but which we have not been able to specify in this analysis.

Simply knowing how many people a country has and how fast the numbers are growing has obvious implications for population policy, but the capacity to monitor change appears to have other types of impact as well. We can suggest only one here, which we suspect is of great importance. This is the impact monitoring can have on specific program performance.

The operations of all large-scale organizations have a tendency to become self-serving for the members of the organization itself. Thus, it is not uncommon to find that a program designed to serve the general public increasingly tends to be subverted and to serve the officials more effectively than the clients. One of the major forces for client service may be the capacity to monitor program performance, especially changes in the environment at which the program is aimed. That is, monitoring helps to obstruct the growth of privilege and to sustain pressures toward performance in large-scale organizations. Thus, in effect, the issue of monitoring the political-ecological adjustment takes us from the diffuse area of the impact on general policy to the more specific area of its impact on program or organizational performance. To say that we know little of how or why public programs perform as they do in high-fertility countries is almost to state a truism. Here we simply argue that further examination of the impact of monitoring capacity on population planning is an area of inquiry with high significance for both analysts and policy makers.

5. The final issue we can identify from our model concerns its generalizability beyond the Asian region. Our brief comparison of Asia with the three other high-fertility regions has suggested that the model of the political-ecological adjustment holds across regions. Many questions remain, however. Are the same political components important in all regions? Are the linkages between political conditions, policy decisions, and program actions similar across regions, or do things work differently in other regions from the way they work in Asia?

The question is of more than theoretical interest. For example, if our model holds, then we can expect increasing demands for more and for different kinds of resources in the high-fertility world outside of Asia. In chapter 2 we suggested that Africa is now absorbing resources primarily for basic data gathering, and that this could well lead to new policy decisions, implying an increased demand for funds for fertility limitation programs. We are already beginning to witness this shifting and increasing demand, as the large number and the vocal character of African political units make their weight felt in the United Nations.

In a more general sense as well, our model suggests that we can expect a secular increase in the demand for resources directed at fertility limitation throughout the high-fertility world. As information is gathered, policies become more developed and articulated, and programs proliferate. World financial resources for population activities have grown very rapidly over the past two decades, but they are still only a minute fraction of the resources mobilized for development assistance. Our model suggests only that the demand for population funds will continue to grow. Whether the world community will continue to mobilize such resources is, of course, a question for which answers are not readily available.

CONTROVERSIES

Malthus's first essay on population in 1798 was directed against the rationalistic utopian dreams of Godwin and Condorcet. That was not the first time, of course, that population issues proved to be controversial. It was, however, the beginning of a controversy that has continued almost unabated over two centuries. The current policy revolution indicates that it still rages. The antinatalist policy revolution has implied a massive mobilization of resources in the world community as a whole to address the problems of rapid population growth in the high-fertility world. Controversy continues to surround both the issues and the mobilization itself. It may be only a slight exaggeration to say that until 1965 the objections to public activity in fertility limitation overwhelmed the mobilization; from 1965 to about 1980 the mobilization overwhelmed the controversy. Now the pendulum swings again, and a large and highly articulate series of objections is rising, which threatens to slow the mobilization.

The many objections to modern population planning can be classified under four major headings.[9] First, some object to population planning in general, arguing that there is no population problem at all. Second, some object to international assistance in population planning, arguing that this is simply a case of the imposition of Western values and aims on the Third World. Third, there are objections to the manner in which population assistance is offered. Paralleling John Stuart Mill's indictment of British colonialism as a marvelous form of outdoor relief for the unemployable British gentry is the argument that modern population assistance is merely a form of indoor air-conditioned relief for a new class of world bureaucrats, employable, perhaps, but not very effective. Fourth and finally, there is objection to the character of family planning programs themselves as inappropriate and ineffectively organized. This constitutes a substantial list of charges. We believe that our political-ecological perspective, both derived from and reflecting our own experiences with population planning in Asia, provides some basis for commenting on these charges and, more generally, on the controversies. Let us close this study by taking our perspective into the arena of these current controversies.

1. *Is there a population problem?* The population literature is replete with doomsday predictions. Paul Ehrlich gave currency to the term "population bomb," and it continues to evoke images of doom. Future generations are already consigned to death by massive famines, if not worse. The doomsayers have, however, consistently been countered by those who see people as the most precious resource. There can never be too many, for people are strength, people are the most adaptive and productive of all resources, they are human resources. Mao Tse-tung was a well-known advocate of this position, and the most recent proponent of one variant is American economist Julien Simon.[10] From this perspective, there is no population problem.

Two variants of this argument have persisted, though in many different guises. There is no problem because there are sufficient resources and enough space to accommodate many times the current population (whatever it happens to be). A second variant holds that there is no problem because it will solve itself. Population growth may indeed be too rapid at any one time, but natural conditions will reestablish an ecological balance, and population growth will cease.

The first version of this argument holds only in the short run. The logic of compound interest, or exponential growth, very soon places severe limits on any continued growth. Mongolia provides a useful illustration. With only one person per square kilometer of arable land, it would appear to have room for almost unlimited growth. And so it does, almost. As we saw, Mongolia's pronatalism makes a great deal of sense, given its low agricultural density. But its current growth rate, somewhere between 2 and 3 percent per year, is something that simply cannot last very long into the future. At just 2 percent growth per year it would take Mongolia less than four centuries to reach the population density of Hong Kong. Such calculations are, of course, completely unreal. They speak only of the logic of exponential growth, leaving all human institutions and behavioral changes out of the picture. Nonetheless, the cold calculations suffice to permit the judgment that even if Mongolia has no population problem, whatever that is, its current rate of growth cannot continue for very long under anything like current conditions.

The argument that there is no problem because it will solve itself raises the question of how the current high rates of population growth that abound in Asia will be reduced. What will be the price of those reductions? Further, who will bear the cost? The grim answer to that question suggested today by the Asian scene is that the cost will be heavy in human health and welfare, and that it will be borne by those least able to complain: poor rural women and children.

Family planners, especially those as interested in spacing as in fertility reduction, are fond of arguing that pregnancy is not a disease and that population planning programs should not treat reproducing human beings as though they were in some way deviant. True enough. Far from being a disease, pregnancy and birth are certainly among the most profoundly creative and productive of human behaviors. But while pregnancy may not be a disease for the individual, it is possible to argue that high fertility is an epidemiological disease for a population as a whole.

It is quite clear, for example, that high fertility implies that women begin childbearing early, that they bear children frequently, and that they cease bearing children late in their reproductive lives. It is also clear that all three conditions are killers. They are all closely associated with infant and maternal diseases and deaths. To be sure, high fertility does not necessarily imply early, frequent, and late childbearing. It is statistically possible to have high fertility along with relatively late first births, relatively long spacing, and relatively early cessation of births. This is, unfortunately, only a statistical possibility. Empirically, high fertility is associated with childbearing patterns that are very costly for women and children. Even more unfortunately, these are precisely the people least likely to be heard when we ask who bears the costs of high fertility, or the costs of self-adjusting processes.

One of the early trial family planning programs in Asia, the Pothram project in Thailand, showed clearly that these perceptions and calculations of costs were very much in the minds of rural women who came long distances to be fitted with IUDs. In Malaysia, Indonesia, and the Philippines we have heard rural women affirm the common saying that men want more children for the glory, but women want fewer for the burden. There is much laughter surrounding these public discussions when they occur, but they reflect a genuine understanding on the part of rural women of the costs to themselves and their children of high fertility. If this were not enough, the prevalence of abortion, often involving great pain and great risk of death, should tell us that for some substantial numbers of people, high and uncontrolled fertility is indeed a problem.

Rapid population growth presents a very real problem in quite another way as well. We have seen that in Asia antinatalist programs emerged out of the process of economic planning and found especial urgency when the planners made projections of the costs of education, health, housing, and employment. That is, rapid population growth is very much of a problem for people in positions of responsibility for mobilizing resources for what is coldly called human capital formation.

Finally, population growth may be seen as unproblematic because all societies have deeply embedded ways of controlling their fertility. This is a point made by Abernathy, and one recounted most recently by William Petersen in his broad attack on fertility limitation programs.[11] Abernathy recognizes, however, what Petersen failed to consider. She noted that all societies have effective homeostatic mechanisms that control fertility, unless they experience profound changes in their perceptions of scarcity. It is, of course, precisely this perceptual change that modernization, or the expansion of the world capitalist economy, has brought to the current high fertility societies. Tokugawa Japan may have had effective mechanisms for controlling fertility, since it maintained its population at about thirty million for more than a century. Now, Japan's population is no longer thirty million; it is nearing four times that level. The populations of India and China are no longer at the roughly (and only probably) fifty million they had when older homeostatic mechanisms were at work. In this respect there is a current problem of rapid population growth precisely because the world has undergone vast and radical changes over the past two or three centuries. It is difficult to find a region in which those problem-producing changes have been more profound than in Asia.

2. *Is international population assistance necessary, ethical, and justified?* Especially given the energetic leadership in US AID'S Office of Population in its first decade, it is quite easy to argue that population planning or, more specifically, fertility limitation, represents only a narrow set of Western values that is being forced upon unwilling leaders and peoples in the high-fertility world. When US leaders pressed the IUD upon unwilling, and as it turned out far more rational, Indian leaders, and then tied grain assistance to Indian family planning commitments, the signs of Western pressure were strong indeed. There has also been a substantial amount of arm twisting in the form of political and fiscal pressure, especially from the US to promote fertility limitation in Asia. Thailand and the Philippines have experienced such pressures, as has Nepal.

Memories are short, however. When Western powers are accused of these pressures, one speaks only of the late 1960s and the early 1970s. We have shown that Asian leaders pressed the United Nations for fertility limitation assistance when America's President Eisenhower rejected the use of foreign assistance for such ends. The United States stood with other Western nations in precluding discussion of such issues in the United Nations, and all were implicated in the resistance the Indian head of the United Nations' Food and Agricultural Organization, B. F. Sen, experienced when he attempted to use his office simply to promote open discussion of the issues. It should also be remembered that Sen lost his job as well for his efforts. It is important to recall that Asian nations led the world in attempts to mobilize the international community for work on the problem of high fertility. We have shown that half of the Asian nations, representing about two billion people, made their own antinatalist decisions for their own internal reasons before either the United Nations or the United States admitted that such programs were legitimate.

If it was not Western governments, then surely Western intellectuals were involved in spreading the fear of high fertility among the Asian leaders. Again, such an argument is attractive, especially given current perceptions of the power of the core capitalist countries, but again, the argument runs afoul of the facts. Western intellectuals saw grave dangers in the low fertility of the Western countries prior to World War II, and not, as Napoleon had it, for fear of the yellow horde. They were concerned with the weakening of economic demand from slow or zero population growth.[12] Even before this, as early as 1916 the Indian demographer P. K. Wattal called attention to the growing Indian population problem, and that at a time when much of the British elite concerned with India continued to believe that population growth reflected the benevolence of British rule.

Finally, our analysis of the flow of funds for population activities in Asia calls for some caution in attributing heavy financial pressure to the Western assistance. As we saw in India, the program organization, strategy, and funding were overwhelmingly Indian. This was even more so in the case of China, where external assistance has been totally absent until only recently.

Foreign assistance of any sort always looks different to the source than it does to the recipient. It is not unusual that perceptions and evaluations of such assistance are greatly inflated at the source. Much of the current discussion in Washington, for example, makes United States foreign assistance, and especially population assistance, appear far more weighty, either for good or for evil, than it appears from the field. It is a common, if not very attractive trait of world capitals, and especially of the people who inhabit those capitals, to see themselves as the centers of the universe. Our view from Asia indicates that regional initiatives have been strong, and they have been quite strongly antinatalist. There is a far more convincing case to be made that international population assistance is a set of values and demands that Asians have foisted upon the rest of the world than the other way around. Neither argument can be taken seriously, of course, but it is useful to permit the Asian experience to be heard in this controversy.

3. *Are international population assistance strategies effective, appropriate, and defensible?* It is not difficult to argue that they are not, and it is easy to point to many cases of waste and inefficiency. Unfortunately, most criticisms of assistance strategies seldom get beyond the ad hoc listing of illustrations of such weaknesses. There is usually little attempt at systematic analysis of either weaknesses or strengths, or the balance between the two. From our experience it is first necessary to make an important distinction between multilateral and bilateral population assistance. Each is embedded in very different organizational environments, which present very different types of constraints. Each also shows specific types of weakness, which are usually the substance of popular criticisms.

On the multilateral side, it is often noted that the United Nations is an exceptionally weak organization, with little effective political direction. An organization with more than 150 heads is one without any effective head at all. Thus, it is subject to various political pressures that continually undermine its technical competence and efficiency.[13] Its major activities, according to many detractors, lie in meetings and conferences that provide high life styles and symbiotic relationships between national and international civil servants. Conferences are called; the host country and the other participants obligingly follow the agenda and dutifully resolve that the office convening the conference proceed with additional work. The resolution then provides the leverage by which the office gains more resources and convenes more meetings.

Although it may be possible to characterize some United Nations meetings in this manner, our analysis of the processes of the development of a regional community in Asia presents a rather different picture. Here we saw leaders in the Asian region pressing the world organization for greater recognition of its problems. When the United Nations was dominated by the United States and other North Atlantic powers, Asia demanded greater attention to Asian development problems. It was precisely the multinational nature of the world organization that gave Asian leaders some political leverage. Later, we saw that giving attention to the problems of regional development provided at least some of the force for creating a regional community in which nations could assist one another in identifying and addressing their problems. It was out of that emergence of a regional development-oriented community that some of the pressures for rational and humane population policies have come.

Bilateral forms of population assistance often come under attack for being heavy-handed, and for being more concerned with the interests of the donor than of the recipient nation. Where national security interests are at stake, for example, major donors might use population assistance as nothing more than a mechanism to pay off part of an indigenous elite. Grand buildings, beautifully paneled and inhabited by banks of attractive and uniformed, but not terribly busy, secretaries, are not unknown in the region's population programs. Nor are those where supplies and equipment remain trapped in the capital and cannot find room to trickle down to the provinces.

There are, of course, villains in plenty in such bilateral population assistance, but there are heroes as well. Many efforts, of course, are neither villainous nor heroic. They are simply modest attempts to provide assistance in situations that do not by any means fully support honest effort. From the Asian experience, let us us cite only two of the more effective types of bilateral assistance. Thailand showed a substantial increase in contraceptive acceptance and use when US AID provided contraceptives that the Thai government agreed to distribute free of charge.

The cost to the United States was small (and even smaller than the absolute funds involved, since this was also a form of subsidized export for American drug companies), but the value to the poor Thai women was substantial.[14] Their rapid acceptance of the free contraceptives gave ample evidence of this. If one of the stated goals of recent United States foreign assistance has been to provide help to the poorest of the poor, one could scarcely have found a better program.

US AID's assistance to the Indonesian family planning program provides another case of modest heroism, though both AID and Indonesian actors in this project reject such a laudatory appellation. In providing funds for the Indonesian program, AID and the Indonesian officials worked out a simple procedure that would ensure the rapid flow of funds from the center to the provinces. Provincial and district officials could generate experimental or routine family planning projects, make a request to Jakarta, and reasonably expect to have actual funds in their hands within three or four months. Anyone familiar with the problems of financing development projects will recognize both the rarity of this situation and its importance for stimulating local initiative in addressing any problem.[15] The fast funding procedure was generally recognized as a critical determinant for obtaining local support and thus for increasing the capacity of the program for providing effective services to the rural poor.

Nor are these two examples isolated cases of good and effective foreign assistance in population affairs. Examples of such efforts could be cited many times over in Taiwan, South Korea, and especially in India. Our experience in Asia and our analysis of the population assistance processes have shown us that there are both villainous and heroic efforts. Most are neither. There are weak strategies and strong strategies, and most projects as well as the overall effort itself are some mixture of both. Blanket condemnations are as undefensible as are blanket claims of success.

Most of the criticism of population assistance is focused on family planning programs alone. We have seen in Asia that this omits much other assistance that we believe is of a greatly liberating character. We refer especially to training in the social sciences and demography and, to a lesser extent, in the biological sciences as well. It is striking to observe that it was an Indian demographer who first called attention to that country's population problem. When the thrust for modern economic development was getting under way in Asia in the decade following World War II, it was primarily Western social scientists who were identifying problems and proposing solutions. Asia lacked the scientific personnel to examine Asian problems with the technical competence needed to speak to Western social scientists and policy makers. This was especially true in population affairs, the role of India's Dr. Wattal notwithstanding. This is certainly no longer the case. Asia is now well supplied with indigenous social scientists who can examine the region's conditions and identify its problems with great skill. This rapid development of human scientific talent is the result of large investments in training for Asian scholars. International population assistance has played a major role in this training, even before the United Nations or the United States formally recognized the need for public intervention into population affairs. Now we find that ESCAP divisions, and in particular the Population Division, are staffed with Asian social scientists. Even more important is the fact that the individual countries of the region now have substantial numbers of their own trained professionals working in their own population programs. It is no longer necessary for Asians to listen to Western experts on population affairs, and this, of course, has had a greatly liberating influence. It gives Asian nations greater leverage in determining what policies will be adopted and how programs will be implemented.

4. *Are family planning programs themselves appropriate and effective, or useless, wasteful, and even hurtful?* They are all, of course, but at different times and in different settings. Indian attempts in the 1950s to promote the use of the rhythm method with colored beads were certainly useless and wasteful. The more recent attempt to force sterilization upon unwilling males was hurtful and stupid. East Java experienced some forced IUD recruitment campaigns. Any revolutionary regime has great capacity for coercion, and some have used coercion in official fertility limitation campaigns. Projects that inappropriately attempt to use male field workers to recruit female acceptors are not unknown, nor are those that attempt to promote sterilization among Muslims, against strong religious proscriptions on such an operation. Examples of waste and ineffectiveness are also legion. Overcentralized administrative systems that generally fail to deliver any form of effective social service to the rural poor generally fail in family planning as well. Often where success is documented in increases of acceptors there is deceit in reporting, or acceptors who accept contraceptives but do not use them. At other times success in recruiting more acceptors means no real change in reproductive habits, only a substitution of program supplies or services either for traditional fertility limitation (often abstinence) or for supplies obtained through other channels. Such program success is, of course, nothing of the sort.

The list of inappropriate, wasteful, and hurtful experiences could go on for a long time. Some can be found even in the best of programs, and there are many very good programs in Asia. It need not go on, however, as our point is only to recount the empirical programmatic weaknesses that fuel the controversy over the utility of family planning programs.

The weaknesses of family planning programs are immensely important for providing some understanding of the determinants of performance, but the weaknesses are unfortunately seldom used in this manner. They are more often used to support blanket judgments of inappropriateness than to examine conditions of performance. Such an examination can be useful and valid if it searches for systematic variance among countries and programs. We have found, for example, that among the states of India those that manage to fill existing rural family planning positions manage to gain more acceptors than those that do not. We are not sure what determines the administrative capacity to fill positions, but we can describe a plausible scenario by which this capacity leads to the provision of more effective service to poor rural women.

In examining twenty-one states of Asia, we also observed that stronger political-administrative systems and earlier antinatalist policy decisions were important in explaining both family planning program strength and the rates of fertility decline. That is, there is something in the strength of a political-administrative system that permits it to do a better job of providing family planning services to the large mass of poor rural women, doubly isolated by poverty and physical distance from public assistance.

We sat once in a small clinic in Taiwan talking with one of the women field workers who had worked at recruiting family planning acceptors for the past few years. During our discussions a young woman appeared at the clinic door. The field worker excused herself, left us, and went to talk with the young woman. They sat together on a bench in the corner talking quietly and earnestly. Soon a doctor appeared, a curtain was drawn around a cot in another corner, and the young woman was escorted to the cot for an IUD insertion. From our perspective the field worker appeared warm and reassuring, comforting and friendly.

After the insertion our field worker returned, apologized for leaving, and explained what had happened. The young woman in the door was the wife of a poor day laborer in the town. She had recently given birth to her fifth child. The field worker visited the woman every time she was in that part of the town with information and persuasion about the use of the IUD. The woman had hesitated largely out of fear. On this occasion, she came to the clinic only to see if it would be possible to make an appointment for the insertion. The field worker managed to mobilize a doctor to do the work at that moment. It was difficult not to see in that situation the impact of a program that was well designed to provide effective service to poor women.

We had a very different experience at a clinic in Iran. When we entered, as honored foreign guests, the doctor leapt to his feet, shouted orders to clear the office of waiting women, and sent nurses scurrying for tea. It is not difficult to see in this experience some confirmation of our deviant case analysis in chapter 4, nor to see that there is substantial difference between countries in their capacities to provide effective service to the poor.

The issue of substitution also calls for some comment. It is, to be sure, evident that many of the "acceptors" by which a program measures its success are not new acceptors reacting to the unique and initial work of the public program. Thus, using acceptors as a quantitative measure of success is at least partly flawed. This is probably true to a certain extent in all programs, and it is often impossible to tell to what extent the measure is flawed in this manner. Nor is this the only way in which program statistics are suspect. There is, however, another dimension of substitution that deserves mention. For many rural women family planning services are quite obviously substituting for abortion as a means of fertility limitation. This was perhaps most clear in the early years of the South Korean program and in the rapid downturn of fertility in Japan. Although this is certainly a substitution for methods of fertility limitation that have traditionally been practiced in all societies to some extent, it is difficult to see in this substitution anything other than an advance in the assistance offered, especially to poor rural women.

One of the dimensions of appropriateness that we have not been able to examine systematically concerns the technology of contraception. At this time a relatively wide range of the technology—new and not so new—is available to the Asian population through both public and private, legal and illegal, channels. It is evident that this technology is differentiated by its appropriateness for different people at different times. Sterilization is for cessation of child bearing. The IUD and the pill are effective for postponing the first birth or spacing subsequent births. Commonly, the pill is used by younger women, the IUD by somewhat older women. Other methods are available as well, and all are differentially suited to the special conditions of an individual man, woman, or family. It would seem the most elementary of propositions that a public program would use a wide range of the new technology so as to provide for a more effective adaptation of that technology to these different conditions. What we observe in Asia, however, is something quite less than this rational strategy. India has used sterilization, and for a time, male sterilization, as the principal, or nearly the only widely available, method. Malaysia uses the pill almost exclusively. It is a fair proposition that the wider the range of contraceptive technology a program uses, the more effective it will be. As we have seen for India, however, it is also useful to be sensitive to the political and cultural conditions that determine the range of technology that will be used. Our perspective leads us to believe that the method mix used in a program will be determined more by the program managers than by the clients.

There is one final point to be made about family planning programs. Despite the concerns with appropriateness, despite the charge that they are potentially hurtful public experiments with women's bodies, they do have, and for precisely this reason, a unique and we believe significant characteristic. They are everywhere one of the very few public programs, and often the only one, aimed especially at providing an important social service to the poorest of the poor: poor rural women. Women have often been seen as the world's great underclass. Nowhere is there equality; there is only variance in the degree of female subordination and male dominance.[16] Most public programs have neglected women and have been aimed at serving the interests of men. This is especially true in productive activities, but it is even true in social services such as education and health. The past three decades of independent efforts at economic development have done much to correct this imbalance, but it persists in many places nonetheless. Under these circumstances of inequality and neglect, the family planning programs stand out as unique. They do provide useful services to poor rural women, even though in Asia, as elsewhere, these services are often flawed.

Our observations will not by any means lay all of these controversies to rest. In one form or another they are at least as old as the Malthus-Godwin debate, and we can confidently expect that they will continue well into the future. We do believe, however, that the type of detailed analysis we have provided on Asia, with a perspective that links ecological changes to political conditions, does add some light to those controversies.

Shedding a little additional light on enduring controversies is not a very exciting way to conclude a study of modern population problems. These are dramatic and exciting problems whose resolution, whatever that is, will surely be of great significance for human societies. But perhaps there is already too much drama in the concern for population problems. Perhaps there is reason to aim modestly at a little more clarity, particularly if that also includes helping to illuminate the political conditions and the responsibilities of political leaders in modern population processes.

Afterword

Reflections on Japan from a Political-Ecological Perspective

Minoru Muramatsu
Institute of Public Health
Tokyo, Japan

AUTHORS' INTRODUCTION

We asked Dr. Minoru Muramatsu to consider the case of Japan from our political-ecological perspective. As the only Asian society to have completed the demographic transition (with Singapore as a recent arrival) and to have undergone thorough industrialization and urbanization, Japan is both a unique example of Asian society and a potential model for currently modernizing societies. Dr. Muramatsu has been deeply involved in both the scholarship on Japan's transition and the current discussions of its demographic position. His reflections thus not only help to place Japan in the perspective we have developed, but they also help to place that perspective in the larger Asian experience, possibly pointing to some of the forces that will be manifest in the rest of Asia as it moves forward in this modern political-ecological adjustment.

INTRODUCTION

"Considering the characteristic features of different peoples in the world in terms of cultural values, aspirations, and life styles, where do you put the Japanese people between the two extremes of the West and the East?" This was one of the favorite questions of the late Dr. Irene B. Taeuber. Each time she met a new Japanese friend, she tried it on him. More often than not, the reply was "closer to the West," and this seemed to give her a sense of satisfaction.

In the current behavior patterns of the Japanese people there are many aspects strongly influenced by Western culture, but there are also many differences, especially in those related to family structure and its dynamics.

Japan's past experience in population and family planning can also be said to stand between the Western and Asian experiences. The rapid decline in fertility in postwar Japan was primarily due to the spontaneous adjustment efforts by the people themselves. In this they were like Westerners, responding as individuals and families to profound changes in their social and economic conditions. Unlike Westerners, however, they received much encouragement, help, and direction from their government in reducing their fertility.

Japan is unique in many respects. It is the only industrialized country in Asia. It is the only non-Western country (with the possible recent exception of Singapore) where the demographic transition has been completed. The rapidity with which that demographic transition proceeded in Japan is unprecedented, though it should be pointed out that Japan's birth rates began to decline as early as 1920 rather than in the late 1940s, which all too often is misconstrued as the very beginning of fertility decline in Japan. Traditional disparities in fertility rates between rural and urban areas have existed for as long as adequate measures exist to show them. They have been narrowed down quite precipitously, but there still exist some traces of higher rural fertility.

Perhaps most striking, however, is the fact that in Japan's fertility decline, induced abortion was by far the most important method producing the rapid fall in birth rates, at least for the initial period after the war. Finally, like the West, Japan is today seriously concerned with the rich array of population-related problems, such as the enormous rate of resource consumption, environmental degradation, and the uneven internal distribution of population. And this occurs only three decades after Japan's struggle against the problem of excessive growth of population that characterizes the current situation in the rest of Asia.

In summary, for the most part, Japan's fertility decline has been brought about by the people's initiative, but the political authorities have been quick to grasp changes in the social milieu and to expedite the transition. The whole development can be regarded as an example of a combination of political leadership and people's reaction, or we could turn the formulation around and say that it was brought about by the people's initiative and government response.

HISTORICAL HERITAGE: PRIOR TO WORLD WAR II

During the period of the Tokugawa shogunate (1603–1867), Japan was divided into large fiefs ruled by feudal lords who exercised, at least in theory, absolute authority over their territories. This was a period of relative peace, in which the institutions of Japan developed and matured. In developing suzerainty and maintaining the peace, the Tokugawa attempted to solidify the social structure. There were four social classes with the samurai at the top. Farmers were not regarded as the lowest, but they had to give a substantial portion of their rice harvest as tax to the local lord. In times of crises, such as crop failures due to unfavorable weather, farmers had but little left over, often barely enough for the family's subsistence.

Although the Tokugawa were successful in maintaining the peace, they did not thereby hold time still. Japan developed in its own internal manner. There was agricultural expansion, especially in the lands outside the control of the Tokugawa (the Tozama lands); Osaka grew into a major commercial center, and Tokyo grew into a major political center. Through all this development, however, Japan remained relatively closed to the outside world, giving the nation the opportunity to develop its institutions in a distinctively Japanese fashion.

According to the historical documents available, infanticide and induced abortion were prevalent among farmers, and sometimes even among the samurai. A semi-professional birth attendant often asked the mother if she wanted to have the baby survive or not. It is said that girl babies were more often likely to be victims. In large cities there was a special group of medical people known as professional abortionists. The methods they used for the induction of abortion were undoubtedly primitive, but the abortions they handled were apparently numerous.

The population of Japan grew slowly during the first half of the Tokugawa period (roughly 1600–1700), then stabilized at a level of about thirty to thirty-two million during its latter half (about 1700–1850). Since there was no international migration at that time, artificial checks on population growth were obviously at work, and infanticide and abortion were notable examples of such checks.

This retrospective review of what was occurring in Japan a few centuries ago serves to remind us that many of the population issues we are discussing today are not entirely new. They have significant historical precedents.

The Population Problem Inquiry Council, an advisory committee to the Minister of Health and Welfare, recently came to the conclusion that stabilization of population growth should be a national demographic target. The idea of a nongrowing population, however, had been accepted before, not necessarily voluntarily but rather by virtue of circumstances. Tokugawa society was static in terms of population size, but it was also the time when the spiritual culture of the Japanese people reached its maturity. This was when the tea ceremony, flower arranging, poetry, and music, all of which modern Japanese value as an important part of their heritage, gained their maturity. In addition, the observation that infanticide and abortion were frequently resorted to, harsh and drastic as they were, indicates that fertility limitation was practiced by the population. The existence of strong motivation toward small family size at the grassroots level and the high incidence of induced abortion soon after the war in this century were thus not phenomena suddenly emerging as departures from the past. They can only be fully understood in the light of distinct and longstanding traditions among the Japanese people.

Shortly after the termination of the Tokugawa shogunate in 1867, Japan embarked on a drive to modernization. A number of Japanese young men went to the West. They were enthusiastic, hard working, and much impressed by the marked progress they saw being made in Western civilization. Medicine, legal systems, education, communications, and transportation were among the major fields they studied. On their return home, they brought back with them new knowledge and skills. In this process of transplanting Western civilization, imitation took place in some areas, and modifications of the original form were made in others to suit the different conditions at home. For example, the legal treatment of induced abortion was rather strict in Europe in those days, which to a great extent reflected Christian influence. The Japanese penal code was then formulated on European models, and similar restrictions on abortion were incorporated into it. Some current Japanese critics hold the opinion that this was fundamentally inappropriate. They maintain that Christian laws should not have been introduced into a non-Christian country. They point out that the Japanese people as a whole have been historically tolerant of abortion, and that the laws best suited to them are the ones that allow for such traditional liberalism.

In chapter 2, Ness and Ando argue that Western colonialism exerted a strong influence on the subsequent development of nationalism and the political-ecological adjustment in many of the Asian countries. In the case of Japan, there was no direct colonial rule, but Western civilization in fact significantly influenced Japan through this small corps of elite Japanese citizens. They were elites indeed, in the sense that most of them were chosen from the well-disciplined, highly educated samurai class. Because of their unique personal background, they were fully aware of their responsibility for the modernization of their nation, which they saw to be necessary for its very survival.

During their stay in the West, these elites became familiar with the utility of modern government, with the efficiency and capability of capitalist bureaucratic systems as well as the value of economic rationality. They also saw the value of social mobility and tried to abolish social class differentials. This gave rise to the general perception among the masses that even a man with low social standing could aspire toward a high living standard depending on the skills and knowledge he acquired through education. Western technology and ways of thinking were thus introduced in a manner different from that of most other Asian countries. In any event the fact remains that the transplantation did take place, but it also brought about rapid and penetrating changes as the elite group trained overseas came to hold major positions in the government hierarchy.

All of these developments during the early stage of the Meiji era (which followed on the Tokugawa period) paved the way for the economic and technological progress Japan made in subsequent years. The success in national economic recovery following World War II and the continuous struggle for the betterment of daily life since then owe a great deal to such previous conditioning. Moreover, when people realized the merit of family limitation at both the macro and micro levels for the attainment of these purposes and viewed its practice as an absolute necessity, the historical heritage, coupled with the Japanese tradition of realism, had considerable influence, whether people were aware of this or not.

The population of Japan in 1870 is estimated at about thirty-six million. With the progress of industrialization and subsequent economic growth, the resource base of the country expanded, permitting an increase in population. The stagnation of population growth that marked the last half of the Tokugawa era came to an end, and for the fifty year period after 1870 the population of Japan continued to increase until it reached some fifty-six million in 1920, the year when the first modern census was taken in the country. The rate of population increase, however, was rather slow. In the period 1870–90 it amounted to an annual average of 0.5 percent. Japan's economic takeoff was about to happen in this period, and this low rate was of great help for the speedy completion of the whole process. With the further development of the nation as a result of the economic takeoff, the population grew at a rate slightly above 1 percent a year in the period 1900–1920.

According to the estimates of some Japanese demographers, the first sign of the downward trend in birth rates in Japan came shortly before or around 1920. This was the beginning of Japan's demographic transition, which was, like the Western experience, closely related to modernization. Unlike the Western experience, however, where the decline in the death rate preceded that in the birth rate, both declines almost coincided in Japan. As a result, the rate of natural increase of population remained fairly stable at a level of 1.2–1.4 percent, only slightly higher than in the preceding few decades. In 1940, the population of Japan was registered as seventy-three million, twice as large as that of 1870. (The doubling of population in seventy years implies an average growth rate of about 1 percent per year.)

When the demographic transition began in the 1920s, birth control campaigns were initiated by a small number of enlightened citizens. Many

Figure A.1 Birth, Death, and Natural Increase Rates, Japan 1900–1973

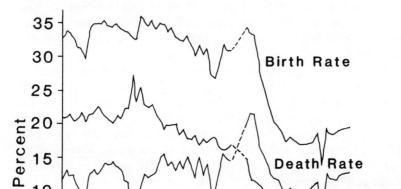

of them were the followers of socialist ideologies, and their effort was concentrated primarily on settlement work and the relief of the poor. Margaret Sanger's first visit to Japan in 1922 was a stimulus, and the movement for birth control in the cause of the emancipation of women also developed. All participants in the campaigns had the same end in mind, but certain differences were discernible in their evaluation of the means: socialists tended to be permissive about induced abortion while those stressing the emancipation of women could hardly free themselves from their strong hatred of it. In any event, the campaigns were successful in the sense that they aroused considerable interest in birth control among the general public. Already in the 1930s, then, Japanese fertility was not uncommonly subject to deliberate control, especially among the upper social groups.

1945–60: PERIOD OF RAPID FERTILITY DECLINE

The defeat in the Second World War brought chaos to Japan. Every aspect of people's lives was seriously affected. Food shortages were acute and housing problems were grave, especially in the cities. Practically all industries were destroyed, and economic activities were severely paralyzed. Though actual cases of starvation were not reported, malnutrition was widespread.

To aggravate the adverse situation, the population of Japan underwent a sudden jump as a result of large-scale demobilization and repatriation. In the three-year period 1945–47, a large number of Japanese nationals, mostly young men, returned to Japan proper from its former colonial territories. This resulted in a net gain in population of some five million. This itself was a significant factor in the population increase, but the ensuing baby boom, which amounted to some 2.7 million births a year, imposed an additional burden on the war-devastated national economy.

Under these conditions, the ecological pressures on the population were intense. It was not merely the condition of high density that produced these pressures, although density was indeed high. It has, however, been high in Japan for a long time. Even a century ago, Japan's overall density was ninty persons per square kilometer, which is more than twice the average for fifty African countries today. Overcrowding in any absolute sense has long been a condition of Japanese living, but this in itself has not had any apparent direct effect on population growth. As we have noted, the Japanese population doubled from 1870 to 1940, but this was under the condition of modern industrial development, when in one sense the ability of the land to support the population increased greatly. When this high density was combined with the severe social and economic dislocation of the post-World War II period, however, it amounted to great ecological pressure. Both the government and the population reacted quickly and strongly to this new stress.

During the decade following the end of the war, a large number of discussions and debates on population took place among both the leadership and the general public. Official committees on population were established one after another and submitted their conclusions to the government. In 1946, a Population Planning Committee was organized with the purpose of investigating the fundamental course and aim of the needed population policy. The committee published a statement in which they noted the problem of overpopulation and urged the government to adopt two countermeasures; one, an increase in the ability to support the population, and the other, the limitation of population growth. Here we see an interesting difference between the condition Ness and Ando expose for the rest of Asia and what we see to be the Japanese experience. In newly independent Asia, the goal of modern social and economic development, which was to increase the capacity to support the population, came first. This was a thrust for modern economic development from which, as Ness and Ando point out, the push for fertility limitation *followed*. In Japan, these two thrusts came simultaneously.

In 1949, a Population Problem Advisory Council was established in order to advise the prime minister on population. As did the above-mentioned planning committee, it called for the policy of birth control as well as the restoration of foreign trade to enhance the country's supporting capacity and emigration to relieve population pressure. In 1951, a quasi-governmental organization concerned with population studies issued a Population White Paper in which they again emphasized the necessity of fertility regulation.

Political authorities and social leaders actively participated in these discussions and debates. In part, they were the parties who led the discussions in favor of birth control, but at the same time it should be noted that they could do so because they believed that the idea of birth control was already favored by the majority of the people. Radio programs and newspaper articles helped a great deal, both in the identification of the current population problems and in the creation of public awareness of those problems. As time went on, certain groups of political leaders and government officials moved ahead to the formulation of actual policy measures in population and family planning. The adoption of the Eugenic Protection Law in 1948 and the adoption of a national family planning program in 1952 are two remarkable examples of such political action.

The Eugenic Protection Law was mostly concerned with the legal bases for the performance of induced abortion, though it also contained some other aspects of fertility regulation such as sterilization. When promulgated in 1948, it displayed a permissive attitude toward abortion. When it was amended in 1949 and 1952, however, it became even more permissive. Economic stress was added to the original provisions as grounds for abortion, and the decision could be made by the woman and only one medical practitioner. People interpreted these moves as an indication of tacit official approval of induced abortion in the interest of family limitation. The number of abortions reported annually rose sharply from 246,000 in 1949 to 1.17 million in 1955.

In October 1951, a cabinet meeting was called in order to discuss the increasing rate of induced abortion. The participants were concerned with the high abortion rate, and wanted to decrease it by encouraging contraception. In the following year, the Ministry of Health and Welfare developed a scheme for the promotion of family planning on a nationwide scale. The entire public health network, including health centers and local midwives, was mobilized for the dissemination of knowledge about the subject.

Even today there are some uncertainties about the underlying rationale for these political actions taken shortly after the war. On the one hand, some reviewers argue that the motive clearly was the serious concern of politicians and economic planners with Japan's overpopulation. They believe that the seemingly drastic measure of liberalizing abortion was taken because of its unquestionable usefulness for population control. On the other hand, a different analysis is offered by others who take the health implications of these measures more seriously. They admit that the population consideration was certainly in the background, but that the real force behind the decision must have been the safeguarding of maternal health, first by eliminating illegal abortions and then by switching from abortion to contraception. In any event, health was presented as a major consideration, while population was treated as secondary in the official government documents produced in those years.

There were two opposing streams of thought regarding the adoption of policies for population control and family planning. On one hand, politicians feared that direct allusion to population control might evoke undesirable antagonism from Marxist ideologists. The left-wing parties were rising in power as a result of political liberation, and the traditional opposition of these parties to neo-Malthusian doctrine would complicate population programing. Also, no government wishes to adopt a policy that has an inherently negative tone, and population control is such a policy. In addition some political leaders feared that antinatalist population policies might be bitterly criticized by the people. After all, pronatalist policies had been advocated during the war years and were strongly associated with the overall policies of the war, which had drastic negative effects. Political leaders feared that Japan's military defeat might have produced a widespread distrust of whatever the government did, and therefore a popular rejection of any type of population policy.

On the other hand, the Japanese suffered greatly in the period immediately after the war. Their standard of living had been cut in half, thus greatly increasing the sense of ecological pressure. Emigration was discussed, but was out of the question, since defeat had made Jpaanese immigrants unwelcome in most countries. Birth control appeared to offer the only solution. Under these circumstances, many political leaders were fairly confident that family planning policies would be accepted by the people who themselves were fully aware of their hardships. Furthermore, despite the possibility of ideological opposition mentioned above, some groups believed their opponents would hardly refuse to support birth control since all the pros and cons were being discussed by what was, after all, a racially homogeneous population.

Because of the mixture of negative and positive thoughts about the issues, official pronouncements based both liberal abortion laws and the promotion of family planning primarily on health considerations. Demographic considerations were also deeply involved, but the political and administrative authorities at that time believed it wiser to direct their efforts to the provision of actual means of birth control in order to meet the people's demands rather than to indulge themselves in a complicated, unfruitful ideological polemic. Thus, a liberal abortion law was enacted in 1948 and was further liberalized in 1949 and 1952. A national family planning program was launched in 1952 which made Japan one of the first nations to adopt such action in Asia, paralleled only by India.

For several years after the implementation of the national family plan-

ning program in 1952, induced abortions were still on the increase. According to the reported numbers of abortions, 1955 was the peak year
followed by a gradual decline. There is, however, some evidence suggesting that induced abortions actually peaked around 1960 if unreported
abortions are taken into consideration as well.

The increasing trend in induced abortion in those years may be explained in part by the related facts that contraceptive devices and chemicals supplied were not of good quality, and that users were not familiar
with these methods of contraception. More importantly, however, it is
suspected that the nation's history and the longstanding realistic philosophy of the Japanese people were important factors in the widespread
resort to induced abortions. The doctrines of Buddhism and Shintoism,
the two major religions of Japan, are clearly opposed to induced abortion. Nevertheless, in countries such as Japan, where the separation of
the laity and sacred power is distinctive, people's behavior in most instances is determined by their own practical calculations. Japanese
women reportedly do not prefer abortion, and their negative feeling is
reported to be greatest just following the operation. Many say they wish
never to repeat it. Yet in the face of an additional unwanted child as a
result of contraceptive failure, women are likely to resort to another
artificial termination of pregnancy. Given the unreliable contraceptive
methods and the still inadequate knowledge about their use, a number of
failures must have occurred. Women in those years, then, tended to
regard induced abortion as a necessary evil.

At any rate, with induced abortion as a major contributing factor, the
birth rate in Japan was brought down quite rapidly from the postwar high
of 34.5 in 1947. By 1960 it fell to 17 per thousand population. A norm of
two to three children per family had been widely accepted. The decline
continued, however, and dropped below replacement levels in 1960.

As has been noted repeatedly in this paper, it is a general consensus
among Japanese demographic scholars that it was the couples themselves
who initiated the moves toward the vigorous practice of family limitation
and the attainment of a small family. Government actions regarding induced abortion and family planning were adopted, in essence, in order to
catch up with the people's desire. No particular effort was needed to
create the basic motivation for family planning since it was already in
existence at the people's level. The main task for which the government
was called upon was only to provide people with practical means necessary for fertility regulation. With very much the same motivation as Japanese women, in the face of the unavailability of an effective contraceptive
technology, the government moved to promote the only effective alternative available to it: liberalized abortion.

This does not necessarily imply, however, that the government's effort
was ineffective. The involvement of the government and political leaders

in this issue gave both psychological support and legal permission to the practice of family planning. In addition, the mobilization of the extensive network of governmental public health organizations made for the quick dissemination of whatever technical knowledge there was about the planning of family size.

It is possible to speculate about what Japan's birth rate might have been in the absence of either the war or any of the postwar private or public family planning programs, by simply extrapolating the prewar fertility trend into the postwar years with a logistic curve. By so doing, a comparison may be made between the expected and the actually registered birth rates to determine how much of the acceleration in fertility decline was contributed by such programs. Figure A.2 is a graphic presentation of such an attempt.[1] For this attempt, we used the three-year moving averages of the recorded birth rates for the period 1921–37 to construct a logistic curve. Extending the curve to 1961 provides a hypothetical path for fertility decline in the absence of major social disturbances such as the war. We then plotted the 1950–65 birth rate on this curve, placing the 1950 actual rate on the 1939 hypothetical rate. By 1950 the demographic abnormalities of the war years had been generally eliminated, and the 1950 and 1939 rates almost exactly coincide.

Recorded birth rates were far below the expected values in the period 1951–64, suggesting the possible effect of external intervention. Admittedly, it is a risky venture to estimate what was likely to happen in this manner since we cannot create an alternative past experience. Nevertheless, this extrapolation does add strength to the argument that the government did exert some influence in accelerating the process of fertility decline in postwar Japan. Even in the absence of organized efforts to promote family planning, the fertility of the Japanese people would have fallen to the same low level anyway, but the number of years required for it to do so might have been greater—possibly ten years or so.

THE POST-DEMOGRAPHIC TRANSITION SOCIETY: 1960–PRESENT

Fertility has declined. Japan has now completed the demographic transition. The sense of urgency over the high rate of population growth has gone. In one sense, the problem that most Asian nations face is part of Japan's past, but that does not mean that the population problem is at an end. It remains with Japan. Population continues to be discussed and to be debated in general public settings, and in the arena of politics as well. If the problem is no longer simply one of rapid growth, it is now a problem of much greater complexity. And it continues to be a "political" problem in the sense that the larger society is involved in the attempt to develop a policy and a general orientation toward the problem.

Figure A.2 Actual Versus Expected Crude Birth Rates, Japan 1950–65

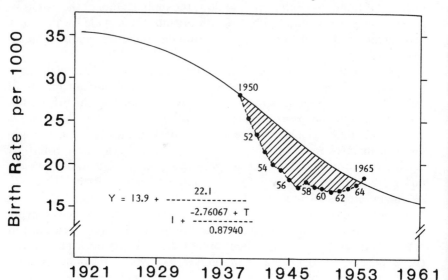

A very brief summary of the issues raised illustrates how complex the problem is. With the decline of fertility, some groups began to worry about the long-term supply of labor. In August 1969, for example, the Population Problem Inquiry Council raised the question of the desirability of raising the fertility level to ensure that the country would have a sufficient supply of young workers for the expanding economy. The issue was raised, but no immediate policy solution emerged.

Then came a series of attempts to change the abortion laws. In 1972, 1973, and 1974, various religious and political groups attempted to change the laws to restrict the use of abortion. Since these were public attempts to change the laws, there was naturally a lively debate about the issue and the problem. The debate was sufficiently heated to cause the Parliament to table the proposals.

The oil crisis and the soybean crisis of 1973 focused attention on the longer-range problems of population growth, resource consumption, and environmental degradation. Again, public discussion was lively. In 1974 the Population Problem Inquiry Council presented a Population White Paper in which the stabilization of Japan's population was proposed. The discussion around this issue also saw the emergence of a proposal to move toward a long-term and gradual decline in population levels in order to improve environmental quality. At this point the country began to question the attachment to a growth value. Japanese leaders toured other

Asian countries and became aware of the intense problem of population growth in the region. This led to proposals to increase Japanese bilateral aid for population assistance. In 1974 a Japanese Parliamentary Federation for Population was formed on a bipartisan basis. It now numbers 129 members and focuses attention on issues of maternal and child health.

These highly abbreviated comments illustrate the extent to which the population issue has become complex and multifaceted, even though the problem of rapid growth has been solved through reduction of fertility and completion of the demographic transition. It is important to note that these issues have become public and are discussed in the arena of national politics. Ness and Ando have suggested that the organization of societies in modern political forms has brought the capacity to perceive population dynamics and their consequences. Japan illustrates how these political forms of organization provide a forum for public discussion as well, permitting population policy to become truly an issue for the nation. It is possible that the Japanese development thus points to some patterns of change that we can expect in the rest of Asia. The antinatalist policy revolution implies that governments take account of population growth and attempt to curb the growth. It also suggests, however, that once the growth is curbed, a larger and more complex series of issues will emerge as problems that will continue to demand attention and public discussion in the future.

Notes

Chapter 1

1. Migration can also be viewed in part as a response to rapid population growth, but the response is only a temporary one. People do move from lands of less to lands of greater opportunities, and for small communities these can be effective responses to rapid population growth. In the final analysis, however, migration is only a temporary solution. It may well be that the world could postpone the need for fertility decline or mortality increase through the colonization of outer space, but even this can only be a temporary solution.

2. Karen Paige and Jeffrey Paige, *The Politics of Reproduction Ritual* (Berkeley and Los Angeles: University of California Press, 1981).

3. The early numbers of the Population Council's *Studies in Population/Family Planning* contain many examples of KAP studies, showing the rich information generated by them. For a brief note on the World Fertility Survey, see Murray Kendle, "The World Fertility Survey: Current Status and Findings," *Population Reports*, series M, no. 3 (Johns Hopkins University, 1979).

4. Ronald Freedman, *The Sociology of Human Fertility* (New York: Irvington Publishers, 1975). The model is produced on page 15.

5. Marriage, conception, and parturition are grouped together and called "the intermediate variables" in the model. The reference is to the seminal work of Kingsley Davis and Judith Blake, "Social Structure and Fertility: An Analytical Framework," *Economic Development and Cultural Change* 4, no.4 (1956): 211–35, which proposed these three conditions as those through which all environmental conditions affect human fertility.

6. Ronald Freedman and John Y. Takeshita, *Family Planning in Taiwan: An Experiment in Social Change* (Princeton: Princeton University Press, 1969).

7. This set of issues has recently been discussed in Ruth Simmons, Gayl D. Ness, and George Simmons, "On the Institutional Analysis of Population Programs," *Population and Development Review* 9, no. 3 (1983): 457–74.

8. The most useful statements of the ecological perspective applied to human populations will be found in Amos Hawley, *Human Ecology* (New York: Rand McNally Press, 1950), and Otis D. Duncan, "Social Organization and the Ecosystem," in Robert E. L. Faris, *Handbook of Modern Sociology* (Chicago: Rand McNally, 1964), pp. 37–82. See also the more recent statement by Hawley,

"Ecology and Population" in *Science* 179 (March 1969): 1196–1201. Virginia Abernathy has also provided a good example of the use of the ecological perspective in *Population Pressure and Cultural Adjustment* (New York: Human Sciences Press, 1979).

9. Max Weber, *Economy and Society,* ed. Gunther Roth and Claus Wittich (Berkeley and Los Angeles: University of California Press, 1978), 2: chap. 11, provides Weber's fundamental statement on bureaucracy.

10. Charles Tilly, ed., *The Formation of National States in Western Europe* (Princeton: Princeton University Press, 1975) provides the major formulation of Tilly's work here. See also the insightful treatment by James Coleman in *Power and the Structure of Society* (New York: W. W. Norton & Co., 1974).

11. See, for example, Etienne van de Walle and John Knodel, "Europe's Fertility Transition: New Evidence and Lessons for Today's Developing World," *Population Bulletin* 31, no. 6 (1980), especially for the role of the polity in limiting marriage. For more general treatments of the demographic transition, see George Stolnitz, "The Demographic Transition: From High to Low Birth and Death Rates," in Ronald Freedman, ed., *Population, The Vital Revolution* (New York: Andover, 1964), and Ansley Coale, "The Demographic Transition Reconsidered," *Proceedings of the IUSSP Conference* 1, no. 53 (Leige, Belgium, 1973).

12. Michael Teitlebaum, "The Relevance of Demographic Transition Theory for Developing Countries," *Science* 188 no. 4187 (1975): 420–25.

13. John Caldwell, "Toward a Restatement of Demographic Transition Theory," *Population and Development Review* 2, nos. 2–3 (1976): pp. 321–66.

14. It is, of course, this opposition that has been crystallized and made problematic in modern constitutional law and political theory. For a recent and highly relevant review of the issues raised here, see Stephen Isaacs, *Population Law and Policy* (New York: Human Sciences Press, 1981), especially chap. 2.

15. Geoffrey McNicoll, "Institutional Determinants of Fertility Change," *Population and Development Review* 6, no. 3 (1980): 441–62.

16. Amitai Etzioni, *The Comparative Analysis of Complex Organizations* (Glencoe, N.J.: The Free Press, 1961), provided a comprehensive theory of organizational analysis that identified compliance structures and power as central elements.

17. See Joseph J. Spengler and Otis D. Duncan, *Population Theory and Policy* (Glencoe, N.J.: The Free Press, 1956) for the most general statement; and Jason L. Finkle and Alison McIntosh, "Policy Responses to Stagnation in Developed Societies", in *Social, Economic, and Health Aspects of Low Fertility*, ed. Arthur A. Campbell (Washington, D.C.: Government Printing Office, 1980), pp. 275–96 for a good review of policy definitions. Isaacs, *Population Law and Policy*, chap. 8, provides another succinct review of policy definitions. For reviews of policies relevant to the high-fertility countries, see Jyoti S. Singh, ed., *World Population Policies* (New York: Praeger, 1979), and Maxwell Stamper, *Population and Planning in Developing Nations: A Review of Sixty Development Plans for the 1970s* (New York: Population Council, 1977).

18. Spengler and Duncan, *Population Theory and Policy.*

19. Finkle and McIntosh, "Policy Responses to Stagnation."

20. Dorothy Nortman and Ellen Hofstetter, *Population and Family Planning Programs*, 10th ed. (New York: Population Council, 1978), p. 17, show half of the developing nations either have official antinatalist policies or support fertility-limiting programs. The sixty-six countries in this category, however, contain 91 percent of the population of the developing countries.

21. Jason L. Finkle and Barbara Crane, "The World Health Organization and the Population Question," *Population and Development Review* 2, nos. 3–4 (September-December 1976): 367–93.

22. The World Plan of Action adopted at Bucharest in 1974 and the Final Act of the Teheran Human Rights Conference in 1968 are among the major statements. For a fuller list of relevant United Nations statements, see UNFPA, *The United Nations and Population: Major Resolutions and Instruments* (New York: UNFPA, 1974).

23. Isaacs, *Population Law and Policy*, chap. 8, provides a good review of the two sides.

24. Kingsley Davis, "Population Policy, Will Present Programs Succeed?" *Science* 158, no. 3082 (November 1967): 730–39.

25. See the various reviews in the Population Council's periodically revised *Induced Abortion*, the third edition of which appeared in 1979.

26. Ronald Freedman and Lolagene C. Coombs, *Cross Cultural Comparisons: Data on Two Factors in Fertility Behavior*, Occasional Paper (New York: Population Council, 1974).

27. Indonesia and Thailand are only two of the more dramatic cases where modest initial targets or efforts in contraceptive distribution were almost swamped with population demand. See, for example, Chulalongkorn University, Institute of Population Studies, *The Pothram Report*, 2d ed., Research Report no. 4, Bangkok, 1966, for the Thai experience. For the Indonesian experience, where the target for acceptors in the first year was 200,000, and actual acceptors numbered 500,000, see Population Council, "East Asia Review," *Studies in Family Planning* 3, no. 7 (July 1972): 128.

28. John Aird, "Population Studies and Population Policy in China," *Population and Development Review* 8, no. 2 (June 1982): 267–97.

29. See the brief but perceptive treatments in William Petersen, "Malthus and the Intellectuals," *Population and Development Review* 5, no. 3 (September 1979): 467–78, and Mogens Boserup, "Fear of Doomsday: Past and Present," *Population and Development Review* 4, no.1 (March 1978): 133–43.

30. Ronald Freedman and Bernard Berelson, "The Record of Family Planning Programs," *Studies in Family Planning* 7, no.1 (January 1976): 1–40; Bernard Berelson and W. Parker Mauldin with Zenas Sykes, "Conditions of Fertility Decline in Developing Countries 1965–75," *Studies in Family Planning* 9, no. 5 (May 1978): 90–147; and K. S. Srikantan, *The Family Planning Program in The Socio-Economic Context* (New York: Population Council, 1977).

31. Donald J. Hernandez, "The Impact of Family Planning Programs on Fertility: A Critical Evaluation," *Social Science Research* 10 (1981): 32–66.

32. Robert Cuca, *Family Planning Programs: An Evaluation of Experience*, World Bank Staff Working Paper no. 345 (Washington, D.C.: The World Bank, 1979).

33. Immanuel Wallerstein, following Fernand Braudel, is one of the leading proponents of this perspective. See *The Modern World System* (New York: Academic Press, 1976) and *The Modern World System-II* (New York: Academic Press, 1980).

34. Nicholas J. Demerath, *Birth Control and Foreign Policy* (New York: Harper, 1976), presents an analysis of the "capitalist core network" in population planning, which is a favorite topic of those holding this perspective. A more radical position is stated in Lars Bondestam and Staffan Bergstroem, eds., *Poverty and Population Control* (New York: Academic Press, 1980).

35. See, for example, the brief and partisan treatment in James W. Brackett, "The Evolution of Marxist Theories of Population: Marxism Recognizes the Population Problem," *Demography* 5, no. 1 (February 1968): 158–73.

CHAPTER 2

1. Dorothy Nortman, "Population and Family Planning Programs: A Factbook," *Reports on Population/Family Planning* (New York: Population Council), various years 1970 through 1978.

2. For this analysis, we use the numbers of nations in existence during the 1960s. In the 1970s the number of Asian nations was greatly increased by the inclusion of the new ministates of the Pacific. During the decades of the most significant policy changes, however, these new ministates were not independent and thus were not in a position to make political decisions based on forces perceived within their own boundaries.

3. See, for example, the analysis of Bernard Berelson, W. P. Mauldin, and Sheldon Segal, "Population: Current Status and Policy Options," Population Council/Center for Policy Studies, *Working Papers*, 44 (May 1979), pp 6, 16.

4. John B. Calhoun, "Population Density and Social Pathology," *Scientific American* (February 1962): 138–48. For reviews of density and human behavior see Virginia Abernathy, *Population Pressure and Cultural Adjustment*; Jonathan Freedman, *Crowding and Behavior: The Psychology of High Density Living* (New York: Viking Press, 1975); and Omer R. Galle and Walter R. Gove, "Overcrowding, Isolation, and Human Behavior: Exploring the Extremes in Population Distribution," in *Social Demography*, ed. Karl E. Taeuber, Larry Bumpas and James L. Sweet; (New York: Academic Press, 1978): pp 95–132.

5. J. Mayone Stycos, *Ideology, Faith and Family Planning in Latin America* (New York: McGraw-Hill Book Co., 1971).

6. Our evaluation of the Chilean government as "progressive" refers to the period of the late 1960s, when the policy decision was made.

7. Ibid., p. 33.

8. Gayl D. Ness, "The Ethnic Numbers Game and Population Policy in Malaysia," Paper presented at the American Political Science Associations meetings, Chicago, September 1976.

9. Edward Shils, "Political Development in the New States," *Comparative Studies in Society and History* 2 (1959–60): 265–92, 379–411.

10. Ramiro Guerra y Sanchez, *Sugar and Society in the Caribbean* (New Haven: Yale University Press, 1964).

11. E. Stokes, *The English Utilitarians in India* (Oxford: Clarendon Press, 1959).

12. H. A. Miller, "The Nationalist Epidemic," in *The World Trend Toward Nationalism*, Annals of the American Academy of Political and Social Science (July 1934): 9–14; Royal Institute of International Affairs, *Nationalism* (Oxford: Oxford University Press, 1939). When nationalism is mentioned in connection with Africa, it is European nationalism that is the issue. Nationalist movements in Germany and Italy constituted major elements in the intra-European conflicts whose resolution included the penetration and division of Africa in the late nineteenth century.

13. See Gayl D. Ness and Jeannine R. Ness, "Metropolitan Power and the Demise of Overseas Colonial Empires," paper read before the American Sociological Association, New Orleans, August 1972, for an argument that links this

process of colonial breakup to a similar process occurring in Latin America following the Napoleonic Wars.

14. We deal with this comparison in detail in Chapter 3.

15. See especially the argument of the "Economic Nationalists" presented in B. T. McCully, *English Education and the Origins of Indian Nationalism* (New York: Columbia University Press, 1940), pp. 241–95.

16. See Richard Koebner and Helmut D. Schmidt, *Imperialism, the Study and Significance of a Political Word* (Cambridge: Cambridge University Press, 1964).

17. See, for example, Gayl D. Ness, *Bureaucracy and Rural Development in Malaysia* (Berkeley and Los Angeles: University of California Press, 1967), for a detailed account of this discussion in Malaysia, which was a relative latecomer to the nationalist independence fervor.

18. Some observers have noted that private family planning associations provided important stimuli for public antinatalist policies. This was especially true of the Commonwealth countries, where private associations had often been active since the early 1930s. We shall show, however, that in India the major theoretical and political arguments for fertility limitation were developed in the Planning Commission. In Malaysia, Sri Lanka, and Indonesia the links to economic planning were far more powerful than those to the private associations. Taiwan, South Korea, and North Vietnam all came to antinatalist policies without prior experience with private associations. Finally, the prior existence of private associations in Hong Kong and the Philippines did not move those governments to explicit antinatalist policies until other significant changes had taken place.

19. Halvor Gille, "What Asian Censuses Reveal," *Far Eastern Economic Review* 29 (June 1961): 653–61.

20. Even in India, where population planning was initiated as early as 1952 with the first five-year plan, the real emphasis dates only from the early 1960s, after the first decade of development planning demonstrated the importance of population growth as an obstacle to progress. See Chapter 3 below.

21. Barbara Ward, *Spaceship Earth* (New York: Columbia University Press, 1966).

22. Amos H. Hawley, "Ecology and Population."

23. For a detailed history of the UN and population affairs, see Richard Symmonds and Michael Carder, *The United Nations and The Population Question, 1945–1970* (New York: McGraw Hill Book Co., 1973); and Gayl D. Ness, "Organizational Issues in International Population Assistance," in *World Population and Development*, ed. Philip Hauser (Syracuse: Syracuse University Press, 1979).

24. United Nations, General Assembly Resolution 2211 (21), "Population Growth and Economic Development," 1497th Plenary Meeting, 17 December 1966.

25. United Nations, Report of the United Nations World Population Conference, 1974 (New York: United Nations, 1975).

26. Jason L. Finkle and Barbara B. Crane, "The Politics of Bucharest: Population, Development and the New International Economic Order," *Population and Development Review* 1, no. 1 (September 1975): 87–114. See also W. Parker Mauldin, Nazli Choucri, Frank Notestein, and Michael Teitlebaum; "A Report on Bucharest," *Studies in Family Planning* 5, no. 12 (December, 1974): 357–95.

27. Rafael M. Salas, "Asia: An Area Assessment," Statement to the Second Asian Population Conference, Tokyo, November 1972.

28. ESCAP Secretariat and United Nations Population Division, *Report of the*

Post World Population Conference Consultation Meeting (Bangkok: ESCAP, January 1975).

29. This population figure includes China, of course. UNFPA did not provide any financial assistance to mainland China until the end of the 1970s, thus we could count the Asian population minus the near one billion in China. We include the entire total, however, to make the argument more conservative.

30. See Rafael M. Salas, *People: An International Choice* New York: Pergamon Press, 1976), for a personal account of the UNFPA by its executive director.

CHAPTER 3

1. Gunnar Myrdal coined the term "soft states" in his *Asian Drama,* 3 vols. (New York: Pantheon, 1968), p. 66, by which he meant a state whose government was unwilling to demand disciplined action of its citizens or unable to enforce those disciplining laws it had enacted. His reference was directed largely at India, whose evolutionary parlimentary development was in effect responsible for the "weakness" of state government.

2. There is now a rich literature on the Chinese fertility limitation program. Chen Pi-chao provides a detailed account from a review of documents and from personal interviews in China in, *inter alia,* his *Population and Health in the People's Republic of China* (Washington, D.C.: Smithsonian Institution, Interdisciplinary Communications Program, 1976). See also Leo Orleans, *China's Experience in Population Control: The Elusive Model* (Washington, D.C.: Government Printing Office, 1974) and the more recent series of papers from the 1980 East-West Population Institute's *China Population Analysis Conference,* which is extensively used later in this chapter.

3. Bernard Berelson, "Programs and Prospects for Fertility Reduction: What? Where?" *Population and Development Review* 4, no. 4 (December 1978): pp. 579–616. Since this review, it appears that the crude birth rate in China may already have dropped below 20.

4. B. D. Misra, Ali Ashraf, Ruth Simmons, and George Simmons, *Organization for Change: A Systems Analysis of Family Planning in Rural India* (Ann Arbor: Center for South and Southeast Asian Studies, 1982) present the fullest account of the political and organizational aspects of family planning that is now available. The study refers to Uttar Pradesh.

5. Berelson, "Programs and Prospects for Fertility Reduction."

6. Major sources that review the events in this section are as follows: Lucien Bianco, *Origins of the Chinese Revolution* (Stanford: Stanford University Press, 1971); Wolfram Eberhard, *A History of China* (Berkeley and Los Angeles: University of California Press, 1977); Francine Frankel, *India's Political Economy 1947–1977: The Gradual Revolution* (Princeton: Princeton University Press, 1978); Barrington Moore, *The Social Origins of Dictatorship and Democracy* (Boston: Beacon Press, 1966); Rhodes Murphey, *The Outsiders: The Western Experience in India and China* (Ann Arbor: University of Michigan Press, 1977); Franz Schurmann, *Ideology and Organization in Communist China* (Berkeley and Los Angeles: University of California Press, 1968).

7. The present Chinese government does not define Manchus as foreigners, but as a minority of the nation. This is not, however, a view that was shared by early twentieth-century nationalists.

8. The impact of these ecological conditions has led to extensive controversies over whether or not this constituted a unique form of Oriental despotism

manifested in a centralized bureaucracy built on the demands of water control. Karl Wittfogel's *Oriental Despotism* (New Haven: Yale University Press, 1957) is the principal anti-Marxist work in this controversy. Wolfram Eberhard presents a divergent view in his *Conquerors and Rulers* (Leiden: E. J. Brill, 1952). It is immaterial to our argument how or whether this controversy is settled, but for a useful summary, see S. M. Eisenstadt, "The Study of Oriental Despotism as Systems of Total Power," *Journal of Asian Studies* 17, no. 3 (May 1958): pp. 435–46.

9. It is important to note the greater weight of organizational than of technological superiority, though the West held both types. The point is examined on the military side in Gayl D. Ness and William Stahl, "Western Imperialist Armies in Asia," *Comparative Studies in Society and History* 19, no. 1 (January 1977): 2–29.

10. There is controversy over the degree of Western economic penetration into China. Murphey, *The Outsiders*, chaps. 10–12, emphasizes the limitations more than other observers. The point of relative penetration is scarcely debatable, however; it was far greater in India than in China.

11. The phrase is from Eric Stokes, *The English Utilitarians in India* (Oxford: Clarendon Press, 1959).

12. Bianco, *Origins of the Chinese Revolution,* pp. 49–50.

13. Pare Kishen Wattal, *The Population Problem in India* (Bombay and London: Bennett, Coleman & Co., 1934), p. 10. (This volume was originally published under the same title in 1916, revised in 1934, and revised again in 1958.) The reference, of course, is to pre-partition India, which includes what is now Pakistan and Bangladesh. The three together had an estimated population of 878 million in 1981. ESCAP, Population Division, *1981 Demographic Estimates for Asian and Pacific Countries in the ESCAP Region* (Bangkok: ESCAP Population Division, 1981).

14. Kingsley Davis, *The Population of India and Pakistan* (Princeton: Princeton University Press, 1951), pp. 26–29.

15. Albert M. Hanson, *The Process of Planning; A Study of India's Five Year Plans* (London: Oxford University Press, 1966), p. 30.

16. National Planning Committee, *Population (A Report of the Subcommittee)* (Bombay: Voral and Co., 1957), p. 145.

17. Government of India, National Planning Commission, *First Five Year Plan* (Delhi: GOI Printing Office, 1947), p. 145.

18. Ho Ping-ti, *Studies on the Population of China, 1368–1953* (Cambridge: Harvard University Press, 1959), p. 256.

19. Ibid., p. 95.

20. Austin Coates, *India and China and the Ruins of Washington* (New York: John Day Co., 1972), pp. 34 ff. See also Christopher S. Wren, "Old Nemesis Haunts China on Birth Plan," *New York Times,* 1 August 1982.

21. Martin Whyte and William Parish, *Village and Family in Contemporary China* (Chicago: University of Chicago Press, 1978).

22. L. Silberman, "Hung Lian-chi,'A Chinese Malthus,'" *Population Studies* 13, no. 3 (March 1960): 257–65.

23. Cited in Rusikesh M. Maru, "Birth Control in India and The Peoples Republic of China: A Comparison of Policy Evolution, Methods of Birth Control, and Program Organization" (Ph.D. diss., University of Michigan, 1976), p 46. This is probably the most cited reference to population policy in China.

24. S. Chandrasekar, "Communist China's Demographic Dilemma," in *Asia's Population Problems*, ed. S. Chandrasekar (New York: Praeger, 1967), p. 62.

25. Irene B. Taeuber, "Population Policies in Communist China," *Population Index* 22, no.4 (1956): pp. 263–4.

26. M. Freeberne, "Birth Control in China," *Population Studies* 18 (1964): 6.

27. Minami, Ryozaburo, *Chugoku no Jinko* (Population of China), (Tokyo: Ajia Keizai Kenkyu-sho, 1970).

28. Maru, *Birth Control in India and the Peoples Republic of China*, p. 48.

29. Yoshida Tadao, "Chugoko no Jinko to Minzoku" ("Chinese Population and Race") in *Chugoku Seiiji Keizai Soran* (*Annals of Chinese Politics and Economy*), ed. by Ajia Seikei Gakkai, (Tokyo: Hitotshubashi Shobo, 1960) pp. 39–55.

30. Minami, *Chugoku no Jinkozoka to Keizaihatten*, p. 214.

31. Kan Majima, Gekido o Itkita Otoko (An Autobiography of Dr. Kan Majima) (Tokyo: Japanese Family Planning Association, 1971), pp. 246–8.

32. Leo Orleans, *China's Experience in Population Control: The Elusive Model.*

33. Maru, *Birth Control in India and in the Peoples Republic of China*, p. 53.

34. Freeberne, "Birth Control in China," pp. 8–9.

35. An unofficial report of the UNFPA mission to China, April, 1979.

36. Edgar Snow, "Chou Shusho Tono 5 Jikan" ("Five-Hour Interview with Premier Chou"), Asahi Shimbun, 11 February 1964.

37. People's Republic of China, Documents of the First Session of the Fifth National People's Congress of the People's Republic of China (Peking: Foreign Languages Press, 1978), p. 14.

38. David Bonavia, "Astonishing Reversions to pre–1966 Social Policies," *Far Eastern Economic Review,* 5 October 1979, pp. 51–52; Stewart E. Fraser, "One Is Fine, Two Is More Adequate," *Far Eastern Economic Review,* 5 October 1979, p.61.

39. Bonavia, "Astonishing Reversions," p. 51.

40. Quoted by Fraser, "One Is Fine, Two Is More Adequate," p. 61.

41. Ibid.

42. For more on this point see, for example, John P. Lewis, "Population Control in India", in *Are Our Descendants Doomed?* ed. Harrison Brown and E. Hutchings (New York: Viking Press, 1972), pp. 243–65.

43. UNFPA, *Inventory of Population Projects in Developing Countries Around the World 1976/77* (New York: UNFPA, 1978), pp. 178–94.

44. The 1956–65 figures are drawn from the Five-Year Plans; the 1972 figure is from the Government of India, Department of Family Planning, *Family Welfare Planning Yearbook, 1972–73* (New Delhi: Ministry of Health and Family Planning, 1973); and the 1976 figure is from Dorothy Nortman and Ellen Hofstetter, *Population and Family Planning Programs* (New York: Population Council, 1978).

45. Government of India, *FWP Yearbook, 1972–73,* pp.75–78; Nortman and Hofstetter, *Population and Family Planning Programs,* p. 47.

46. See, for example, the excellent example of such a chart in Piers M. Blackie, *Family Planning In India: Diffusion and Policy* (London: Arnold Press, 1975), p. 272.

47. See Maru, *Birth Control in India and in The Peoples Republic of China*, pp. 291–300.

48. Ibid., pp 301–03.

49. David Mechanic has made this point more generally in his extensive studies of the sociology of health care systems. See his general review in "The Comparative Study of Health Care Delivery Systems," *Annual Review of Sociology*, vol. 1 (Palo Alto: Annual Reviews, 1975), pp. 43–66.

50. Robert Cassen, *India: Population, Economy and Society* (New York: Holmes & Meier Pubs., 1978), Chap. 3, examines this extensively. We have drawn heavily on Cassen's analysis for this section.

51. United Nations, *Report on the Family Planning Programme in India*, TAO/IND/48 (New York: United Nations, 1966). It is important to note that this assistance to India was given pursuant to, and justified by, the ECAFE resolution of March 1964. The same resolution was put to the Population Commission in New York at the same time, but was defeated and was not accepted until the following year. Again, Asia was ahead of the rest of the UN on the population question, and the regional commissions permitted some significant forms of local autonomy from the UN center.

52. Cassen, *India*, p. 360, n. 38.

53. Government of India, *FWP Yearbook*, 1972/3, p. 41; and Nortman and Hofstetter, *Population and Family Planning Programs*, p. 54.

54. Taiwan and South Korea give ample demonstration of this; and Cassen, *India*, pp. 154–56, reviews other clinical evidence as well.

55. As in Chap. 1, nonrational here does not imply that the distrust was *ir*rational, simply that it was not calculated. It was a distrust built upon more or less unquestioned values that were deeply embedded in the political culture.

56. See Maru, *Birth Control in India and in The Peoples Republic of China*, pp. 133–43, for the American role in the India pill decision.

57. Pravin Visaria and Anrudh Jain, *India* (New York: Population Council, 1976), provide a good summary of the Nirodh program. See also Peter King, "The Use of Private Market Mechanisms for the Diffusion of Contraceptive Technology," SEADAG Seminar on Problems of Organizational Control and Coordination in Southeast Asian Family Planning Programs, Washington, D.C., 1972.

58. Visaria and Jain, *India*, p. 51 n. 194, show distribution prices and markups. The government price to distributors was .08 rupees; distributor to outlet, .12 rupees; and outlet to consumer, .15 rupees for a packet of three condoms.

59. Peter King, "Use of Private Market Mechanisms."

60. Ibid., pp. 33–35; also Cassen, *India*, pp. 160–65.

61. Government of India, *FWP Yearbook*, 1972–73, p. 64.

62. Cassen, *India*, pp. 170–75.

63. Nortman and Hofstetter, *Population and Family Planning Programs*, show the eighty high-fertility countries with family planning program information had a population total of 1,467,000,000 persons. Total vasectomies shown for 1975 were 1,545,000 (excluding Sri Lanka, whose 39,000 sterilizations are not differentiated by sex), of which India accounted for 1,438,000.

64. See Simmons for field notes showing villagers often identify sterilization with castration. V. A. Pai Panandiker, et al, *Family Planning under the Emergency*, (New Delhi: Radiant Publishers, 1978), p. 137, also show this identity in the minds of villagers of sterilization with castration.

65. This was first suggested to us in personal communication by Dipak Bhatia, former permanent secretary to the Family Planning Department.

66. UN ESCAP Population Division, *Husband-Wife Communication and Practice of Family Planning*, Asian Population Studies Series no. 16 (Bangkok: ESCAP, 1976), pp. 124–25.

67. Visaria and Jain, *India*, p. 45.

68. Davidson R. Gwatkin presents a general summary of the emergency and its impact on family planning in "Political Will and Family Planning: The Implication of India's Emergency Experience," *Population and Development Review* 6 (1979):

29–60. For a more detailed report of actual field surveys of the impact, see V. A. Pai Panandiker, *Family Planning under the Emergency* (New Delhi: Radiant Publishers, 1978).

69. See Frankel, *India's Political Economy,* p. 548, for electoral figures taken from relevant issues of the *Times of India.* One of the notable old Congress representatives who lost in this election was Subhadra Joshi, whose preelection letter to the party president detailing party abuses under the Emergency is published in *Asia Week,* 13 May 1977, pp. 24–25.

70. V. A. Pai Panandiker, *Family Planning under the Emergency,* pp. 24–50. See also Frankel, *India's Political Economy,* Chap. 13, for a parallel indictment.

71. Frankel, *India's Political Economy,* p. 565.

72. See N. C. Chaudhuri, *The Autobiography of an Unknown Indian* (Berkeley and Los Angeles: University of California Press, 1951), for an examination of the depth of Indian communal hatreds.

73. Maru, *Birth Control in India and in The Peoples Republic of China,* pp. 346 ff.

74. Misra, Ashraf, Simmons and Simmons, *Organization for Change,* pp. 357–82.

75. Government of India *FWP Yearbook,* 1972–73 and Nortman and Hofstetter, *Population and Family Planning Programs* p. 54, 78 are sources for these figures. The Yearbook shows numbers of users of conventional contraceptives. We have divided this figure by 72, which is the estimate used in Indian documents for coital frequency. This provides only a rough estimate, of course, since the coital frequency estimate probably has a substantial error margin, and not all conventional contraceptive use is of condoms.

76. Nortman and Hofstetter, *Population and Family Planning Programs,* p. 78.

77. Ibid., p. 11.

78. Jain and Sharma, *India,* pp. 4, 15.

79. Cassen, *India,* 179–81.

80. Albert I. Hermalin, "Regression Analysis of Areal Data," in *Measuring the Effects of Family Planning Programs on Fertility,* ed. C. Chandrasekar and A. I. Hermalin (Brussels: Ordina Editions, 1975), pp. 245–98.

81. We are fortunate to have available a set of papers from a 1980 East-West Population Institute "China Population Analysis Conference." This provides an economical survey of what is known about China's population and its fertility-limitation program. We have drawn heavily on these papers for this section, since they represent a good summary of some of the leading writers on Chinese population. We shall cite by author's name and CPAC.

82. Li Chou-ming, *The Statistical System of Communist China* (Berkeley and Los Angeles: University of California Press, 1962), pp. 111–12.

83. Leo Orleans, "Twenty-Five Years of Watching China's Population: Some Reflections," CPAC, p. 9.

84. Chen Pi-chao, "The Birth Planning Program," CPAC.

85. Ibid.

86. Katherine Chiu Lyle, "Planned Birth in Tientsin," CPAC, p. 1.

87. Chen Pi-chao has written most extensively on the prescribed character of planned birth in China. From his review of documents and discussions with many elites, including Chou En-lai, we can gain a clear view of how the system is supposed to work. For much of its actual operation, however, other sources must be used as well.

88. See, for example, Reinhard Bendix, *Work and Authority in Industry,* (New

York: John Wiley, 1958), chap. 6 for an early discussion of this political-administrative character as illustrated in the Soviet Union and the German Democratic Republic.

89. Chen Pi-chao, "Birth Planning Program."

90. Martin K. Whyte, *Small Groups and Political Ritual in Communist China* (Berkeley and Los Angeles: University of California Press, 1974).

91. There is a growing literature on health care in the People's Republic of China, but the reorganization of health care and the extensive use of paramedical personnel have been commented upon favorably for some time. For an enthusiastic and supportive view, see Victor Sidel and Ruth Sidel, *Serving the People: Observations on Medicine in the People's Republic of China* (Boston: Beacon Press, 1973). For a more objective and critical treatment, see David M. Lampton, *The Politics of Chinese Medicine* (Boulder, Colo.: Westview Press, 1977).

92. Chen Pi-chao, "Birth Planning Program," p. 7.

93. Chen, "Birth Planning Program", p. 7.

94. Chen, "Birth Planning Program", p. 8.

95. Cited in Chen, "Birth Planning Program", p. 4. A fuller exposition of this distinctive strategy of revolutionary dictatorship along with local adaptive mobilization can be found in Franz Schurmann, *Ideology and Organization in Communist China,* and in Martin K. Whyte, *Small Groups and Political Ritual.*

96. William Parish, "Marriage and Family in the People's Republic," CPAC, especially tables 3 and 8.

97. Katherine Chiu Lyle, "Planned Birth in Tientsin," table 7.

98. Ibid., p. 13.

99. Asok Mitra, *India's Population* (New Delhi: Abhinav Publications, 1978), pp. 230–34; see also chap. 2, pp. 294–370, for data and analysis of the relation between age at marriage and select social variables.

100. Chen Pi-chao, "Birth Planning Program," Table V–2.

101. Katherine Chiu Lyle, "Planned Birth in Tientsin," table 3.

102. John Aird, "Reconstruction of an Official Data Model of the Population of China," CPAC pp. 8, 26; Chen Pi-chao, "Birth Planning Program," tables V–2, V–3; Judith Bannister, "Strengths and Weaknesses of China's Population Data," CPAC, p. 15.

103. Chen Pi-chao, "Birth Planning Program," table V–3.

104. Katherine Chiu Lyle, "Planned Birth in Tientsin," pp. 13–14.

105. United Nations Fund for Population Activities, *India, Report of Mission on Needs Assessment for Population Assistance* (New York: UNFPA, 1979), p. 109, summarized data from 1967 to 1978 showing a rise in the prevalence rate from 4 to 22 percent.

106. Ibid., p. 110, indicates that 90 percent of the effective contraceptive protection is provided by sterilization. This exaggerates the prevalence, since it includes weights for different methods and for attrition rates for mortality and method discontinuation, and it does not distinguish between male and female sterilization. Nonetheless, male sterilization has often counted for more than 50 percent of all acceptors, with female sterilization accounting for another 20 to 25 percent.

107. William Parish, "Marriage and Family," pp. 6, 9–11.

108. R. T. Ravenholt, "The Population of China," mimeographed, 5 February, 1979, pp. 1–3.

109. Chen Pi-Chao, "Birth Planning Program," p. 2.

110. William Parish, "Marriage and Family," p. 3.

CHAPTER 4

1. For other development policies, it is quite conceivable that the level of socioeconomic development will be related to the policy decision. For example, a strong political-administrative system can be expected to develop industrialization or educational policies based on acute perceptions of the level of productivity or social communication. In such cases, the relevant theory would hold that the policy decision is related to the development level, not to the level of population density. For population policies, however, development level appears far less relevant than does the level of density or the fact of political-economic planning.

2. See Virginia Abernathy, *Population Pressure and Cultural Adjustment* (New York: Human Sciences Press, 1979) for an extended and extensively documented argument on this point.

3. It is customary, for example, to insist on a minimum of ten observations per variable in multiple regression analysis. In our three equations for this analysis, however, we can employ only seven, five, and four observations per variable. Although this weakens the statistical base of our argument, we believe that the use of the historical analysis of deviant cases, or multivariate outliers, provides an adequate and quite appropriate compensation.

4. See above, Chap. 2. We also developed some of these ideas in an earlier comparative analysis of Malaysia and the Philippines. See Gayl D. Ness and Hirofumi Ando, "The Politics of Population Planning in Malaysia and the Philippines," *Journal of Comparative Administration*, 3 (November 1971):296–329.

5. Ibid.

6. Their standardized residuals are two standard deviations or more from the mean of the residuals.

7. See James Heiby, Gayl Ness, and Barbara Pillsbury, *AID's Role in Indonesian Family Planning*, AID Program Evaluation Report no. 2, Washington, D.C.: Agency for International Development, December 1979, for a recent analysis supporting this interpretation.

8. See, for example, John K. Friesen and Richard V. Moore, "Iran," *Country Profiles* (October 1972).

9. See, for example, Terence H. Hull, Valerie J. Hull, and Masri Singarimbun, "Indonesia's Family Planning Story: Success and Challenge," *Population Bulletin*, 32, no. 6, (Washington, D.C.: Population Reference Bureau, 1977).

10. Both are Muslim countries, although, to be sure, Iran is Shi'ite and Indonesia Sunni. Even this does not adequately reflect the full differences in the two countries. Islam, like all world religions, is differentiated by national experiences as well as by doctrinal characteristics. Our only point here is that the two countries are not radically divided by religion.

11. Elaine Zeighami, Bahram Zeighami, Iraj Javidian, and Susan Zimmer, "The Rural Health Worker as a Family Planning Provider: A Village Trial in Iran," *Studies in Family Planning* 8, no. 7 (July 1977): 184–87; Roy C. Treadway, Robert Gillespie, and Mehdi Loghmani, "The Model Family Planning Project in Isfahan, Iran," *Studies in Family Planning* 7, no.11 (November 1976): 308–21. Bernard Berelson and Ronald Freedman, "The Record of Family Planning Programs," *Studies in Family Planning* 7, no.1 (January 1976) give figures of 14 percent for contraceptive user rates (p. 16) and 10.8 percent for acceptors as the percentage of estimated nonusers in 1973 (p. 15). *The Agency Report, 1975* (Washington, D.C.: AID, 1976) states that 700,000 Iranian couples practiced family planning in 1974, implying a 12.8 percent acceptance rate based on the Population Council's estimated 5.5 million married women of reproductive age.

12. David Wightman, *Toward Economic Cooperation in Asia: the United Nations Economic Commission for Asia and the Far East* (New Haven: Yale University Press, 1963), p. 266.

13. Ibid., pp. 12–20.

14. We must neglect here many of the details of the international debate through which ECAFE came to identify its major tasks. Asians proposed representative committees to be concerned with technical issues of reconstruction and development, but the Western powers resisted, arguing for expert groups—largely, it would seem, to preclude the development of a strong political center in Asia. Whether this saved ECAFE from destructive internal political conflicts or weakened it in its relations with the industrial powers cannot be determined, but it did focus most of ECAFE's energies on information gathering. For the first two years of its existence, ECAFE's attention was directed to reconstruction, paralleling the activity of the Economic Commission for Europe; but by 1950 Asian thinking was dominated by issues of economic development. See ibid., chap. 4.

15. See Gayl D. Ness, *Bureaucracy and Rural Development in Malaysia* (Berkeley: University of California Press, 1967), chap. 4, for a detailed exposition of this common change in one new nation of that region.

16. Richard Symonds and Michael Carder, *The United Nations and The Population Question 1945–1970* (New York: McGraw-Hill Book Co., 1973) pp. 135–36.

17. The $1.05 billion figure is reported in *World Population Growth and Responses 1965–1975* (Washington, D.C.: Population Reference Bureau, 1976), p. 20 and comes originally from US AID. The $1.402 billion is from UNFPA, as reported in Rafael Salas, *International Population Assistance: The First Decade* (New York: Pergamon Press, 1979), p. 391.

18. Bhagwati, for example, has estimated that between 40 and 60 percent of all foreign assistance goes to export subsidy or to institutional support to the donor country. J. N. Bhagwati, *Amount and Sharing of Aid* (Washington, D.C.: Overseas Development Council, 1970).

19. Hong Kong Family Planning Association, annual reports 1965 through 1975.

20. UNFPA, *Inventory of Population Projects in Developing Countries Around the World 1973/74 and 1976/77.*

21. The broadening base of support for population assistance is examined in Gayl D. Ness, "Organizational Issues in International Population Assistance," in *World Population and Development,* ed. Philip Hauser (Syracuse: Syracuse University Press, 1979), chap. 17.

22. Ness and Ando, "The Politics of Population Planning in Malaysia and the Philippines"

23. For Indonesia, see Heiby, Ness, and Pillsbury, *AID's Role in Indonesian Family Planning.* The Community Based Family Planning Program is Thailand's most well-known private effort in family planning. It has received substantial financial assistance from the International Planned Parenthood Federation and appears to have made an appreciable impact in gaining acceptance for fertility limitation among the Thai rural population. The program has also been closely associated with the government's effort, to the extent that its acceptors are counted as acceptors of the government's program. For a general view, see UNFPA, *Thailand,* Population Profiles 8 (New York: UNFPA, n.d.).

24. On the Philippines Gayl D. Ness, "Philippine Political Dynamics and Population Policy: Some Provocative Observations," in *Population and Politics in the Philippines,* ed. George A. Fauriol (Washington D.C.: Georgetown University

Center for Strategic and International Studies, 1979) presents an argument in this direction. Family Health Care, *A Review of the Philippines Population Program* (Washington, D.C.: Family Health Care, 1977) provides a more detailed review of the program, which sustains Ness's indictment. On Pakistan, see Controller General of the United States, *Report to the Congress; Impact of Population Assistance to an Asian Country* (Washington, D.C.: GAO, 1977), which questions the commitment, and by inference the organizational competence and integrity, of Pakistan's government in the area of family planning.

25. See Jason Finkle and Barbara Crane, "Organizational Impediments to Development Assistance: The World Bank's Population Program," *World Politics* Vol 33, no. 4 (July 1981): 516–53.

26. A. Laquian, "Planned Population Distribution: Lessons from Malaysia and Indonesia," UNFPA University of Singapore/University of Michigan Working Group on Planned Population Distribution, Singapore, 1979.

27. Especially in the use of field experiments to manage public programs, the Taiwan family planning program is a superb example of the utilization of social science for public policy. Unfortunately, the full story of this policy effort, and the close collaboration of the Population Council, the University of Michigan, and the Taiwan family planning program has not yet been written. One of the major architects of this collaboration is Ronald Freedman, who with John Y. Takeshita presents an introduction in their *Family Planning in Taiwan* (Princeton: Princeton University Press, 1969).

28. Even the assessment of quantity is subject to considerable error, as we shall show in work that is currently in progress. In the case of Taiwan, however, Professor Freedman has noted in a personal communication that after the formal withdrawal of foreign assistance, the family planning program continued to draw support from counterpart funds that were a residual of the initial foreign assistance. It is as yet unclear whether such residuals in local currencies should be counted a part of foreign or domestic funds. Although they originate abroad, they become resources substantially controlled by the host government, as the Indian experience so clearly demonstrates.

29. Heiby, Ness, and Pillsbury, *AID's Role in Indonesian Family Planning*.

30. Morris D. Morris, *Measuring the Condition of the World's Poor* (New York: Pergamon Press, 1979).

CHAPTER 5

1. See, for example, Ronald Freedman and Bernard Berelson, "The Human Population," in The Scientific American, *The Human Population* (San Francisco: Freeman Publishing Co., 1974), pp. 8–9.

2. Tokugawa Japan is a notable exception. Population equilibrium appears to have been a goal of the government, expressed in a variety of policies that had that effect, at least in part.

3. See the analyses in ESCAP, Population Division, "Comparative Analyses of Family Planning Programme Performance." *Asian Population Studies Series* no. 27, Bangkok, 1977; and Gayl D. Ness, "The Ethnic Numbers Game and Population Policy in Malaysia," paper delivered at the American Political Science Association meeting, Chicago, 1976.

4. On the very successful Malaysian Federal Land Development schemes, see Colin MacAndrews, *Mobility and Modernization,* and Tunku Shamsul Bahrin and P.D.A. Pereira, *Twenty Years of Land Development* (Kuala Lumpur: FELDA, 1977).

5. ESCAP Population Division, "Regional Seminar on Evaluation of Schemes and Strategies for Integrated Family Planning Programmes with Special Reference to Increased Involvement of Local Institutions," *Asian Population Series*, no. 51, Bangkok, 1982.

6. Arthur Stinchcombe, *Creating Efficient Industrial Administration* (New York: Academic Press, 1974). Stinchcombe's observations are based on analysis of steel plants in Venezuela, Chile, and Argentina, but the argument on the strength of regimes is a generally applicable one.

7. Gunnar Myrdal, *Asian Drama* (New York: Pantheon, 1968), pp. 707–900.

8. The debate is often titled as one between Malthus and Marx, although William Petersen has shown that this is an incorrect attribution. See William Petersen, "American Efforts To Reduce the Fertility of Less Developed Countries," in *Fertility Decline in Less Developed Countries* ed. Nick Eberstadt (New York: Praeger Publishers, 1981), pp. 355–358. See also the recent collection by Lars Bondestam and Staffan Bergstron, eds., *Poverty and Population Control* (New York: Academic Press, 1981).

9. Jason Finkle's extended observation of modern population problems has led to this specific formulation, with its insightful classification of the controversies. We happily record our debt to our colleague.

10. Julien Simon, *The Ultimate Resource* (Princeton: Princeton University Press, 1981). For a sensitive and highly literate critique of Simon's controversial book, see Garrett Hardin, "Dr. Pangloss Meets Cassandra," *The New Republic* 185, no. 17, issue 3 (28 October 1981): pp. 31–34.

11. See Virginia Abernathy, *Population Pressure and Cultural Adjustment* (New York: Human Sciences Press, 1979) for a broad-ranging and sensitive presentation of a homeostatic theory. Petersen, "American Efforts to Reduce Fertility," has produced one of the most recent attacks on American population assistance in the Third World. We find Petersen's argument flawed by his failure to consider the differences between country experiences, which is, of course, the heart of our analysis.

12. Petersen, "American Efforts to Reduce Fertility," does well to remind us of this point.

13. See Gayl D. Ness, "Organizational Issues in International Population Assistance," *World Population and Development,* ed. Philip Hauser (Syracuse: Syracuse University Press, 1979).

14. US AID, *Third Evaluation of the Thailand National Family Planning Program*, AID Program Evaluation Report no. 3 (Washington, D.C.: US AID, February 1980).

15. Gayl D. Ness, *Bureaucracy and Rural Development in Malaysia* (Berkeley and Los Angeles: University of California Press, 1967), argues that precisely the rapid flow of funds to closely monitored local projects accomplished both the rapid advance of public infrastructure development and the increased popularity of the government.

16. Asia is no exception, although we do have in Asia great variance in the levels of female subordination. It is probably greatest in western Asia, followed by southern and eastern Asia, with Southeast Asia showing remarkable conditions of female autonomy and near equality.

AFTERWORD

1. Minoru Muramatsu, "Changing Public Attitudes toward Population Growth in Japan," in *Are Our Descendants Doomed?* ed. H. Brown and E. Hutchings, Jr. (New York: Viking Press, 1970), p. 276.

Index

All entries appear with single page numbers; in some cases discussion continues on succeeding pages.

GAYL D. NESS is professor of sociology and population planning at the University of Michigan and is director of its School of Public Health's Program in Population Planning. His many publications on population planning and economic development in Asian countries include two books, *The Sociology of Economic Development, A Reader* and *Bureaucracy and Rural Development in Malaysia.*

HIROFUMI ANDO is chief of the Asia and Pacific Branch, Programme Division, United Nations Fund for Population Activities. For the past twelve years he has worked in the area of population planning.

The Johns Hopkins University Press

THE LAND IS SHRINKING

This book was composed in Lonotron Times Roman
by Huron Valley Graphics, Inc., Ann Arbor, Michigan
from a design by Gerard A. Valerio.

It was printed on 50-lb. Sebago Eggshell paper and
bound in Holliston Kingston cloth by
The Maple Press Co., York, Pennsylvania.